Vol. XCV   No. 1

Bible Expositor and Illuminator

WINTER QUARTER   December 2022, January, February 2023

God's Great Blessings

UNIT I: Blessing of a Saviour

UNIT II: Blessing of the Gospel

UNIT III: Blessing of Grace in Christ

Editor in Chief: Kenneth Sponsler

Edited and published quarterly by
THE INCORPORATED TRUSTEES OF THE
GOSPEL WORKER SOCIETY
UNION G_____ ____ESS DIVISION
____an, Founder
____quarter*

Union
Go
Pre

*ing extra

5-310-5

LOOKING AHEAD

This quarter's lessons are devoted to studying God's great blessings to us in Christ. The first unit begins our survey of God's blessings with the greatest blessing of all, the blessing of His sending us a Saviour in the person of the Lord Jesus Christ. Lesson 1 examines the promise of the one who would be the herald of the coming Christ, John the Baptist. Lesson 2 takes us back to the time of King David and the Prophet Nathan's prophecy of God's covenant with David. Lesson 3 deals with the angel Gabriel's announcement to Mary that she would bear the Son of God, Jesus Christ. Then, in lesson 4, we study the actual birth of the Saviour from Luke chapter 2. Born in humble circumstances, His birth was gloriously announced by a multitude of angels!

Our second unit of study for this quarter examines the great blessings of the saving gospel message. Through faith in that message, we are made heirs of God in Jesus Christ, receiving the promise of eternal life. Lesson 5 looks at our reconciliation with God through Jesus Christ and our calling to be His ambassadors to bring the message of reconciliation to the world. In lesson 6, we study the blessings of forgiveness and new life from I John. When we sin as Christians, God promises to forgive us and cleanse us if we confess our sins to Him. In lesson 7, we look at the blessing of Christ as our intercessor before the very throne of God. Lesson 8 takes us to Paul's letter to the Galatian churches and the blessings of our liberty in Christ.

Our third unit of study examines the blessings of the amazing grace that God has provided for us in Jesus Christ. Lesson 9 looks at the blessing of being members of Christ's body, the church. In lesson 10, we are encouraged by James to count all our trials and temptations as joy because our enduring them will bring us a crown of life. In lesson 11, we will study the blessings of God's comfort toward us in the midst of our trials so that we might be equipped to comfort others. Lesson 12 looks at the blessing of our growth in godliness as the Holy Spirit works in us to produce Christian virtues. Our final lesson for this quarter examines the blessing of the fruit of having the Holy Spirit indwelling us and conforming us to the image of Christ.

I hope our studies this quarter will be an additional blessing to all the many blessings that God has already blessed us with.

—*The Editors.*

EDITORIALS

The Blessing of Trusting God

REGINALD COATS

Choosing whatever delectables you desire from the menu of your choice and chasing your meal down with ice cream for dinner every night would seem like a tremendous blessing for most children. The knowledge and wisdom acquired by most adults, however, teaches that such a meal plan is more likely to cause eventual problems than be a blessing.

God has no need to acquire knowledge and wisdom because He already has all of it. This is an important truth to bear in mind when giving consideration to God's blessings. As His children, God has the best intentions and a perfect plan for each of our lives even when our present situations suggest otherwise.

Years of being unable to conceive must have felt the exact opposite of being blessed for Elisabeth and Zacharias (Luke 1:7). By the time God blessed them with a child, their desire had no doubt dwindled into the despair of nothing more than a distant unfulfilled dream. God had other plans, however, and their earlier disappointment gave way to eventual jubilation as they welcomed into the world their son, John, who was chosen by God to pronounce the arrival of the much-anticipated Messiah (Matt. 11:10-11).

The intentions behind the timing of God's blessings will not necessarily be in line with what makes His people comfortable or instantly gratified. God's desire is to work through the events of human history, including our lives, for the sake of bringing glory to Himself (Rev. 4:11). Just as a child might not immediately recognize and appreciate the good intentions of a parent who does not consent to a daily diet of fast food, God's people can fail to see the true blessing that accompanies His perfect timing.

Every one of God's promises comes equipped with His faithfulness. Any inclinations to doubt what He is doing can therefore be directed to what He has already said and faithfully done (cf. Josh. 21:45; Matt. 1:22-23).

The promised Saviour, who would be a descendant of David (II Sam. 7:12-16), did in fact come even though He did so hundreds of years after David had died. Despite the seeming delay, David and numerous other people we encounter in Scripture experienced the blessing of trusting the Lord while He worked through them to bless and make Himself known to others.

The greatest of all God's blessings is the gift of His Son, who came into the world wrapped "in the likeness of sinful flesh" (Rom. 8:3). God's good intentions could not have been expressed more emphatically. Jesus' willingness to make the ultimate sacrifice of laying down His life to save us brings the blessing of God's salvation to all who put their trust in Him as Saviour.

By not withholding the most precious of gifts from us, God has clearly shown His immense love and that He will continue to bless us with all we need (Rom. 8:32). Having died for our sins and been raised from the dead, Jesus is living proof that God cares for us.

In addition to the wonderful realities of being reconciled to God and having Jesus to intercede with the Father on

(Editorials continued on page 186)

SCRIPTURE LESSON TEXT

LUKE 1:8 And it came to pass, that while he executed the priest's office before God in the order of his course,

9 According to the custom of the priest's office, his lot was to burn incense when he went into the temple of the Lord.

10 And the whole multitude of the people were praying without at the time of incense.

11 And there appeared unto him an angel of the Lord standing on the right side of the altar of incense.

12 And when Zacharias saw *him,* he was troubled, and fear fell upon him.

13 But the angel said unto him, Fear not, Zacharias: for thy prayer is heard; and thy wife Elisabeth shall bear thee a son, and thou shalt call his name John.

14 And thou shalt have joy and gladness; and many shall rejoice at his birth.

15 For he shall be great in the sight of the Lord, and shall drink neither wine nor strong drink; and he shall be filled with the Holy Ghost, even from his mother's womb.

16 And many of the children of Israel shall he turn to the Lord their God.

17 And he shall go before him in the spirit and power of Elias, to turn the hearts of the fathers to the children, and the disobedient to the wisdom of the just; to make ready a people prepared for the Lord.

18 And Zacharias said unto the angel, Whereby shall I know this? for I am an old man, and my wife well stricken in years.

19 And the angel answering said unto him, I am Gabriel, that stand in the presence of God; and am sent to speak unto thee, and to shew thee these glad tidings.

20 And, behold, thou shalt be dumb, and not able to speak, until the day that these things shall be performed, because thou believest not my words, which shall be fulfilled in their season.

NOTES

4

The Promise of Messiah's Forerunner

Lesson Text: Luke 1:8-20

Related Scriptures: Genesis 18:9-15; 25:20-28;
Malachi 4:1-6; Matthew 11:9-15

TIME: 7 or 6 B.C.

PLACE: Jerusalem

GOLDEN TEXT—"Thy wife Elisabeth shall bear thee a son, and thou shalt call his name John. And thou shalt have joy and gladness; and many shall rejoice at his birth" (Luke 1:13-14).

Introduction

The faith of even the most godly people can sometimes falter. Elijah experienced a great spiritual victory on Mount Carmel (I Kgs. 18:17-46), but soon after he fell into despair when Queen Jezebel sought his life (19:1-4). Peter drew his sword, ready to defend Jesus to the death in the garden (John 18:10), but only hours later he denied knowing the Lord (vss. 17-18, 25-27).

We believe in God and acknowledge that God is all-powerful, but His work is not always readily visible to our eyes. As a result, we often become discouraged. Zacharias the priest is an interesting case study. He knew God, but when he was given a promise that seemed impossible of fulfillment, his faith failed him. The good news for both him and us is that one person's failure does not thwart the purpose and plan of God.

LESSON OUTLINE

I. THE PRIEST AND THE PEOPLE—Luke 1:8-10

II. THE ANGEL AND THE MESSAGE—Luke 1:11-17

III. THE RESPONSE AND THE REPERCUSSIONS—Luke 1:18-20

Exposition: Verse by Verse

THE PRIEST AND THE PEOPLE

LUKE 1:8 And it came to pass, that while he executed the priest's office before God in the order of his course,

9 According to the custom of the priest's office, his lot was to burn incense when he went into the temple of the Lord.

10 And the whole multitude of the

people were praying without at the time of incense.

Zacharias's ministry (Luke 1:8-9). After his introduction to his Gospel (vss. 1-4), Luke began his account of Jesus Christ. But he led off not with the birth of Christ but with the birth of the Saviour's forerunner, John the Baptist. Actually, the account begins more than nine months before John's birth.

Luke 1:5 introduces us to the Jewish priest Zacharias and his wife, Elisabeth. Both are described as "righteous before God" (vs. 6). They diligently obeyed His commands. By this time both were advanced in age, and they had never been able to have children (vs. 7).

The story begins with Zacharias executing his priestly service in the temple according to the set rotation. There were many priests in Israel—too many, in fact, to keep them all occupied in temple service. Therefore, the priests had been organized into twenty-four groups, or courses (I Chr. 23-24; Luke 1:5). Twice a year, each course would serve in the temple for one week, with specific duties being assigned by lot.

On this occasion Zacharias had been chosen to burn incense inside the temple. {This was a great privilege and a once-in-a-lifetime opportunity, since according to historical records, "a priest could not offer incense more than once in his entire lifetime" (Morris, *Luke,* InterVarsity). Thus, it was at the pinnacle of his priestly career}[Q1] that Zacharias received both the greatest promise to him personally and the greatest challenge to his faith.

The people's anticipation (Luke 1:10). Only Israel's high priest could enter the Most Holy Place, or Holy of Holies, in the temple, and he did so only once a year on the Day of Atonement. Separated from the Holy of Holies by a tall, heavy curtain, or veil (cf. 23:45), was the holy place.

It was into the holy place that Zach-arias entered to offer incense on the golden altar. This offering, symbolic of prayer, was presented both in the morning and in the evening each day. We do not know whether this was the morning or evening offering, but a large crowd of faithful Jews was gathered outside in the temple courtyard, praying and anticipating the reappearance of the priest when his duties were concluded.

THE ANGEL AND THE MESSAGE

11 And there appeared unto him an angel of the Lord standing on the right side of the altar of incense.

12 And when Zacharias saw him, he was troubled, and fear fell upon him.

13 But the angel said unto him, Fear not, Zacharias: for thy prayer is heard; and thy wife Elisabeth shall bear thee a son, and thou shalt call his name John.

14 And thou shalt have joy and gladness; and many shall rejoice at his birth.

15 For he shall be great in the sight of the Lord, and shall drink neither wine nor strong drink; and he shall be filled with the Holy Ghost, even from his mother's womb.

16 And many of the children of Israel shall he turn to the Lord their God.

17 And he shall go before him in the spirit and power of Elias, to turn the hearts of the fathers to the children, and the disobedient to the wisdom of the just; to make ready a people prepared for the Lord.

Fear of the angel (Luke 1:11-12). As Zacharias stood in the holy place, an angel appeared before him, standing beside the altar. This angel would later identify himself as Gabriel (vs. 19), the same angel who would appear to Mary in Nazareth six months later (vs. 26).

{The priest's initial response was similar to Mary's: "he was troubled, and fear fell upon him" (vs. 12).}[Q2] With his holy moment of divine service interrupted by this sudden appearance, it was only natural for Zacharias to be agitated and fearful, not knowing what the angel's presence meant.

Promise of a son (Luke 1:13-14). The angel quickly assured Zacharias that his presence meant only good news for the priest. There was no reason to fear, for {the angel was there to announce the answer to Zacharias's prayer: his wife, Elisabeth, would bear a son.}Q3

There is no specific prior mention of the two praying for a child or specifically a son, but this had surely been their prayer for many years. Yet it is also quite possible that this request had not been voiced for some time; the hope of being parents might have given way to hopelessness now that they both were getting well on in years (Luke 1:7).

Their desire and prayer for a child, however, was now about to be fulfilled in an even greater way than they could have imagined. Moreover, Gabriel even told Zacharias what the child was to be named (vs. 13). It was not to be a family name, as we learn later (vss. 59-63), but its significance apparently was in its meaning. This child, miraculously given to a previously barren mother now beyond normal childbearing age, would be named {John, which means "the Lord is gracious."}Q4

The angel's words in Luke 1:14 seem rather obvious and could apply to most any parents who welcome the birth of a child: "Thou shalt have joy and gladness." Yet the joy that John would bring to his parents would extend far beyond them. Not only would family and friends rejoice with them at his birth, but so also would many others who understood or would come to understand the role he would play in God's plan of salvation.

Prophecy concerning the son (Luke 1:15-17). The son who would be born to Zacharias and Elisabeth would bring joy to many people, and he would be "great in the sight of the Lord." No higher praise could be given to a person than this, and {years later Jesus essentially repeated it, saying, "Among them that are born of women there hath not risen a greater than John the Baptist" (Matt. 11:11).

In the description that follows, John's greatness is presented in terms of his character and his role in preparing the way for the Messiah's coming.}Q5

First, the angel said that John would drink "neither wine nor strong drink" (Luke 1:15). While this was a requirement for a Nazarite—a person specially set apart to God's service by a vow (Num. 6:2-6)—it does not necessarily mean that John was one since other requirements for a Nazarite are not mentioned. It does, however, suggest a special mission for John (cf. Luke 7:33).

{That unique mission also would be indicated by the work of the Holy Spirit in his life even before birth.}Q6 John would be filled with the Spirit "from his mother's womb" (Luke 1:15). This expression, which is applied to no one else in the New Testament, "emphasizes the fact that God chose him and equipped him from the very beginning" (Morris).

To be filled with the Spirit is to be controlled and empowered by God the Holy Spirit. John experienced this from the very beginning of His existence. Luke described Jesus Himself as "full of the Holy Ghost" (Luke 4:1). All others Luke described as being filled with the Spirit publicly proclaimed Jesus as Saviour, Lord, and Messiah (1:41-43, 67-75; cf. 2:25-32). And so it would be for John.

{John's future ministry, Gabriel said, would involve turning many people in Israel to "the Lord their God" (Luke 1:16). The Greek word for "turn" here is a word commonly used in the New Testament for spiritual conversion, or salvation (cf. Acts 9:35; 11:21; II Cor. 3:16; I Thess. 1:9).}Q7

The Jewish people were privileged

to have God's revelation in the Old Testament Scriptures, but the New Testament clearly indicates that the majority of them were blind to the revelation of God in Jesus Christ. Still, there were some—even many—of his fellow Jews whom John would turn back to the true God.

The angel then spoke words to Zacharias that were certainly familiar to this godly priest. He invoked the prophecy of Malachi 4:5-6, applying it to John. {John would go before the Lord—that is, Jesus the Messiah—in the spirit and power of Elijah. Like Elijah, John would be empowered by the Spirit of God.}Q8 While—unlike Elijah—John performed no miracles, "there was clearly present in his ministry and preaching the power of the Spirit" (Stein, *Luke,* B&H).

{The Spirit's power would be plainly evident in John's ministry, for his preaching would turn "the hearts of the fathers to the children, and the disobedient to the wisdom of the just" (Luke 1:17; cf. Mal. 4:6). What seems to be in view here are the results of people turning to the Lord,}Q9 with family relationships being restored and the formerly wicked, or "disobedient," humbly submitting to the wisdom that characterizes the righteous.

Interestingly, the prophecy in Malachi that Gabriel applied to John in Luke 1:17 is originally presented as referring to Elijah. This is why the Jewish people expected Elijah to return before the Messiah's arrival (cf. Matt. 17:10). John denied that he was Elijah (John 1:19-21), yet Jesus later identified John as Elijah (Matt. 11:12-14).

This mystery deepens in Matthew 17, where Jesus said that Elijah *will* yet "come, and restore all things" (vs. 11), but He also said that Elijah had already come and been rejected (vs. 12). The disciples understood this last comment to be a reference to John the Baptist. Some hypothesize that Jesus was saying that in some way, *"John could have been Elijah if Israel had accepted his message"* (Whitcomb, *The Rapture and Beyond,* Kainos). According to this theory, because John's message was rejected by the nation as a whole, Elijah will yet come at a later time just before Christ's return.

The result of John's ministry would be a people who were ready for the Lord's arrival. His primary work would be calling people to repentance so that they would be prepared to recognize and receive Israel's Messiah and Saviour, whom John would precede and introduce (cf. Matt. 3:1-12; Luke 3:1-18). John would be the one crying in the wilderness, preparing the way of the Lord (Luke 3:4-6; cf. Isa. 40:3-5).

THE RESPONSE AND THE REPERCUSSIONS

18 And Zacharias said unto the angel, Whereby shall I know this? for I am an old man, and my wife well stricken in years.

19 And the angel answering said unto him, I am Gabriel, that stand in the presence of God; and am sent to speak unto thee, and to shew thee these glad tidings.

20 And, behold, thou shalt be dumb, and not able to speak, until the day that these things shall be performed, because thou believest not my words, which shall be fulfilled in their season.

Answer of unbelief (Luke 1:18). We might think a message delivered by an angel of God would surely be believed immediately, but Zacharias could not escape the physical reality that both he and his barren wife were now old, and having a son at this stage of their lives seemed impossible. He wanted to believe the angel's words, but {he wanted a sign that would assure him that the joyous message was true.}Q10

Because we too are human, we can

fully understand Zacharias's doubts; but the demand for a sign revealed a significant lack of faith.

The realities of this life often challenge our faith. But when things seem impossible and hopeless and we are tempted to give up, we can still trust God and His Word. Even in the bleakest times, we can boldly and thankfully let our requests be known to God and be certain that "the peace of God, which passeth all understanding, shall keep [our] hearts and minds through Christ Jesus" (Phil. 4:7).

Consequence of unbelief (Luke 1:19-20). At this point the angel identified himself as Gabriel, one who stands "in the presence of God." Gabriel had been sent from God's very presence to bring this good news to Zacharias. Such "glad tidings" deserved a better response than Zacharias's doubt.

Zacharias would have immediately recognized the name Gabriel from Daniel 8:16 and 9:21, and any doubt about the genuineness of his message certainly must have dissolved. Still, there was a price to pay for the initial expression of unbelief.

Zacharias had requested a sign that the angel's words would be fulfilled. Now he was given a unique sign: he would be unable to speak until the day came that the things declared to him were accomplished. This indeed would be a sign, but it would also be a punishment, or chastisement, for his failure to believe the divine message, which certainly would be fulfilled at the proper time. That time came a little over nine months later when the newborn son of Zacharias and Elisabeth was to be named (Luke 1:59-64).

Hendriksen noted that God's justice was "tempered with mercy" (*Exposition of the Gospel According to Luke,* Baker). Because he did not believe the Lord's words given by Gabriel, Zacharias would suffer muteness, but it would be only

for a time. Like David and others who suffered for their sins, he was not abandoned by the God he loved and served.

This portion of Luke's Gospel sets the stage for the presentation of Christ's birth, as well as the beginning of His ministry, which was introduced by the divinely prepared forerunner. It gives us a glimpse of how God's eternal plan was carefully laid out and His instruments were chosen and prepared in accordance with what had already been prophesied. Nothing happens by chance in the world God sovereignly rules.

These verses also provide a gracious reminder that God's plan involves faithful but flawed people. We are all flawed, but let us be sure we always remain faithful followers of the Lord.

—Jarl K. Waggoner.

QUESTIONS

1. What made burning incense in the temple the pinnacle of Zacharias's priestly work?

2. How did Zacharias react to the angel's appearance?

3. What prayer did the angel say had been heard?

4. What does the name John mean?

5. How did the angel express John's greatness? How did Jesus later reaffirm this?

6. What evidence would point to the unique ministry of John in God's plan?

7. What would John's ministry entail?

8. To what Old Testament prophet did the angel liken John? Why?

9. What would result from John's ministry?

10. How did Zacharias respond to Gabriel's message?

—Jarl K. Waggoner.

Preparing to Teach the Lesson

This may be one of the most important and practical lessons of your teaching career. It bears on believing God and His truth in the face of impossibility. It may be that one of your students will come to faith in Christ and His Word through what you teach and the way you teach it. This is a great opportunity for you as a teacher and facilitator of God's Word. This lesson can really make a difference in your students' lives.

It may well be that all of us struggle with believing God. After all, much of what He tells us in His Word is counter to our culture's teaching and our own experience. But even just the reading of spiritual truth can be used by God to bring people to immediate faith. One thing our lesson shows us is that God will not let even our doubts overturn the blessings He has planned for us.

TODAY'S AIM

Facts: to see God at work in Zacharias's life in bringing him to faith in the angel's message.

Principle: to realize that God will work in our hearts to help us understand and receive His Word.

Application: to learn to respond to God's Word in faith quickly and consistently.

INTRODUCING THE LESSON

The Bible is the story of God and of humanity's relationship to God. We can learn a lot by seeing the dynamics of this relationship and its outcomes.

Much of the Bible is prophecy. In fact, God repeatedly says that prophecy and its fulfillment are a sure mark of the authenticity of His Word. No one but God can foretell an event and cause perfect and complete fulfillment every time. God could have simply carried out His plan to have John the Baptist born to this couple, but He chose instead to give them this prophecy, let them anticipate the birth, and live through the events that fulfilled the prophecy.

DEVELOPING THE LESSON.

1. God's hand in ordinary circumstances (Luke 1:8-10). Zacharias and Elisabeth were special in some ways, but in others were ordinary people like you and me. Zacharias was a priest, and he and Elisabeth were an exceptionally godly couple. They were older and past childbearing age, so Zacharias must have been functioning as a priest for a long time. It is thought that Zacharias had never handled the duty of offering the daily incense offering in the temple. Our text says he was chosen by lot to do it on this particular day.

Proverbs 16:33 says, "The lot is cast into the lap; but the whole disposing thereof is of the Lord." The Lord determined the outcome of the "lot," or in modern terms, the "coin toss." So what looked like an ordinary event was really a divine appointment. Scripture says that all our days were written in His book before we were born: "In thy book all my members were written . . . when as yet there was none of them" (Ps. 139:16). There is no such thing as a random happening. Our average day may be just the time for God to break through to us with a divine encounter of great significance and personal growth.

2. God's message at the perfect time (Luke 1:11-17). Zacharias was stunned and shaken by the appearance of an angel. He was rightly afraid. Have you ever noticed that the first words out of an angel's mouth tend to be along the lines of, "Do not be afraid"? The angel said that Zacharias's prayer had been heard. We have no scriptural mention of it, but it is probable that the godly couple had prayed for a child for years. We know they had prayed at least once, and it had been heard. Now was God's sovereign time to answer the prayer and send the forerunner of the Lord Jesus into this godly home. The answer was to be far bigger than the prayer!

We must keep praying. The circumstances of how it will be answered are not up to us. Our job is to pray. What a shame it would be to miss this golden opportunity!

3. God's proof to help the doubtful believe (Luke 1:18-20). Zacharias's answer to the angel was not total skepticism, but a cry for understanding. He could not see how this could happen. God does not mind helping us with believing. What the angel foretold seemed impossible from a human viewpoint (Zacharias and Elisabeth were beyond childbearing age), so Zacharias wanted to know how it could be so.

Furthermore, the angel had foretold that they would have a son and gave his name. He had also given instructions and an indication of John's ministry and purpose in being born as a forerunner of the Messiah.

The angel said his name was Gabriel. (He and Michael are the only two angels whose names are given in Scripture. They both are archangels of the highest rank.) Gabriel told Zacharias that he stood in the presence of God. In other words, Gabriel's normal position was beside the throne of God. His name, rank, and position meant he had to be speaking the truth.

Gabriel gave Zacharias a miraculous sign of the truth of the message. Zacharias would not be able to speak until he had given his newborn son the name "John." Every word of the angel's prophecy came true at the proper time.

ILLUSTRATING THE LESSON

God's messages to us can be communicated through life's daily circumstances.

GOD ANSWERS PRAYER

CONCLUDING THE LESSON

We should remember that the Scriptures were given to us for our instruction and training (II Tim. 3:16). This lesson has shown us once again that the ordinary, seemingly random happenings of life can suddenly become part of a divine encounter. In His infinite wisdom and power, God may choose to bring about something special and life-changing. It may result in a spiritual rebirth. We should always be open to His leading. A great way to do this is to make a daily habit of reading Scripture and praying. We can open ourselves to hearing a verse in a way that we have not previously done. We do not need a new revelation or new doctrine. Every word we think is from God must meet the test of compliance with the written Word of God.

ANTICIPATING THE NEXT LESSON

In our next lesson, we take a look at God's promises to David.

—*Brian D. Doud.*

PRACTICAL POINTS

1. Dependability pleases God; He rewards faithfulness (Luke 1:8-10; cf. Matt. 25:23).
2. We must keep an attitude of hospitality, always welcoming God (Luke 1:11).
3. Fear and anxiety blind us to the fact that God's timing is perfect. He is a good Father (Luke 1:12-13; cf. Isa. 65:24).
4. We should make sure our motivation is to please God (Luke 1:14-16).
5. We cannot serve the Lord without prepared hearts (vs. 17).
6. We do not please God when we ignore the facts, avoiding the truth before us (Luke 1:18-20; cf. Matt. 16:4; 17:17).

—Lendell Sims.

RESEARCH AND DISCUSSION

1. According to custom, Zacharias was chosen to burn incense in the temple. How did God use tradition and custom to foster His work?
2. Contrast the appearances of the Angel Gabriel to Zacharias and Mary. How are the two appearances similar and different?
3. What is the significance of Elijah being the point of reference in Luke 1:17?
4. Who in the Old Testament questioned a pronouncement from God? Does such questioning necessarily indicate a failure of faith?
5. Does the penalty given Zacharias seem unduly harsh?

—Lendell Sims.

ILLUSTRATED HIGH POINTS

In the presence of God (Luke 1:19)

Gabriel's purpose is to stand in the presence of God, as well as to speak to whom he is sent. This is much like the duties of a simple page. For years the page program in Congress used young men and women who assisted on the House floor or ran errands for the senators and representatives.

In the United Kingdom, a "Page of Honour" has the duty of carrying Queen Elizabeth's eighteen-foot train for the State Opening of Parliament. He then drapes her long train down the steps below her golden throne and takes his place standing beside her.

Like the angels, we were created with a simple purpose—to stand in God's presence (cf. Rev. 7:9-12) and speak to whom we are sent. Unlike the United Kingdom pages, the train we carry is not made of mere cloth but of the glory of God (cf. Isa. 6:1; John 12:41).

Because thou believest not my words (vs. 20)

Like the angels, priests were called to enter into God's presence (in the holy place) and then go out to minister.

On Tuesday, April 22, 2013, the Dow Jones Industrial Average took an alarming dive, falling 134 points in seconds. What had happened? A moment before, a tweet seemingly by the Associated Press read that there were two explosions in the White House and that the president was injured. The Associated Press computers had been hacked.

God could not allow the false report that might flow from Zacharias's unbelieving heart. False, unbelieving reports had repeatedly crippled the progress of Israel (cf. Num. 13:32, 14:36). How tiny yet world-altering is the human tongue (cf. Jas. 3:5)!

—Therese Greenberg.

Golden Text Illuminated

"Thy wife Elisabeth shall bear thee a son, and thou shalt call his name John. And thou shalt have joy and gladness; and many shall rejoice at his birth" (Luke 1:13-14).

This text concerns the birth of John the Baptist, who was another important part of God's messianic plan. God determined that the Saviour would benefit from a forerunner who would prepare the world for His entry. Our text points to two mighty effects of John's ministry—first in the lives of his family and then in the lives of the wider world, since many would rejoice over his birth.

Obviously, John's parents, Zacharias and Elisabeth, were greatly blessed to have a role in the fulfillment of God's promise to send the Saviour. Joy and gladness came to them; this was personal. We cannot look at these Bible characters merely as passive instruments in the hand of God. They were real people, and they personally received the grace of God in their lives. Let us always take the grace of God to heart in our lives so that it might instruct us in God's love and hold us strong in His mercy.

But the wider concern here is the joy and rejoicing that John's birth would bring to the many. His birth would have a widespread impact. His whole life and ministry would have a powerful role in preparing the way for the Lord Jesus. John's ministry exalted Christ, and the blessing of God's salvation came to many in those days.

John preached Christ, always making a clear distinction between himself and Jesus. He pointed others to the Lord, saying that he was not worthy to untie the sandal of the One who would come after him. In his day there was no greater preacher in the land than John, but his only intent was to point to the Messiah.

John served Christ, even though it ended up costing him his life. He willingly dropped back into obscurity after the Lord came on the scene, and then he was willing to pay the ultimate price of his own life for the sake of the truth.

After John's death, the Lord eulogized him as the greatest man ever born of a woman (Matt. 11:11). His was a life of willing service to Christ. Our world has many ideas of greatness, but in God's kingdom the greatest are those who willingly and sacrificially serve, as John did.

So John's whole life was consecrated to Christ. This is what led him to deemphasize the marks of earthly success. His modest diet and rough clothing were only reflections of a life that turned away from worldly success. He was unwavering in living for Christ. John the forerunner teaches us what being a follower of the Lord Jesus is all about. It is about consecration to the things of Christ, leaving in our wake a compelling and countercultural statement of the necessity of salvation and the ultimate futility of devotion to earthly attainments.

Let us be like John, a bold and burning light for Christ in the world (John 5:35). This is how to bring joy to a troubled and sad world. John pointed people to the joy of salvation. So today we are challenged to be lights to the world, bringing the joyful news of salvation to as many needy souls as we can.

—*Jeff VanGoethem.*

Heart of the Lesson

God always prepares the way for us. Sometimes He sends people ahead of us to pave a road for our easy travel. At other times He leads us by His Spirit so that we can make a way for others. John the Baptist was guided by the Holy Spirit; he prepared the way for Jesus.

1. Right place and right time (Luke 1:8-12). Our times and seasons are in God's hands. By God's divine plan He placed Zacharias in the temple, seemingly alone, to give him an encounter that would change his life forever. Zacharias went into the temple to burn incense while people outside the temple were praying. Incense is often symbolic of prayers. As incense burns, the fragrance rises upward, just as our prayers rise to heaven.

Zacharias and Elisabeth had been unable to conceive a child. In a culture that based one's worth on the ability to produce an heir, imagine the number of times they must have prayed for a child. As Zacharias was performing his priestly duty and burning the incense, an angel appeared. God had arranged for Zacharias to be in the temple at that time (cf. vs. 9).

God knew Zacharias was praying when He sent a messenger to him. We would expect prayer to be a two-way conversation. We want God to answer our prayers. He may not answer immediately. He may not answer in the way that we expect. Nevertheless, when God answers our prayers, it is always for a greater purpose than solely fulfilling our desires.

2. Great joy and gladness (Luke 1:13-14). As Zacharias began to catch his breath, he heard the angel speaking to him. "Zacharias: . . . thy prayer is heard; and thy wife Elisabeth shall bear thee a son, and thou shalt call his name John." The angel continued by telling Zacharias that he would have great joy and gladness and that many would rejoice at John's birth.

When you have a child, the birth affects others as well. His or her addition changes the world of your relatives, your friends, and most significantly, your world. In most cases, when friends and family learn of the pregnancy, they are overjoyed and excited in anticipation of the birth of this bundle of joy.

3. Anything but ordinary (Luke 1:15-20). Even before his conception, John the Baptist was destined to be anything but ordinary. The Angel Gabriel announced his birth to Zacharias, told him to name the boy John, and stated that he would be great in the sight of the Lord. The angel also declared that he would "go before [the Lord] in the spirit and power of Elias, to turn the hearts of the fathers to the children, and the disobedient to the wisdom of the just; to make ready a people prepared for the Lord."

Because Zacharias did not believe the words of the angel, he was unable to speak until the day John was circumcised. This was a sign in and of itself that the words Gabriel spoke were true. Can you imagine the stories Zacharias and Elisabeth told John as he was growing up about how his birth and his destiny had been foretold by God?

After four hundred years of God's silence, John the Baptist was given the privilege of awakening the hearts of God's people and preparing the way for Jesus. We too need to make a way for God in our lives.

—*Kristin Reeg.*

World Missions

In the human experience there is always a first. Someone or something is at the head of every line. Inventors always have a prototype. Businesses have founders, industries have pioneers, nations have forefathers, and all people have Adam as their common ancestor.

Zacharias and Elisabeth were chosen to give birth to the most important herald in history. Their son John would proclaim the coming of the Messiah, the Lamb of God. As Zacharias listened to the angel, he had difficulty believing that he, an old man, had been selected to bring such a prominent prophet into the world. Because of his unbelief, Zacharias was made unable to speak until his son was eight days old (Luke 1:59-64).

Being first is often a difficult position. Missionary trailblazers often face dangers, diseases, the unknown, and often violence. As they scout foreign lands to find unreached tribes and nations, they are exposed to these and other risks. Because of their efforts, millions have heard, responded to, and further spread the message of our Lord Jesus Christ.

Will and Paula accepted the challenge of becoming missionary pioneers in a country that was known to be hostile to Christians. Amid reports of persecution, this couple insisted that God had laid this nation on their hearts and that He was sending them there to fulfill their missionary assignment. Many in their home church attempted to talk this courageous couple out of their intentions, but Will and Paula were steadfast in their resolve. Much like John the Baptist, Will and Paula were confident in their missionary calling and determined to complete their work, despite the danger.

Will and Paula landed in their target nation only weeks after its government had declared a non-Christian faith as their national religion. Local authorities were allowed to harass, threaten, and even arrest those who held to unsanctioned beliefs.

The first objective was to locate Christian pastors in a particular urban area. God provided miracles as Will met three pastors within the first week. Most church groups had been driven underground, having only secret meetings in house churches. Their aim became to teach, build up, and supply these pastors. They held conferences for leaders in the city to help them support and network with one another. They also kept a running list of the physical and financial needs of the churches in the area. God blessed the efforts of Will and Paula throughout their six-week stay.

When Will and Paula returned to their home church, they reported several instances of the dangers they had faced. The home they had lived in was damaged by vandalism, and windows were broken by rocks. Will was once stopped by two policemen and detained for what turned out to be mistaken identity. They accused him of a serious crime, and one of the officers pointed a gun at him and threatened to shoot him.

God showed many times that His hand of protection was upon Will and Paula. His miraculous providence for them can remind us of the miracle He performed when He caused an old man and a barren woman to give birth to the forerunner of Jesus Christ. God has not changed, so we can believe that He will perform amazing works for us today.

—*Beverly Medley Jones.*

The Jewish Aspect

Zacharias the priest served at a very exciting time in the history of Israel and of the world. It is important to note that he and his wife had been filled with the Holy Spirit (Luke 1:41, 67). Their son, John, the Messiah's forerunner, was filled with the Holy Spirit from his mother's womb (vs. 15).

The filling of the Spirit in Zacharias and Elisabeth is suggestive of a small coterie of believers centered on the temple, nearly all of whom shared the uncommon filling of the Holy Spirit. They seemed to share a ministry of keeping the covenant promises of the King before the righteous.

Simeon, a righteous layman filled with the Spirit, was charged with bearing witness to the Christ Child, Jesus, born under the law as Saviour and Lord (Luke 2:27-30). Anna, a prophetess, served a similar function. She "departed not from the temple, but served God with fastings and prayers night and day" (vs. 37). She gave testimony of the promise of the Messiah (vs. 38).

The high priesthood was in the hands of the Sadducees. Sadducees were aristocrats who wielded much political power in Israel. The Sadducees accepted the authority of the Torah, the first five books of Moses, and held that the sayings of the fathers were without authority (Schurer, *A History of the Jewish People in the Time of Jesus Christ,* Hendrickson).

The Sadducees' doctrine generally alienated them from the traditionalist Pharisees. However, the two sects could cooperate when necessary. Some scholars suggest that they together incited Herod to slay John the Baptist (cf. Matt. 14:1-12).

In places the Old Testament speaks of "priests" without mention of the order of priests, the sons of Aaron, or the Levites in lesser service positions. Zacharias belonged to the sons of Aaron, "of the course of Abia" (Luke 1:5; cf. I Chr. 24:10). Elisabeth "was of the daughters of Aaron" (Luke 1:5), which shows that both were of Aaron's lineage.

The godly couple lived in the high country of Judah, mere miles from Jerusalem. Because there were so many priests at the time of Jesus' birth, Zacharias probably had only one day in a lifetime career to actually serve in the temple worship. Residing outside Jerusalem spared Zacharias a good deal of the pseudo-spiritual chicanery of the Pharisees and Sadducees.

The Sadducees of Jesus' day were opposed to belief in miracles or angels. This antisupernaturalism fits into the popular heresy of no life after death, and, of course, no Messiah. Sadduceeism is attractive to Reform (liberal) rabbis of our day.

The high priest was often both the spiritual and the civil ruler of the people, except when they were under foreign rulers, like the Roman authorities. Life was good for the high priest, for he was required to preside only on the great Day of Atonement. The rest of the year, he could sacrifice or leave it to others as he chose (Schurer).

The high priest's robes were beautifully made and of rich material. They were to speak of the holiness of the high office. On the solitary day he entered the Holy of Holies, the high priest wore a simple, well-made robe.

The temple was a repository of great riches. Stacks and stacks of gold and silver utensils were held in reserve. Priests' robes were also plentiful. Great sums of money were in the treasury, and other nations knew of this and were anxious to plunder the riches.

—*Lyle P. Murphy.*

Guiding the Superintendent

Each January, the president of the United States presents his annual State of the Union address. Prior to his presentation, the sergeant-at-arms of the United States House of Representatives introduces the president. The sergeant-at-arms announces the president by saying, "Mister (or Madam) Speaker, the President of the United States."

This week's lesson shows the Lord's preparation for the Messiah's coming. We will be reminded that a forerunner was put in place to lead the way for the Saviour's ministry.

DEVOTIONAL OUTLINE

1. The promise of a son (Luke 1:8-14). Zacharias was a priest. As had been determined by lot, Zacharias was assigned to burn incense in the sanctuary. Exodus 30:7-8 gave the significance of this burning of incense. As Zacharias did this, people were praying outside the temple.

While Zacharias was completing his priestly responsibilities, he had an angelic encounter. When this happened he understandably was overcome with fear. The appearance of an angel was no doubt an overwhelming experience.

Understanding Zacharias's situation, the angel attempted to calm him. The angel told him that there was no reason to fear. The angel informed him that God had heard the prayers he and Elisabeth had spoken. God was giving them a son. He assigned the child a name—he would be called John. The angel promised Zacharias that John's birth would bring joy and excitement.

2. The promised forerunner (Luke 1:15-17). The angel provided Zacharias with more detailed information concerning John. In the Lord's eyes, John would be great. He would not drink wine or alcoholic beverages. He would be filled with the Holy Spirit even before he was born.

John's ministry pricked the hearts of the Jewish people. As the result of John's ministry, many would turn to God. John would be similar to Elijah in his tenacity, power, and anointing. He would have a commanding impact, preparing Israel for Christ's ministry. People's lives would change from rebellion to willingly hearing words of godly wisdom.

3. Zacharias's doubt (Luke 1:18-20). After hearing the angel's message, Zacharias expressed doubt. He could not fathom how someone the age of Elisabeth and himself could have a son.

The angel identified himself as Gabriel. He indicated that God sent him to tell Zacharias the good news. However, because Zacharias doubted the message, he would be stricken, unable to speak until after John was born.

CHILDREN'S CORNER

Show children the care God took to prepare for Jesus' coming. Explain to them how God used John to announce Jesus to the world.

Children can also learn that God can use even them if they are willing to trust Him and be His helpers. They do not have to know a lot to have an impact on their friends and other people. They can simply talk about Jesus and what He means to them. If they have memorized some Bible verses, they may have opportunities to share those with some people. God is pleased to use the simple faith of little children to accomplish His will.

—*Tyrone Keith Carroll, Sr.*

SCRIPTURE LESSON TEXT

II SAM. 7:4 And it came to pass that night, that the word of the LORD came unto Nathan, saying,

5 Go and tell my servant David, Thus saith the LORD, Shalt thou build me an house for me to dwell in?

6 Whereas I have not dwelt in *any* house since the time that I brought up the children of Israel out of Egypt, even to this day, but have walked in a tent and in a tabernacle.

7 In all *the places* wherein I have walked with all the children of Israel spake I a word with any of the tribes of Israel, whom I commanded to feed my people Israel, saying, Why build ye not me an house of cedar?

8 Now therefore so shalt thou say unto my servant David, Thus saith the LORD of hosts, I took thee from the sheepcote, from following the sheep, to be ruler over my people, over Israel:

9 And I was with thee whithersoever thou wentest, and have cut off all thine enemies out of thy sight, and have made thee a great name, like unto the name of the great *men* that *are* in the earth.

10 Moreover I will appoint a place for my people Israel, and will plant them, that they may dwell in a place of their own, and move no more; neither shall the children of wickedness afflict them any more, as beforetime,

11 And as since the time that I commanded judges *to be* over my people Israel, and have caused thee to rest from all thine enemies. Also the LORD telleth thee that he will make thee an house.

12 And when thy days be fulfilled, and thou shalt sleep with thy fathers, I will set up thy seed after thee, which shall proceed out of thy bowels, and I will establish his kingdom.

13 He shall build an house for my name, and I will stablish the throne of his kingdom for ever.

14 I will be his father, and he shall be my son. If he commit iniquity, I will chasten him with the rod of men, and with the stripes of the children of men:

15 But my mercy shall not depart away from him, as I took *it* from Saul, whom I put away before thee.

16 And thine house and thy kingdom shall be established for ever before thee: thy throne shall be established for ever.

NOTES

God's Promise to David

Lesson Text: II Samuel 7:4-16

Related Scriptures: I Chronicles 17:1-15; I Samuel 16:1-13;
Psalm 89:1-5; I Kings 8:12-26; Psalm 132:1-18

TIME: about 1000 B.C.

PLACE: Jerusalem

GOLDEN TEXT—"He shall build an house for my name, and I will stablish the throne of his kingdom for ever" (II Samuel 7:13).

Introduction

There are many remarkable evidences that the Bible is the inspired Word of God, but one of the most striking is the fulfillment of Old Testament prophecies.

Among the multitude of fulfilled prophecies are those related to the first advent of Jesus Christ. The Gospel writers and apostles have pointed out numerous ways He fulfilled prophecy given from the time of Adam and Eve to the book of Malachi. Our lesson this week will examine one of the most striking prophecies, a promise of great blessing to come.

Jesus was not only the divine Son of God but also the human descendant of King David. For centuries the Jewish people longed for the reign of the Davidic Messiah.

These hopes were based on a covenant God had made with David and his offspring. This covenant was given by the Lord at the height of David's reign, and its terms were repeated in numerous psalms and prophecies thereafter. Here we look at God's original promise.

LESSON OUTLINE

I. DAVID'S OFFER DECLINED— II Sam. 7:4-7

II. DAVID'S FORTUNES PROTECTED—II Sam. 7:8-11a

III. DAVID'S DYNASTY ESTABLISHED—II Sam. 11b-16

Exposition: Verse by Verse

DAVID'S OFFER DECLINED

II SAM. 7:4 And it came to pass that night, that the word of the Lord came unto Nathan, saying,

5 Go and tell my servant David, Thus saith the LORD, Shalt thou build me an house for me to dwell in?

6 Whereas I have not dwelt in any house since the time that I brought up the children of Israel out of Egypt, even to this day, but have walked in a tent and in a tabernacle.

7 In all the places wherein I have walked with all the children of Israel spake I a word with any of the tribes of Israel, whom I commanded to feed my people Israel, saying, Why build ye not me an house of cedar?

The Lord's question for David (II Sam. 7:4-5). David was by this time well established as king (vs. 1). He had earned the approval of all the tribes of Israel, had defeated his major enemies, and was living in his own house in Jerusalem. He had also assigned the ark of the covenant a place in the city.

But David was not satisfied with this. He thought the ark deserved a better dwelling place (vs. 2). His own house was a luxurious dwelling of cedar, while God's ark was only surrounded by curtains. Curtains had been fine for the nomadic life of the wilderness, but surely the ark deserved a better place now.

{David implied to Nathan the prophet that he intended to build a proper house for God, and Nathan hastily agreed}Q1 (vss. 2-3). He was touched by the sincerity of David's intentions. But he had not consulted the Lord about the matter, and that night the Lord spoke to him and corrected his advice (vs. 4). The rest of our passage, then, is God's revelation to David through Nathan.

This revelation began with a question: "Shalt thou build me an house for me to dwell in?" (vs. 5). This question anticipated a negative answer (cf. I Chr. 17:4). It implied that the initiative for building a temple should come from God Himself, not a king. This is evident from the verses that follow. If He had needed or wanted a temple, He would have asked.

The question also implied that if a temple was to be built, {David was not the one to do it. The Lord was not opposed to the idea (cf. II Sam. 7:13), but He reserved the right to designate both the person and the time to do it. David was unsuitable for building a temple

because he was a man of war who had shed much blood (I Kgs. 5:3; I Chr. 22:7-8; 28:2-3).}Q1 God wanted it to be a house of peace, so Solomon, a man of peace, would build it in a tranquil time.

The Lord's previous dwelling (II Sam. 7:6-7). The Lord reminded David that He had been satisfied with the place of worship already designated. More than four hundred years had passed since the Exodus from Egypt. After the Exodus, He had given specific instructions about the place He wanted for worship (Deut. 12:5-14). There He would live among His people.

{"In a tent and in a tabernacle" (II Sam. 7:6) can be translated "in a tent as a dwelling." There God "walked" with Israel as they traversed the desert.}Q2 He went wherever they went, giving guidance, protection, provision, and discipline. And after they had reached their land, His ark of the covenant remained with them, though no temple then existed.

In light of this history, the Lord asked another question: In all the places He had accompanied them, had He ever asked why the tribes of Israel had not built Him a house of cedar? David was invited to review every location in which God had walked with them. He would look in vain for any command to build a luxurious temple.

There is some question about the words "the tribes of Israel, whom I commanded to feed my people Israel" (vs. 7). We have no record that God ever assigned a shepherding role to the tribes of Israel. The passage parallel to this in I Chronicles 17:6 uses the word "judges" instead of "tribes." There is a difference of only one letter in these two Hebrew words, so perhaps our text originally read "judges." The tribes, of course, could have acted as shepherds through the judges who arose from within them.

In any case, the Lord made it clear

that He had never demanded of former leaders that they build Him a temple. He had been satisfied with the tabernacle, and He still was. The time for a temple had not yet come. He had a dwelling among His people, and that was the most important thing. It is worthwhile for us today to reflect on this when considering whether imposing structures are significant to God.

DAVID'S FORTUNES PROTECTED

8 Now therefore so shalt thou say unto my servant David, Thus saith the Lord of hosts, I took thee from the sheepcote, from following the sheep, to be ruler over my people, over Israel:

9 And I was with thee whithersoever thou wentest, and have cut off all thine enemies out of thy sight, and have made thee a great name, like unto the name of the great men that are in the earth.

10 Moreover I will appoint a place for my people Israel, and will plant them, that they may dwell in a place of their own, and move no more; neither shall the children of wickedness afflict them any more, as beforetime,

11a And as since the time that I commanded judges to be over my people Israel, and have caused thee to rest from all thine enemies. Also the Lord telleth thee that he will make thee an house.

The Lord's care for David (II Sam. 7:8-9). The Lord now began to reveal what He really had in mind for David and Israel. He had something even better for him and his descendants—an eternal covenant. Though this passage does not use the word "covenant," other texts that refer to these promises do (cf. II Sam. 23:5; Ps. 89:3).

{God first reviewed all He had done for David to bring him to this point. He referred to him as "my servant" (II Sam. 7:8)—a title reserved for a select few, such as Abraham, Moses, and Caleb. Thus, although it appears to be a humbling title, it actually was a term of honor. To raise him to this position, God had taken him from the "sheepcote" (pasture), where he had been caring for sheep.

From that humble status, the Lord had promoted David to be "ruler over my people, over Israel." "My people" emphasizes that Israel was not an ordinary nation; it belonged to God. And David was chosen to shepherd this chosen people. What a contrast to watching over the sheep—and what an honor!}^Q3

Since the day Samuel anointed David, the Lord had been with him wherever he went. He not only preserved him from his enemies; He had defeated them all. The Amalekites, Philistines, Jebusites, Saul, and all other foes had been removed or subdued. For many years, David's anointing might have appeared meaningless, but the One who promised him the kingdom preserved him until he had actually obtained it.

Now the Lord promised to increase David's stature even more. "Have made thee a great name" (vs. 9) should probably read "*will* make thee a great name." David's name would come to be honored among "the great men that are in the earth." He would be remembered as one of the giants of history. Unlike Saul, David never sought this reputation for himself. His promotion had come about solely through the sovereign will of God.

The Lord's care for Israel (II Sam. 7:10-11a). God's promotion of David was part of His larger purpose to preserve and bless Israel. He would "plant them, that they may dwell in a place of their own, and move no more." There they would be secure; their enemies would not "afflict them . . . as beforetime." "Beforetime" refers to the chaotic time of the judges, when foes had attacked relentlessly.

{The promise of a land for Israel had been a prominent feature of God's covenant with Abraham (Gen. 15:7- 21). David's conquests had secured much of this territory, but peace was still not a reality. It would remain for Solomon to achieve this promised goal (cf. I Kgs. 4:21-25).

But our text implies that Israel's rest in their own land would be permanent: they would move no more, and their enemies would afflict them no more (II Sam. 7:10). This was not achieved in Solomon's day. Since then they have been exiled twice, and enemies still threaten them to this day. Later prophets continued to tell of a final restoration and peace for Israel (cf. Jer. 32:37-44; Ezek. 39:25-29; Zech. 10:6-12), and this has not yet been completed. It remains for the Messiah to accomplish.}[Q4]

DAVID'S DYNASTY ESTABLISHED

11b Also the Lord telleth thee that he will make thee an house.

12 And when thy days be fulfilled, and thou shalt sleep with thy fathers, I will set up thy seed after thee, which shall proceed out of thy bowels, and I will establish his kingdom.

13 He shall build an house for my name, and I will stablish the throne of his kingdom for ever.

14 I will be his father, and he shall be my son. If he commit iniquity, I will chasten him with the rod of men, and with the stripes of the children of men:

15 But my mercy shall not depart away from him, as I took it from Saul, whom I put away before thee.

16 And thine house and thy kingdom shall be established for ever before thee: thy throne shall be established for ever.

The promise of a ruling house (II Sam. 7:11b). There is now a play on the word "house." {David wanted to *build* a house for the Lord (a tem-

ple), but the Lord declared that He would *make* David a house (a ruling dynasty).}[Q5] Not content to make David a great king personally, He would guarantee the continuation of the throne to his posterity as well. And the promise was unconditional, an exhibition of sheer grace.

The promise of an approved heir (II Sam. 7:12-15). God now looked beyond David's lifetime. He promised, "I will set up thy seed after thee, which shall proceed out of thy bowels, and I will establish his kingdom." {The Lord would install an heir who had not yet been born. David knew by this that none of his existing sons, who at that time numbered at least six and possibly even nine (cf. I Chr. 3:1-9), would succeed him. As revealed later, Solomon would be his heir.}[Q6]

"I will establish his kingdom" (II Sam. 7:12) uses a verb that speaks of bringing something into being and making it certain. It is especially used of God's works, such as Creation, which stand firm (cf. Pss. 24:1-2; 119:90; Prov. 3:19). But it also is used of His direction in establishing kingdoms, kings, and dynasties (cf. I Sam. 13:13; II Sam. 5:12; Ps. 89:4). So here God committed Himself to making the kingdom of David's heir certain and steadfast (cf. I Chr. 17:11; 22:10).

{The Lord declared that this heir "shall build an house for my name" (II Sam. 7:13).}[Q7] Here "house" is used of a literal building, and it would be a temple for the Lord. In Scripture, "name" usually signified the person himself. Thus, a house for God's name was one in which His very presence dwelled. Though He is omnipresent, He condescended to live in a special way among His people.

Solomon fully understood the role the Lord had given him. When negotiating with Hiram of Tyre for materials for building the temple, he recalled God's promise to his father (I Kgs. 5:2-5).

And when he dedicated the completed structure, he recalled before all the people the covenant that had prepared the way for this joyous day (8:15-20).

The Lord also promised David that He would "stablish the throne of his (Solomon's) kingdom for ever" (II Sam. 7:13). Although Solomon would eventually die, his "throne," or dignity and power, would never end. {The right to the Davidic throne would continue to the rest of David's descendants perpetually and, eventually, eternally in Christ (cf. Luke 1:31-33). This was possible because Christ Himself is eternal.}[Q8]

Regarding Solomon, the Lord also promised, "I will be his father, and he shall be my son" (II Sam. 7:14; cf. I Chr. 22:9-10). With all the tenderness of a father, God would establish an intimate relationship with him. {Yet as a father has to chastise a son when he goes astray, so God promised to chastise Solomon.}[Q9] He would use other men to discipline him for his sin.

Solomon did, indeed, suffer "the stripes of the children of men" (II Sam. 7:14) when he sinned (I Kgs. 11:14, 23, 26). But the Lord also vowed, "My mercy shall not depart away from him, as I took it from Saul" (II Sam. 7:15). Saul had been rejected and his dynasty cut off because he disobeyed God (I Sam. 13:13-14; 15:22-28). But God promised He would not reject Solomon—though he might have deserved it.

The promise of an eternal kingdom (II Sam. 7:16). On this note of covenant faithfulness, the Lord concluded His message to David through Nathan. His "house," "kingdom," and "throne" would be established and remain fixed forever. Because of apostasy there were long stretches during which no king occupied David's throne. But there was always a Davidic descendant *available* to occupy it. David's dynasty culminated with Jesus, God's Son and David's son, appeared and claimed the kingdom.

Jesus claimed the legal right to the throne through His legal father, Joseph, who had descended from David through Solomon (Matt. 1:6-16). But He claimed lineal descent from David through His mother, Mary, who had descended from another son of David, Nathan (Luke 3:23-31). Through Him alone could the kingdom be eternal, as Gabriel told Mary (1:32-33).

{The climax of Jesus' reign is still future, awaiting His return (cf. Isa. 11:1-10; Dan. 7:13-14; Rev. 19:11-16). But its fulfillment is just as certain as His first advent, for it is based on the covenant faithfulness of the God of David.}[Q10]

—Robert E. Wenger.

QUESTIONS

1. Why did David want to build a temple for the Lord? Why was he not the right person to do so?

2. How had God lived among His people before David's time?

3. Summarize what the Lord had done for David to this point.

4. What did God plan to do in the future for David and Israel? When will Israel's goal be reached?

5. What did God mean when He promised to make David a house?

6. How do we know David's heir was not one of his older sons?

7. What work did God say David's heir would accomplish?

8. How was it possible for David's dynasty to be eternal?

9. What would happen to David's heir if he should go astray?

10. Has Jesus yet fulfilled the Davidic covenant? Explain.

—Robert E. Wenger.

Preparing to Teach the Lesson

The prophecies of Israel's coming Messiah picture Him as Israel's anointed King. A vital element in this role is that He would be of the lineage of King David. In this lesson your class should gain an understanding of how this promise began.

We will also examine how this future King will reign forever on David's throne. We still await the day when Christ will fulfill this promise.

TODAY'S AIM

Facts: to show that when David sought to build a temple for God, God instead promised to build a dynasty for him—an eternal kingdom ruled over by His Son, the eternal King.

Principle: to show that the coming of Christ was in keeping with God's covenant with David, a covenant that pointed the way toward the Messiah's arrival.

Application: to show that as God prepared for the coming of Christ by means of His covenant with David, we can be assured that He is in control of history and that all that He has promised will come to pass.

INTRODUCING THE LESSON

David was secure in his kingdom. He had successfully transported the tabernacle and the ark of the covenant to Jerusalem. He was living in his royal residence. Jerusalem could now officially be recognized as the capital of Israel.

As David enjoyed this time of peace, he expressed his desire to replace the tabernacle with a permanent temple. God used this opportunity to establish one more step in His plans to send the Messiah. By making His covenant with David, He established that the lineage of David would be the line through which the Messiah would come and upon whose throne He would sit.

DEVELOPING THE LESSON

1. God's response to David's plan (II Sam. 7:4-7). Nathan the prophet was initially in agreement with David's desire to build a temple for the Lord. David was a godly man who had repeatedly exhibited faith and dependence on the Lord and upon whom the Lord's blessings had been clearly evident. Nathan saw no reason to dissuade the God-centered plans of a godly king. He encouraged David to pursue his plans.

Discuss what God revealed to Nathan. What was God's main point? Even though David's plans were well-intentioned, what do we need to learn about God's greater plans and will? What does this tell us about our own plans?

God began His message with a rhetorical question on the order of "Can you build a house for God?" It is not possible to build a structure that can contain God. David's intention was to build a proper, permanent building for the worship of God that would replace the tabernacle, which was temporary and portable in nature. His own house was more sturdy and permanent than that within which the priests ministered. However, God's intention was to narrow even further the human lineage through which He would fulfill His promises.

David lived until 971 B.C. The Exodus from Egypt took place in 1445 B.C., with the construction of the tabernacle taking place in 1444 B.C. God told Nathan that He had met and led Israel by means of the tabernacle. At any point in that period, God could have instructed His people to build a more permanent structure. However, the tabernacle had served His purposes.

Draw a time line on the board. First, track the time from the Exodus to David. Next, track the time from David to the birth of Christ, around 6 B.C. Finally, track the time from Christ to the present, noting that the fulfillment of the Davidic covenant with Christ's reign being fully manifest is yet future.

2. Appointment of kings for God's people (II Sam. 7:8-11*a*). God reminded David of his humble beginnings as a poor shepherd. He had raised David to be the king over Israel, God's chosen people. God also had continually watched over him. Since the days of the judges, God had placed His leaders in position. He was about to reveal to David His plans for His future King, who would come through David's line.

Point out to your class that God orders history to fulfill His plans. When He told David through Nathan that He was now going to build a house for David, He was further laying in place His plans for the coming of Christ.

Long before He had given directions to Moses about the construction of the tabernacle and its furnishings, God had made His covenant with Abraham, promising to make him a blessing to all the world (Gen. 12:1-3; 13:14-17; 15:18-21; 17:1-8).

From the beginning God had promised to send His Messiah, who would redeem mankind (Gen. 3:15). Over time, the prophecies of the Messiah became more specific and narrow. First God selected Abraham. He then narrowed the promise through Isaac and then through Jacob (Israel). Next, He narrowed the promise to the tribe of Judah, and now, by Nathan's prophecy, to David.

3. An eternal covenant with David (II Sam. 7:11*b*-16). God's covenant with David extended far beyond his own life. His seed, or descendant, would inherit an eternal throne. God promised him a dynasty on the throne. From here on, the Messiah would be identified as the Son of David. This term became synonymous with the Messiah (Matt. 1:1; 9:27; 12:23; 15:22; 20:30-31; 21:9; 22:42). Have your students look up these verses.

Isaiah wrote that the Messiah would reign "upon the throne of David" (Isa. 9:7). The coming millennial kingdom will be ruled over by a Davidic king (Jer. 30:4-11; Ezek. 34:23-24; 37:24-25).

David's final words recalled God's promise (II Sam. 23:1-5).

ILLUSTRATING THE LESSON

When God reveals that He has a plan for us, He will fulfill that plan. Count on it.

GOD WILL FULFILL
HIS PROMISES

God's
Promises

COUNT ON THEM

CONCLUDING THE LESSON

God revealed to David a narrowing of His focus for sending the Messiah. The coming Redeemer would be a King of David's descent and would reign from his throne forever.

ANTICIPATING THE NEXT LESSON

In the next lesson we will examine the unfolding of God's covenant with David through the birth of Christ, the King whose reign will one day be fully manifest.

—*Carter Corbrey.*

PRACTICAL POINTS

1. The Lord is always ready to guide us as He works out His plans (II Sam. 7:4-7).
2. God's perfect character means He provides everything we need, since we can do nothing on our own (vss. 8-9).
3. We trust our Heavenly Father more when we realize how He fulfills His promises to us (vss. 10-11).
4. The Lord provides for us in even the smallest ways (vss. 12-13).
5. If God disciplines us, it is because, as His children, we have a family relationship with Him (II Sam. 7:14; cf. Heb. 12:6).
6. The Lord's consistent care for us provides stability in an unstable world (II Sam. 7:15-16).
—Anne Adams.

RESEARCH AND DISCUSSION

1. Was David disappointed when God did not allow his temple plans? Why or why not? Have you ever felt God's leading to cancel your plans in favor of His? How did you feel? What did you learn?
2. Is God's power restricted geographically? How does that affect your Christian life? Does God's great power reassure you or frighten you?
3. In II Samuel 7:10, God promised that Israel would never again be troubled by evil men or displaced from their land. How will this promise be kept? Discuss.
4. God's promises concerned David's spiritual heritage. How do you define your spiritual heritage?
—Anne Adams.

ILLUSTRATED HIGH POINTS

Build me an house? (II Sam. 7:5)

Sometimes God overrules our plan to bless Him with His own plan to bless us. As a new Christian, I wanted to reach my community for Christ. I set out to start a dial-a-prayer line.

Thankfully, my plan failed. Weeks later, I felt a strong desire to walk our city's streets and tell strangers about Jesus. God's plan began to unfold for me. I met Christians who helped me organize and expand the street ministry. Three decades later, I direct Reach and Rescue Ministries, an evangelistic outreach to the homeless.

King David sincerely desired to build God a house. But God had plans to build David a house—an eternal lineage that would include the Messiah Himself.

Shall be established for ever (vs. 16)

A fifth-grade class in Medina, Ohio, planted a time capsule in 1968 to commemorate the town's sesquicentennial. It was ceremoniously buried in the lawn of the town square, to be opened at the bicentennial in 2018. Pictures, newspaper articles, and the personal writings of the ten-year-olds would be revealed then.

Multiple changes have occurred since the time capsule was buried. Hairstyles and fashions have morphed over the decades. The lawn of the town square has been transfigured, becoming a meeting place for festivals, markets, and art shows. And untold transformations have occurred in the minds and bodies of those fifth-graders.

Everything on earth undergoes change. But the Word of God does not alter at all. God's promise to David established his kingdom forever. It was fulfilled in Jesus Christ, whose throne will endure throughout eternity.
—Beverly Jones.

Golden Text Illuminated

"He shall build an house for my name, and I will stablish the throne of his kingdom for ever" (II Samuel 7:13).

With this promise to David, God gave His final covenantal clue about the lineage of His coming Messiah. These clues began in the Garden with the promise that the woman's seed would crush the head of the serpent (Gen. 3:15). Each additional clue narrowed down through whom the seed would come: Abraham, Isaac, Jacob, Judah (Gen. 17:7, 19; 26:4; 28:14; 49:10).

In this week's golden text, God announces His plans for David's kingdom. To David, this promise surely was one of great comfort. After all, Israel's first king, Saul, was removed without ever having a son on the throne, let alone any kind of dynasty (house). Now God was saying David's son would have a never-ending kingdom. Who was this son of whom God spoke?

We learn later that Solomon is the son that built the first temple (I Kgs. 8:20, 27), yet he was soon unfaithful to God, being distracted by the blessings God had given him. Solomon's son Rehoboam saw the nation split under his rule. The dynasty was on shaky ground. Who was this son of whom God spoke?

Despite a divided kingdom, God was faithful to His promise to David. Throughout the historical accounts in Kings and Chronicles, David had an heir to the throne. A few followed in the footsteps of David, seeking to rule in a godly way (II Kgs. 18:1-8; 23:1-27). But none totally fulfilled the promise.

Upon the return from Babylon, David's descendant Zerubbabel oversaw the building of the second temple (Ezra 3:8; Zech. 4:9); yet he never became king. He was only a governor appointed by Darius. Who was this son of whom God spoke?

In the Psalms, the promise to David is recalled several times. In Psalm 89, the promise to David is a sign of the steadfast and faithful love of God toward His people. In Psalm 132, the psalmist is asking the Lord to remember the work David did to prepare for the building of the temple (vss. 1-5) and for the Lord to uphold His promise of a Davidic dynasty (vss. 10-12). All of Israel looked for this promised son.

As we come to the New Testament, we learn who this promised son of David is! He is made known in Gabriel's announcement to Mary. The son that she bears would be given the throne of David and his kingdom would be eternal (Luke 1:32-33). Matthew opens his Gospel account by establishing Jesus as a son of David and therefore a rightful heir to the throne. Matthew reinforces this with the arrival of the Magi looking for the King of the Jews (Matt. 2:1-12).

Israel's religious leaders had not lost sight of this promise to David (Matt. 22:41-46). The Jewish leaders wanted a sign from Jesus showing that He had the authority to cleanse the temple. He responded that He would raise a new temple (His body) three days after it was destroyed (John 2:13-22).

Thanks be to God for the blessing that Jesus is the promised Son of David (Rev. 5:5-14; 19:11-16), and He himself is the perfect temple built for God's name (Rev. 21:22). Today believers around the world reap the benefit of God's fulfilled promise to David.

—K. Hawver.

Heart of the Lesson

"On November 25, 1895, a cornerstone of ice was laid in Leadville, Colorado— the beginning of the largest ice palace ever built in America. In an effort to bolster the town's sagging economy, the citizens staged a winter carnival.

"On New Year's Day of 1896, the town turned out for the grand opening. The immense palace measured 450 x 320 feet. The towers that flanked the entrance were 90 feet high. Inside was a 16,000-square-foot skating rink. But by the end of March the palace was melting away, along with the hopes of Leadville. The thousands of visitors had spent very little" (*Today in the Word,* August 4, 1993).

The temporal nature of life on earth always tempers any fascination that the Christian may have for even the best this world has to offer. In this week's lesson, we become fascinated with God's promise to David because of its eternal nature.

1. God's communication with Nathan (II Sam. 7:4-7). King David had established a luxurious home in which to live and experienced a season of comfortable peace (vs. 1). In the midst of this, David was concerned that the worship of the Lord was centered in the tabernacle, a temporary, tent-like structure.

King David then called in Nathan the prophet and shared his concern (II Sam. 7:2). Nathan encouraged King David to fulfill the desires of his heart (vs. 3). That night the Lord corrected Nathan, reminding him that He had never commanded anyone to build Him an earthly house.

The struggle that the Christian experiences on earth between temporal, earthly desires and eternal, spiritual realities is incredibly tenacious. What is even more tenacious is God's intervention in this struggle as He lovingly and tenderly challenges the believer to embrace His eternal nature and live with an energetic passion fueled by eternal hope.

2. God's covenant with David (II Sam. 7:8-16). The remainder of this week's lesson text summarizes God's unconditional covenant promise to King David, which included the following provisions: (1) David would have a son who would succeed him on the throne; (2) the earthly house that David desired to build would be constructed by his son; (3) the throne of David's kingdom would be continued forever.

In summary, Nathan revealed God's words that King David's house, kingdom, and throne would be established forever. God's covenant promise was partially fulfilled in Solomon, David's son. But the promise goes far beyond Solomon in that King David's kingdom, throne, and house were established forever. The ultimate fulfillment of God's covenant promise to King David is satisfied in the Person and work of the Lord Jesus Christ.

God's Word reveals that followers of Jesus Christ experience life on the earth as foreigners in a strange and temporary place (cf. Heb. 11:13; I Pet. 2:11). God's Word also reveals that followers of Jesus Christ have received mercy that has extracted them from a life of evil darkness and transferred them into a life of spiritual light. With this comes the responsibility to proclaim the excellent character of their Saviour (cf. I Pet. 2:9-10).

Fulfilling this holy responsibility requires that the follower of Jesus Christ prioritize the eternal above the temporal. Christians should joyfully seek first God's eternal kingdom (cf. Matt. 6:33).

—*Thomas R. Chmura*

World Missions

It is easy for us Christians to forget that we are part of a great covenant between God and man. God always keeps His word, but as sinful human beings, we tend to forget to keep our part, and often we break our promises. This breaks the heart of God as He waits for us to return to Him. A covenant is more than a contract; it is a binding promise. When our good God is part of this plan, we can be sure that all faithful parties will benefit. This week He reminds us of what lies ahead for the faithful.

Church history is dotted with many martyrs who gave up their lives for their faith in Jesus. One such man was the bishop of Smyrna named Polycarp. When he was told that he would soon be burned at the stake for his faith in Jesus, he replied, "But why do you delay? Come do what you will." One must then ask what gave this ordinary man such courage in the face of death. The simple answer is that he was living for an eternal kingdom. This life was just a bridge to that eternal kingdom.

As believers in Jesus, it is so important for us to realize that our stay on this earth is only temporary and that we have a destination of more importance beyond this life. Sometimes, despite its hardships, this world glitters a little too much, and we easily lose sight of that greater goal. We are called to give this message to the world. We are to show them that the hardships of this world hardly compare to the glory that lies ahead that God has already prepared for us (Rom. 8:18).

We will remember the idea of covenant that we mentioned at the beginning. This has to do with the character of our God, who loves us so much and, yes, keeps His promises. When God tells us something, we can trust Him. We cannot see what He is preparing for us in the future, and we may ask ourselves whether it is worth waiting for. Those who have already trusted Him know the truth. It is now our task to spread the good news of this gospel to the rest of the world so that they know the truth too.

Only this past weekend, I took a group of adult students to observe how people of some other religions worship. What strikes me is that although they are truly committed to what they believe, they often have no hope and no assurance like what we receive when we believe in our Lord Jesus. Our task in this world, once we have trusted in Jesus, is to provide to others the news of the sure hope that is found in the covenant-keeping God who loves us so much. He is preparing an eternal kingdom for us. It is worth telling others about it.

Before his execution for his faith, Polycarp stated, "Eighty-six years have I served [Christ] and He has done me no wrong. How can I blaspheme my King and my Saviour?" Such an example of courage and conviction, of experiential faith in our Lord, may fan the world's desire to know our Lord Jesus.

As followers of Jesus, we are part of this great mission to share the gospel with a world that is hurting. The God who keeps covenant with His people is worth dying for. After all, did not Jesus die on the cross for us? He was God in the flesh, incarnated for us. It is this unique and selfless act that makes life worthwhile. Now we must share with the world the good news of an eternal kingdom that is prepared for us. He will soon take us home.

—A. Koshy Muthalaly.

The Jewish Aspect

Saul, Israel's first king, was a miserable failure. He had done the unthinkable. He had offered a priestly sacrifice, and he did not belong to the priesthood. The Prophet Samuel had to tell Saul he was finished as ruler, for "the Lord hath sought him a man after his own heart" (I Sam. 13:14).

The man God sought was David. Many a Sunday school teacher has had to grapple with the story of a shepherd boy who became a king—a king who murdered a faithful soldier and friend, stole his wife, and tried to hide the whole thing.

Thomas Carlyle, no friend of godly righteousness, had this to say about David: "All earnest souls will ever discern in it (David's life) the faithful struggle of an earnest human soul towards what is good and best. Struggle often baffled, sore baffled, down as into entire wreck; yet a struggle never ended; ever with tears, repentance, true unconquerable purpose, begun anew" (*On Heroes, Hero-worship, and the Heroic in History,* Bibliolife).

David was certainly a man after God's own heart, and through David's family line God gave an eternal King, a throne for that King, and an imperishable kingdom. If David came back today, he would be shocked at how cold and indifferent the Jewish people are to the great covenant promises we find in this week's text.

Most Jews have no expectation of a ruler on David's throne. Some Jews believe the kingdom is being fulfilled in a worldly way.

How did the Jews lose sight of the promises made to David? About forty years after the Lord went back to glory in the ascension (Acts 1:9-11), Jerusalem came under siege by the Roman army (A.D. 70). Local Christians had been warned in Luke's Gospel that a siege was coming (chap. 21). Jewish historians tell us that the "Nazarenes, that is, those who accepted Jesus of Nazareth as the Messiah, indifferent to the national cause, sought safety in flight from Jerusalem; the small community settled in Pella beyond the Jordan" (*Margolis and Marx, A History of the Jewish People,* Jewish Publication Society of America).

Rabbi Ben Zakkai, a Pharisee, was persuaded that Jerusalem and the temple were doomed. He boldly asked the Romans for the privilege of opening a Jewish center for studying the Torah in peace. The wish was granted.

Judaism soon was based on a forced misreading on sacrifices in Hosea 6:6. "For I desired mercy, and not sacrifice; and the knowledge of God more than burnt offerings" (Margolis and Marx).

The way was opened to change Old Testament texts that spoke of a Messiah who would come to sit on David's throne. The prophecies of the coming King-Messiah go untaught. The Talmud (the often disturbing sayings of the rabbis) has taken the place of Old Testament history and prophecy. The result is religious Jews who do not know much of what was promised to their fathers and who seem unwilling to listen to the truth.

This blind indifference does not prevent all Jews from coming to the Saviour-Messiah. A new report tells of 14 Jewish missionaries in the land of Israel who have won 112 Jews to the Messiah. Good numbers are also being reached in our own country.

A recent conference of missionaries to the Jews of North America had ninety-two workers in attendance. Every possible way of reaching Jews is under way today. God will indeed fulfill His promises to David.

—Lyle P. Murphy.

Guiding the Superintendent

How is it that the finite mind of man thinks that he can help our infinite God? We conceive grandiose plans, thinking they will excite God, when living a life of faith and obedience to His holy commandments is what gets God's attention. From this week's lesson we can learn that there are man's ideas and then there are God's eternal purposes and plans for His covenant people.

DEVOTIONAL OUTLINE

1. David's plan to build God a temple (II Sam. 7:4-7). Considering how mightily the hand of God was at work in his life, it is commendable that David desired to provide a fitting place for the ark of the covenant, the dwelling place of God. Perhaps this was the Prophet Nathan's rationale for encouraging David to proceed without having consulted God.

David lived and rested from war in a magnificent royal palace that had been built for him. He wanted no less for God, whose ark remained in a tent. But God revealed through Nathan that from the Exodus until then, He had had no desire to reside in an extravagant cedar house; nor had He asked the earlier Israelite leaders why they had not built Him such a house.

2. God's plan to make David a kingdom (II Sam. 7:8-11). A close study of the Bible will confirm that from the beginning of time, God was preparing a people for Himself—as what He did for David and the Israelites exemplifies. God elevated David from following sheep to shepherding His chosen people. The nation praised David and sang songs about his conquests, but the reality was that God put David's enemies in his hands. It was God who gave rise to David's legacy, which would live on long after he died. God gave Israel the land of Canaan for a permanent possession and kept her enemies at bay. God has many mansions prepared for the weary Christians who are in constant warfare with the evil one.

3. God's plans lead to everlasting life (II Sam. 7:12-16). God chastises those He loves, and He reproved Nathan for his nod to David's desire to build God a temple. God proceeded to outline how He would execute His greater plan for the building of the temple. Although David was a man after God's own heart, he was also a man of war; therefore, God chose Solomon, the seed of David, to build the temple. God would guide, direct, and chide him as a father loves and nurtures his son.

God rejected David's sins, but He did not reject David. He committed to establishing David's dynasty, and this was accomplished with the coming of our Lord Jesus.

As Nathan told David the full account of his encounter with God, so every believer must share God's plan to extend the gift of eternal life through the shed blood of Jesus Christ, His only begotten Son.

CHILDREN'S CORNER

Teach the children that heaven is God's home and that by faith they can go to live with Him in His eternal kingdom. They need to believe in Jesus, His Son, and trust Him as their Saviour. Make sure they also know that He is with them while they live here on earth. They do not have to wait till they get to heaven to be with Jesus. They cannot see Him now, but He is there and will be guiding them through His Word.

—Jane E. Campbell.

SCRIPTURE LESSON TEXT

LUKE 1:26 And in the sixth month the angel Gabriel was sent from God unto a city of Galilee, named Nazareth,

27 To a virgin espoused to a man whose name was Joseph, of the house of David; and the virgin's name *was* Mary.

28 And the angel came in unto her, and said, Hail, *thou that art* highly favoured, the Lord *is* with thee: blessed *art* thou among women.

29 And when she saw *him,* she was troubled at his saying, and cast in her mind what manner of salutation this should be.

30 And the angel said unto her, Fear not, Mary: for thou hast found favour with God.

31 And, behold, thou shalt conceive in thy womb, and bring forth a son, and shalt call his name JESUS.

32 He shall be great, and shall be called the Son of the Highest: and the Lord God shall give unto him the throne of his father David:

33 And he shall reign over the house of Jacob for ever; and of his kingdom there shall be no end.

34 Then said Mary unto the angel, How shall this be, seeing I know not a man?

35 And the angel answered and said unto her, The Holy Ghost shall come upon thee, and the power of the Highest shall overshadow thee: therefore also that holy thing which shall be born of thee shall be called the Son of God.

36 And, behold, thy cousin Elisabeth, she hath also conceived a son in her old age: and this is the sixth month with her, who was called barren.

37 For with God nothing shall be impossible.

38 And Mary said, Behold the handmaid of the Lord; be it unto me according to thy word. And the angel departed from her.

NOTES

God's Promise of a Saviour

Lesson Text: Luke 1:26-38

Related Scriptures: Isaiah 7:14; Genesis 49:8-12;
II Samuel 7:25-29; Hebrews 1:1-8

TIME: 7 or 6 B.C.

PLACE: Nazareth

GOLDEN TEXT—"Behold, thou shalt conceive in thy womb, and bring forth a son, and shalt call his name JESUS" (Luke 1:31).

Introduction

Even before God created heaven and the earth, His plan of salvation was in place. In eternity past, that plan was established and sure—so much so that in Revelation the Apostle John described Jesus as the "Lamb slain from the foundation of the world" (13:8), and the Apostle Paul could speak of believers being chosen in Christ "before the foundation of the world" (Eph. 1:4).

God's plan to redeem His fallen creatures, however, was worked out in human history, beginning immediately after the sin of Adam and Eve with the promise that One would come to crush the serpent's head (Gen. 3:15). Many centuries and many prophecies later, God's promise came to fruition with the announcement to Mary of the Saviour's imminent birth.

LESSON OUTLINE

I. AN ANGELIC APPEARANCE—
Luke 1:26-30

II. A DIVINE MESSAGE—
Luke 1:31-37

III. A HUMBLE RESPONSE—
Luke 1:38

Exposition: Verse by Verse

AN ANGELIC APPEARANCE

LUKE 1:26 And in the sixth month the angel Gabriel was sent from God unto a city of Galilee, named Nazareth,

27 To a virgin espoused to a man whose name was Joseph, of the house of David; and the virgin's name was Mary.

28 And the angel came in unto her, and said, Hail, thou that art highly favoured, the Lord is with thee: blessed art thou among women.

29 And when she saw him, she was troubled at his saying, and cast in her mind what manner of salutation this should be.

30 And the angel said unto her, Fear not, Mary: for thou hast found favour with God.

The angel's objective (Luke 1:26-27). Luke's Gospel is addressed to Theophilus, a man who apparently was a Greek and thus a Gentile. Luke's goal was to set forth in orderly detail the facts about the earthly life of Jesus Christ in order to encourage and strengthen the faith of Theophilus and his other readers (vss. 3-4). He began with events leading up to the birth of Christ, specifically the miraculous conception by Elisabeth, who would be the mother of John the Baptist (vss. 5-25).

{Mary, the mother of Jesus, is introduced in the sixth month of Elisabeth's pregnancy. At that time an angel was sent from God to Mary's hometown, Nazareth of Galilee}[Q1] (vs. 26). The angel was Gabriel, the same angel who had previously appeared to Elisabeth's husband, Zacharias, in Jerusalem, announcing the coming birth of John the Baptist (vss. 13-19). Now, six months later, Gabriel had a similar task in Galilee, about seventy miles to the north.

{Nazareth was a small village on a hilltop about eighteen miles west of the southern tip of the Sea of Galilee. The town apparently was of little significance, as it is not mentioned in the Old Testament. Furthermore, Nathanael's comment in John 1:46 suggests Nazareth did not have a good reputation.}[Q2]

God, however, had chosen a special person in that village, and He had an important message for her—one important enough to be delivered by an angel. {That person was Mary, a virgin, who was "espoused to a man whose name was Joseph" (Luke 1:27).

Espousal was somewhat akin to our engagement, but it was much more binding. It was a formal marital agreement that continued for about a year before the official marriage took place. However, "the parties during this [espousal] period were considered husband and wife" (Stein, *Luke,* B&H).}[Q3]

Joseph and Mary clearly had not yet "[come] together" (Matt. 1:18), and Mary was still a virgin. Joseph was a descendant of David (Luke 1:27), but he was a common man who would pass on to Jesus the carpenter's trade (cf. Matt. 13:55). {Mary, who was probably still a teenager at this point, apparently did not enjoy great status, either (cf. Luke 1:48), and we know from the couple's later offerings in the temple that they were poor (Luke 2:24; cf. Lev. 12:6-8).}[Q2]

The angel's greeting (Luke 1:28-29). Gabriel's appearance to Mary was accompanied by comforting and reassuring words. {He declared her "highly favoured," or graced by God, indicating that she was the special object of God's grace and that the Lord was with her.}[Q4] {While Mary is consistently presented in Scripture as a godly young woman, the Lord's special presence with her was an act of grace.}[Q5]

{Mary's immediate response was not fear, as we often see in the Bible when people encountered angels (cf. Luke 1:12; 2:9). Gabriel's reassuring words may have allayed any fears she naturally might have had at the angel's appearance, but they also perplexed her. Luke 1:29 says Mary was "troubled at his saying" and wondered about this greeting. "Evidently in her modesty she did not understand why a heavenly visitant should greet her in such exalted terms" (Morris, *Luke,* InterVarsity).}[Q4]

If there was any fear in Mary, it came not from the angel's appearance but from his words. Why would this heavenly messenger come to such a lowly young woman in such an obscure village with such words of blessing?

The angel's encouragement (Luke 1:30). While Mary did not respond verbally, Gabriel saw her uneasiness and told her not to fear. He then reassured her that she had in fact "found favour with God." The emphasis here is again on the Lord's favor, or grace, not on Mary or her righteousness. Knowing she rested in God's grace meant there was nothing about which she needed to be anxious.

We too would do well to heed the words of the angel. If we have experienced God's grace in salvation through faith in Christ, any time we spend worrying about what might or might not be is wasted time. His grace is sufficient for whatever we might experience in this life (cf. II Cor. 12:9).

A DIVINE MESSAGE

31 And, behold, thou shalt conceive in thy womb, and bring forth a son, and shalt call his name JESUS.

32 He shall be great, and shall be called the Son of the Highest: and the Lord God shall give unto him the throne of his father David:

33 And he shall reign over the house of Jacob for ever; and of his kingdom there shall be no end.

34 Then said Mary unto the angel, How shall this be, seeing I know not a man?

35 And the angel answered and said unto her, The Holy Ghost shall come upon thee, and the power of the Highest shall overshadow thee: therefore also that holy thing which shall be born of thee shall be called the Son of God.

36 And, behold, thy cousin Elisabeth, she hath also conceived a son in her old age: and this is the sixth month with her, who was called barren.

37 For with God nothing shall be impossible.

A son promised (Luke 1:31). The grace of God would be especially revealed in Mary's life through the birth of a son. The angel's message was simple and direct: Mary would conceive, she would bear a son, and her son's name was to be Jesus. While it took only seconds for Gabriel to speak the words, they must have taken Mary aback and caused her mind to race with the implications.

That her son was to be named Jesus also must have raised questions. "Jesus" is the Greek equivalent of the Hebrew name Joshua. The name was not unique, but it was uniquely given, and this must have been a hint to Mary of the special nature of her son.

Joseph also was told later that Mary's son was to be named Jesus, which means "the Lord saves," but he was told more about the significance of the name: "He shall save his people from their sins" (Matt. 1:21). Mary was not specifically told the significance. Perhaps there was too much other information for her to absorb at this time.

The son described (Luke 1:32-33). Gabriel continued without interruption to describe Mary's son. Just as Gabriel had announced that John the Baptist would be "great" (vs. 15), so he also declared that Jesus would be great. Jesus, however, would be far greater than even John. His greatness speaks particularly of His "being and nature" (Stein), which the angel went on to describe.

{Gabriel added that Jesus would be called the "Son of the Highest," that is, the Son of God, and that the Lord would give Him the "throne of his father David" (vs. 32). As the Son of God,}[Q6] Jesus would be equal with God the Father (cf. John 5:18). This means Jesus is God.

{Whether Mary fully grasped the idea of Jesus' deity at that point is not entirely clear, but she surely understood the significance of His inheriting the throne of King David and reigning forever over the house of Jacob (Luke 1:32-33). These words could only mean that Gabriel was describing Jesus as Israel's promised Messiah (Christ), or Anointed One (cf. II Sam. 7:12-17; Ps. 89:20, 29).}Q7

The Jewish people of Mary's day knew of he Daniel 9:24-27 prophecy, and from that prophecy they may have known that the Messiah's coming was near. There was great expectation as they looked forward to the arrival of their Deliverer and His mighty reign (cf. Isa. 9:7).

What the people failed to understand, however, was the spiritual nature of Christ's work. They would first need to accept their Messiah and be delivered from their sins. Only then could they dwell with Him in His unending kingdom. As they would learn, the fullness of Christ's reign over David's kingdom awaits His second coming (cf. Rev. 19:11—20:6).

The birth explained (Luke 1:34-35). {Mary's first words are interesting. Given the angel's amazing, almost unbelievable, promise, we might have expected words of doubt, as was the case with Zacharias (vss. 18-20). Instead, she fully believed what the angel told her. Still, there was one matter that troubled her. "How shall this be, seeing I know not a man?" (vs. 34), she asked.}Q8 Gabriel had mentioned neither Joseph nor her impending marriage, and Mary had correctly understood that he was saying that her son would not be conceived by the normal means. She believed the Lord's promise given to her by the angel, but she could not see how it could happen.

The Angel Gabriel did not offer a biological explanation; indeed, there was no natural explanation for a supernatural miracle. He simply said that the Holy Spirit would come upon her and she would be overshadowed by the power of God. This was, in fact, the only explanation for what Mary would soon experience. Although a virgin, she would conceive through a mysterious, divine work, ensuring that the child she conceived would be the holy Son of God.

We usually refer to the miraculous virgin birth of Jesus. Aside from the surrounding circumstances, however, Jesus' physical birth was quite natural and no doubt followed the course of childbirth with which we are familiar. It was the virgin conception that was the real miracle and for which there is no natural explanation.

Scripture clearly sets forth the virgin conception and birth of Jesus Christ. The great prophecy of Isaiah 7:14 looks forward to it, and the united testimony of the Gospel writers declares its fulfillment. Mary was Jesus' mother, but God, not Joseph or any other human man, was the true father of Jesus. This truth is foundational and necessary to the Christian faith.

{While we cannot explain the mechanics of the conception of Christ beyond acknowledging that it was a supernatural work, we can understand the necessity of it. A human mother guaranteed that Jesus was fully human. Yet as the Son of God, He remained also fully God. This divine work in Mary's womb also, in some way, preserved Jesus from inheriting sinful human nature. "If he were born of two human parents, it is very difficult to conceive how he could have been exempt from the guilt of Adam's sin" (Elwell, ed., *Evangelical Dictionary of Theology,* Baker). These important doctrinal truths, while perhaps not fully explained by the virgin conception of Jesus, certainly require it.}Q9

The promise confirmed (Luke 1:36-37). {The Angel Gabriel did not simply tell Mary that she would conceive supernaturally; he also gave her confirmation of the work God would do. This was a gracious gift to Mary. She did not express any doubts about

God's plan, though she may still have been perplexed by the details. However, the Lord gave her a sign that would be a source of encouragement to her in the days ahead. That sign was that her "cousin Elisabeth" had "conceived a son in her old age."}Q10

While the word translated "cousin" (vs. 36) can simply mean "relative," it is clear that Mary knew her well. But with Elisabeth in seclusion for five months (vs. 24) and living a considerable distance away in the hill country of Judea (vs. 39), Mary knew nothing about her pregnancy. This exciting news that God had worked miraculously in her relative's life would confirm to Mary the angel's message to her, for it proved that "with God nothing shall be impossible" (vs. 37).

Mary clearly was a woman of great faith. However, as a human being, she was, like all of us, quite capable of becoming discouraged and falling prey to doubt. God's work in Elisabeth's life would be a source of encouragement to remind Mary that He can do anything and that He is faithful to His promises.

God's Word has many wonderful promises for us. We need to review them often to remind ourselves that He loves us, that He hears our prayers, and that He will never forsake us. His promises are often repeated because we are weak and we need reassurance. He also graciously gives us examples of people like ourselves who lived by faith in spite of great hardships.

A HUMBLE RESPONSE

38 And Mary said, Behold the handmaid of the Lord; be it unto me according to thy word. And the angel departed from her.

Mary's last words to Gabriel were words of humble submission to God's will. She called herself the Lord's "handmaid" (vs. 38), or slave girl, a term that "expresses complete obedience" (Morris). She gladly submitted to God's plan, asking that everything be done according to the angel's word.

The divine plan of salvation required a young woman who was willing to submit to God's will despite the hardships it would entail and despite the inability to fully understand everything God had in store. Mary did not know everything, but she did know God, and she knew He was worthy of her trust and complete commitment.

Do we know God in such a way that we will trust Him even when we do not understand what He is doing or where He is leading us? He is a gracious God who is worthy of our complete faith.

—Jarl K. Waggoner.

QUESTIONS

1. At what particular time was the Angel Gabriel sent to Mary?

2. What indicates the lowly status of both Nazareth and Mary?

3. What was Mary's relationship to Joseph at this time?

4. How did the angel greet Mary, and how did she respond? Why did she respond this way?

5. Was Mary's godly character the key to God's choosing her? Explain.

6. What is meant by the title "Son of the Highest" (Luke 1:32)?

7. What in Gabriel's message proved to Mary that her son would be the Messiah?

8. What were Mary's first words in response to the angel's announcement? What was her concern?

9. Why is the virginal conception of Jesus necessary doctrinally?

10. What news did the angel give Mary to confirm the promise?

—Jarl K. Waggoner.

Preparing to Teach the Lesson

Prophecy and its fulfillment are God's hallmark of authenticity. The promises of the coming Saviour are some of the most striking examples of this. God makes prophecies come to pass because He is in control. His plans are set, and He has the power to make events happen, no matter how impossible it seems from our viewpoint. In teaching this lesson, make a strong point that God never fails to keep His promises. He has promised to save us by His grace apart from our works. We can rely on His promises.

TODAY'S AIM

Facts: to see that God makes and fulfills His promises and to realize how completely trustworthy they are.

Principle: to trust every word from God even when we do not understand how or when it will be fulfilled.

Application: to rest confidently in God's promises as the basis of our security in life.

INTRODUCING THE LESSON

We are constantly beset by people who say, "Trust me!" This can include everyone from used-car salesmen to our national leaders. (Be sure to modify this if you have a used-car salesman in your class!) Even well-meaning people who make promises to us are often unable to carry them through. Times change, people change, and the circumstances of life make it nearly impossible to say what will happen next.

When Isaiah prophesied about seven hundred years before the birth of Jesus that a virgin would conceive, give birth to a son, and call Him Immanuel, it may well be that few believed it. Those who read the prophecy over the intervening seven hundred years may have doubted it would happen or questioned how it could possibly be done. Only God could fulfil this prophecy.

DEVELOPING THE LESSON

1. God's promise to Mary through the Angel Gabriel (Luke 1:26-33). We are so used to this story that we may fail to see the wonder and impossibility of the promise to Mary. Still a virgin, she was engaged to Joseph and could not conceive without a man and losing her virginity. Furthermore, in ancient times, one could not know what the sex of the unborn child would be, so there was only a fifty-fifty chance of having a boy.

The angel said that the child would be called the "Son of the Highest" (vs. 32). The religious Jews were fiercely monotheistic, but in their culture the son of anyone was viewed as being virtually the same as his father. So this could only mean that the child would be God come in the flesh. Since He was to reign over the house of David forever, He would be eternal. He would live forever.

2. Mary's response to God's promise (Luke 1:34). The immense and eternal implications of this complex promise of the coming Saviour would bowl over the staunchest of hearts. However, Mary asked only about how she could conceive, since without that, the whole promise could not be fulfilled. This was not a question of unbelief but rather a desire to understand and get the answers she needed for the situation. We can learn from this the principle that if God promises something, He already has the plan and power in place to bring it to fulfillment.

3. God's statement of how this promise was to be fulfilled (Luke 1:35-37). The angel's answer was not a simple "God will do it." The following details were given to Mary: the Holy Spirit would come upon her and the power of the Highest would overshadow her. This would bring about God's unique plan of sending His only begotten Son into the world, the Saviour of mankind. "Therefore also that holy thing which shall be born of thee shall be called the Son of God." This miraculous event had been foretold by the Prophet Isaiah (Isa. 7:14).

Actually, the answer given to Mary is as overwhelming as the miracle of the promise itself. We have no idea how any of this could have been done. The Scripture does not give any more details how or when this happened. We only know that Mary became pregnant with the Lord Jesus.

4. Mary's faithful answer (Luke 1:38). Mary's faith is seen in this verse. She was obviously satisfied with the angel's answer and was perfectly willing to be used in God's plan.

ILLUSTRATING THE LESSON

We can trust God's promises as accomplished fact, even when we cannot understand how He will fulfill them.

ALL THINGS ARE POSSIBLE

GOD'S PROMISE

MARY'S FAITH

MANKIND'S BLESSING

CONCLUDING THE LESSON

God is under no obligation to tell us what will happen in the future. He does not have to make us any personal promises; however, He has given us many great and precious promises in His Word. We can rely on them in the face of events and threats that may seem to contradict the possibility of their fulfillment.

We can look at missions as an example. Missionaries have undoubtedly relied on God's protective presence with them in hostile situations, only to suffer martyrdom at the hands of those they are sent to serve. Does this mean that God has failed to keep His promise that He would be with them and protect them as they carried out His Great Commission? Not at all!

First of all, missionaries are protected eternally. They have gone to heaven, which is far better than being in this world. Also, we have often heard that the lives, and even deaths, of missionaries have been the very catalyst that brought whole people groups to faith in Christ. What looks like a tragedy to us may be God at work fulfilling His greater purposes.

Remind your students that we have neither the authority nor the power to tell God how to fulfill His promises. (People usually do this to try to get God to handle their personal situations in ways of their own choosing.) We need not "remind" God of His promises. We need to remind ourselves of His promises, and there is no better way to do that than to study His Word. We have no idea how God plans to carry out His promises!

ANTICIPATING THE NEXT LESSON

In our next lesson, we will look at the actual birth of our Saviour, Jesus Christ.

—Brian D. Doud.

PRACTICAL POINTS

1. God does not burden us with un-manageable tasks (Luke 1:26-27; cf. I Cor. 10:13).
2. Understand that you are part of God's royal family (Luke 1:28).
3. Trust a true word from God (Luke 1:29; Heb. 4:12).
4. As children of an esteemed and exalted Parent, we are privileged (Luke 1:30-33; cf. John 1:12).
5. Respect the order and timing of God (Luke 1:34).
6. The Holy Spirit's power makes Christians overcomers (vs. 35).
7. Obedience can resurrect dreams (vss. 36-38).

—Lendell Sims.

RESEARCH AND DISCUSSION

1. Why is it sometimes easier to accept words from people rather than the promises of God? How can we strengthen our relationship with God and increase our confidence in Him (Luke 1:29; cf. Matt. 8:8; Col. 1:10)?
2. Why is it important for us to understand and accept that Jesus came as the Second Adam (Luke 1:31; cf. I Cor. 15:45)?
3. Many generations passed after God promised to send David's special Heir. What should believers do while waiting for God to fulfill His promises (cf. Isa. 9:6-7; Heb. 6:12)?
4. Why is it hard for us to keep our promises?
5. What was Mary's reaction to the angel's announcement?

—Lendell Sims.

ILLUSTRATED HIGH POINTS

What manner of salutation (Luke 1:29)

In contrast to the angel's lavish declarations of God's favor toward Mary, a more typical biblical salutation consisted of humbly asking God to bestow His favor (cf. Num. 6:25). Unaccustomed to being noticed, it is no wonder that Mary felt fearful at being showered with such accolades.

Mira is a star that has been studied by astronomers for four hundred years. Yet only recently has NASA discovered that it has an exceptionally long, comet-like tail. This came to light (literally) when, for the first time, a space telescope scanned it with ultraviolet light, thus revealing its previously unnoticed splendor.

God sees us in a different light than people do. Like Mary, may we all leave a legacy of light.

How shall this be? (vs. 34)

As Nicodemus was mystified by rebirth, Mary struggled to understand the concept of the Incarnation. Although the mysteries of God are beyond our natural understanding, we can learn much by observing our physical world (cf. Job 12:8; Rom. 1:20).

Einstein's theory of special relativity, $E = mc^2$, states that "every mass has an energy equivalent and vice versa" (www.wikipedia.com). In other words, they are different expressions of the same essence.

John 1 teaches that Jesus existed from all eternity as the divine Word. Miraculously, when the Holy Spirit came upon Mary, the Word became flesh and a true man was conceived. The formula is: the Word = the God-Man, Jesus!

—Therese Greenberg.

Golden Text Illuminated

"Behold, thou shalt conceive in thy womb, and bring forth a son, and shalt call his name JESUS" (Luke 1:31).

In biblical times the name given to a child was very important. Names were often laden with significance. Today's parents are likely to name a child based on personal preference, sometimes just because they find it superficially appealing. There may be some family meaning perhaps, or some other intended significance, but the import does not run as deep.

In Bible days the name spoke of character and sometimes even had prophetic significance. This was certainly the case when the Lord Jesus was given His name—a name that, as the song says, is the "sweetest name on earth" ("Oh, How I Love Jesus," Whitfield). This week's golden text brings this home to us.

In the prophecy of the visiting angel, the promise of the birth of the long-expected Saviour came to Mary. The context here is both miraculous and amazing. It is hard to fathom the profundity of the virgin birth of our Lord. There were astonishing prophecies made in conjunction with the Lord's birth, an example of which is Luke 1:32-33. Christ's greatness, uniqueness, deity, sovereignty, and Lordship are all conveyed. Clearly no other such person has ever been or ever will be born.

The glory of the Lord Jesus is seen in the name He was given, which is at the heart of this week's text. Interestingly, His parents did not choose the name; rather, the Angel Gabriel announced what it would be. It most certainly came from God Himself. Mary learned from the angel that she would conceive and bring forth a son, but she did not get to pick His name.

The name of the Messiah had its roots in the Old Testament. The original Hebrew term refers to God being deliverance or salvation. The term is used often in the Old Testament. The Lord Jesus' name announces that He brings the promise of salvation to mankind. Jesus was meant to be a deliverer, a rescuer, a savior. That is why He was given this name. Every man, woman, boy, and girl across the earth must turn to this one Saviour in order to receive the gift of eternal life.

We should realize that the Lord's name in the Hebrew language was the name Joshua. It was a common name at the time of the Lord's birth. But in the New Testament, the Lord is always distinguished from any other Joshua. He is Jesus, the unique and only Son of God, the Saviour of the world.

We see Jesus' name in Scripture associated with titles like Christ and Messiah. He was the Lord Jesus, the Anointed One prophesied for centuries. He is the only hope of the world.

It is important to remember that the deliverance the Lord Jesus brings is primarily a spiritual deliverance. Matthew 1:21 makes clear that the Lord came so that sinners could be forgiven before God. Christmas is about Jesus. Jesus provides the forgiveness of sins. The peace, love, joy, and hope of Christmas are found in Him, the unique and only Son of God. He is the one who saves us.

—*Jeff VanGoethem.*

Heart of the Lesson

The word "promise" is defined as "a statement telling someone that you will definitely do something or that something will definitely happen in the future" (www.merriam-webster.com). Nothing warms the heart like a promise fulfilled. Too often we are surprised when people keep their promises to us; however, we should be expectant when God makes a promise to us. We never have to fear that He will go back on His word, for His words are true.

1. An unlikely visitor (Luke 1:26-28). We often base the validity of a promise on the character or authority of the one who made it or the relationship we have with that person. For instance, if we had faithful parents, we could trust them when they made a promise to us. If our boss makes a promise to us, we expect him or her to fulfill the promise based upon the authority of his or her position in the company.

The Angel Gabriel did not just randomly visit Mary. The Bible tells us that he was sent by God. While we are always surrounded by angels, they do not make a habit of revealing themselves to humans unless our Heavenly Father advises them to do so. Therefore, it is imperative for us to understand that Gabriel was sent by God as he gave Mary not just a message but a promise.

2. The promise (Luke 1:29-33). What was the promise that Mary received from the angel? The promise was twofold. First, Mary had found favor with God. The dictionary defines the word "favor" as "friendly regard shown toward another especially by a superior." Because God approved of Mary, she was given this second and much more important promise: "Thou shalt conceive in thy womb, and bring forth a son, and shalt call his name JESUS."

And there was more! Mary was not going to give birth to an ordinary child. No, this child was destined to be great. He would be King, sit on David's throne, and His kingdom would have no end.

3. The promise confirmed (Luke 1:34-38). A promise is communicated either through the spoken word or the written word; however, how the promise comes to pass is often more involved. Mary was perplexed. She asked the angel, "How shall this be, seeing I know not a man?" Gabriel told her that the Holy Spirit would come upon her and God's power would overshadow her.

Mary must have been overwhelmed. At some point perhaps she wanted to pinch herself to make sure she was truly experiencing this angelic visitation.

God is gracious. He always knows how much we can handle and how much we are mentally capable of processing. God always confirms His promises; He did so with Mary. God, through Gabriel, told Mary a secret that she could not have known other than by Him. Her relative Elisabeth was six months' pregnant even though she was thought to be barren! The knowledge of Elisabeth's pregnancy would prove to Mary that the words she heard were true. The angel said, "For with God nothing shall be impossible" (Luke 1:37).

God gave Mary the promise of a son who would be the Saviour of the world. The birth of Jesus Christ shows that God kept His promise. God has made many promises. His Word is full of them. What is even more exciting is that God still keeps His promises.

—*Kristin Reeg.*

World Missions

God takes promises seriously. Every promise He has ever made is true and indisputable (II Cor. 1:20). In God's eyes, we do better to make no vows at all than to make one and break it. The integrity of God is so stellar that we can stake our eternal lives on the flawless accuracy of His message. A young virgin named Mary recognized the veracity of God's word that came to her through the Angel Gabriel. She embraced its truth immediately and received the greatest blessing anyone could receive.

At nineteen years old, Jeremiah believed an inner message that God wanted to use him to bless the people of Haiti. He had visited the island annually on church mission trips from age fourteen and had participated in feeding and teaching the children there. He watched as the church he attended built a school and an orphanage in a particular village. By age nineteen, Jeremiah knew what God had called him to do. His desire was to raise enough money to pay the bills of every patient on the pediatric floor of a hospital the group regularly visited.

Starting with his church, Jeremiah began to solicit funding and volunteers to join him. His group went to family, friends, classmates, coworkers, businesses, foundations, and public agencies seeking finances to help Jeremiah's dream materialize.

Jeremiah made a promise to his group that he would not stop until he had the money to pay the bills for the entire floor of the Haitian hospital. It appeared to be a nearly impossible task, especially for this small team of teenagers and financially struggling young adults. But Jeremiah persevered, serving as an example and encourager for the others. He knew he had received the promise of God that he could do all things through Christ. The effort, which was initiated in the early spring, concluded that same autumn. Jeremiah indeed reached his goal of $9,000 to take to Haiti. He was able to pay every medical bill on the entire pediatric floor of the hospital!

Both the Virgin Mary and Jeremiah believed these words from God: "For with God nothing shall be impossible" (Luke 1:37). Though young, both teenagers understood the integrity of God and committed their futures to the truth of His words. By acting on the promise of God, Jeremiah succeeded in completing a grand missionary effort. Mary believed and gave birth to Jesus, the greatest missionary, who would change the eternal destiny of mankind.

Thank God for His promises. Thank God for our Saviour, Jesus Christ. Thank God for sending His missionaries throughout the world with the gospel. It takes compassion, sacrifice, and great love to go beyond the perimeter of our own areas of comfort to take the love of Jesus to others. Our Saviour left heaven to come to earth to save us. Mary abandoned merely human thinking and safety to embrace the plan of God for her life. Jeremiah forsook the comforts of home to help suffering, needy people in Haiti.

Not all of us may travel far or experience extreme, hazardous conditions, but we each have promises from God. He vows to help us fulfill His plans for our lives. God's plans may at times seem difficult, challenging, or even unreasonable. But as we carry out our assigned missions, we can remember that all things are possible with God.

—*Beverly Medley Jones.*

The Jewish Aspect

Luke was the right man to cover today's theme, "God's Promise of a Saviour," which focuses on the conception of the Messiah Jesus. During Paul's two-year confinement in prison in Caesarea (Acts 24:27), Luke probably treated his number-one patient. This allowed plenty of time for him to interview eyewitnesses to the essential details of the birth of the Lord Jesus (cf. Luke 1:1-3).

Luke related the visit of the Angel Gabriel with an amazing message for a young virgin of Nazareth named Mary. She was a descendant of King David, the royal family to which the Messiah must be born (cf. Luke 3:23-31). Mary was espoused to a man named Joseph. Joseph also was of the house and lineage of David (1:27; 2:4).

The fact that the couple was espoused (Luke 1:27) places us in the heart of Jewish teaching on marriage. Marriages were family affairs, and the uniting of two people required an engagement contract that was as binding as marriage itself. The document, *erusin,* spelled out the biblically based promises that the young couple were bound to until the ketubah, the final marriage contract (Jacobs, *The Jewish Religion,* Oxford University Press).

An important element in Gabriel's explanation of God's plan to Mary is the mention that Elisabeth, her relative, had "also conceived a son in her old age," though she had been "called barren" (Luke 1:36). An earlier note in this chapter states that Elisabeth and her husband, Zacharias, "had no child," and "both were now well stricken in years" (vs. 7). We are to understand that the conception of John the Baptist, Elisabeth's only son, was a miracle of God.

God's governance over childbirth is emphasized throughout the Old Testament. This may have been because childbirth would be the avenue by which salvation would come to man (Gen. 3:15-16).

Hannah is a clear illustration of God's sovereignty over human procreation (I Sam. 1:2). Elkanah had two wives. One was very fertile, producing sons and daughters. The other, Hannah, had no children. Twice we are told that God had closed her womb (vss. 5-6). No reason is given for God's sovereign act, but it clearly was not the right time for the birth of Hannah's son, Samuel, who would play a commanding role in the transition to a monarchy in Israel.

There are other examples of the Lord "closing the womb." Abraham passed off his wife Sarah as his sister to the people of Gerar, for he feared the people might kill him in order to take her. God intervened, and for a period of time, every womb in the king's family was closed by God (Gen. 20:18).

Jacob worked to obtain a wife and received two. Leah was a good wife and had many children. However, her sister Rachel was Jacob's great love. Rachel was barren for some time until God "opened her womb" (Gen. 30:22).

Michal, Saul's daughter and David's wife, saw her husband leading the procession to restore the ark of the covenant to Jerusalem. David was "dancing before the Lord" (II Sam. 6:16). Later, Michal upbraided David for what she considered a disgraceful performance before the women of the city, and God rendered her barren for life (vs. 23).

Luke beautifully relates the planned conception by Mary with the words "Therefore also that holy thing which shall be born of thee shall be called the Son of God" (Luke 1:35). This is a good time to reflect on how Christ came into the world as Saviour.

—Lyle P. Murphy.

Guiding the Superintendent

In 1848, James W. Marshall discovered large quantities of gold at Sutter's Mill in Coloma, California. The news of this discovery traveled throughout the United States and the world. It encouraged people across the world to leave their homes. They came to California with the hopes of becoming wealthy. Unfortunately, only a few people became wealthy, while many others became impoverished. The promise of wealth did not come true. No doubt many people were disappointed at the outcome.

In this week's lesson, we learn about God's promise of a Saviour to bring true riches to a lost humanity.

DEVOTIONAL OUTLINE

1. Gabriel's appearance (Luke 1:26-28). Mary's relative Elisabeth was six months pregnant with John the Baptist (Luke 1:24). The Lord commissioned the Angel Gabriel to go to Nazareth.

Gabriel's assignment was to visit Mary. Mary was a young virgin who was espoused to Joseph. This meant Mary and Joseph were engaged to be married. Joseph's ancestors could be traced back to David. Gabriel appeared to Mary and greeted her with a salutation. Gabriel indicated that the Lord was with her and that she was highly blessed among women. She met with God's favor.

2. Gabriel's announcement (Luke 1:29-33). Gabriel's appearance startled Mary. She was perplexed by his salutation. Gabriel reported that Mary was greatly blessed. Indeed, Mary had found favor with God; God was pleased with her life. Gabriel conveyed to Mary that God had given her a distinct honor—she would be the mother of the Messiah! Gabriel indicated to her the significance of the Messiah's birth. He would be referred to as the "Son of the Highest" (Luke 1:32). Gabriel told Mary of this Son's future supremacy. God would give David's throne to Him. He would reign over Jacob's house. This meant that He would rule over Israel. His kingdom would be perpetual.

3. Gabriel's assurance (Luke 1:34-38). Mary was a virgin. Without sexual relations, she wondered how pregnancy could occur. Therefore, she questioned Gabriel about his announcement.

Gabriel assured Mary that the pregnancy would occur. It would not be a normal one. The Holy Spirit would take control, and God would perform the miraculous. Although naturally impossible, God demonstrated His supernatural power. He would do something beyond explanation or reason. Upon hearing Gabriel's assurance, Mary stated her willingness to be the vessel to bring Jesus into the world, and then Gabriel left Mary.

CHILDREN'S CORNER

It is never too early to expose children to God's promises. They need to know that their Heavenly Father cares about them. Help your children understand that God's promises are indicators of His love and purpose for them.

Some children may find it difficult to trust God's promises, especially if they have experienced mostly broken promises by other people in their young lives so far. Emphasize that God is not like people; He always keeps His promises, and He will never let us down. So it is vitally important that we understand what His promises are. Many people substitute their own desires for what He has actually promised and then are disappointed when their desires are not met. But God is faithful and will fulfill His promises to us.

—*Tyrone Keith Carroll, Sr.*

SCRIPTURE LESSON TEXT

LUKE 2:1 And it came to pass in those days, that there went out a decree from Caesar Augustus, that all the world should be taxed.

2 (And this taxing was first made when Cyrenius was governor of Syria.)

3 And all went to be taxed, every one into his own city.

4 And Joseph also went up from Galilee, out of the city of Nazareth, into Judaea, unto the city of David, which is called Bethlehem; (because he was of the house and lineage of David:)

5 To be taxed with Mary his espoused wife, being great with child.

6 And so it was, that, while they were there, the days were accomplished that she should be delivered.

7 And she brought forth her firstborn son, and wrapped him in swaddling clothes, and laid him in a manger; because there was no room for them in the inn.

8 And there were in the same country shepherds abiding in the field, keeping watch over their flock by night.

9 And, lo, the angel of the Lord came upon them, and the glory of the Lord shone round about them: and they were sore afraid.

10 And the angel said unto them, Fear not: for, behold, I bring you good tidings of great joy, which shall be to all people.

11 For unto you is born this day in the city of David a Saviour, which is Christ the Lord.

12 And this *shall be* a sign unto you; Ye shall find the babe wrapped in swaddling clothes, lying in a manger.

13 And suddenly there was with the angel a multitude of the heavenly host praising God, and saying,

14 Glory to God in the highest, and on earth peace, good will toward men.

15 And it came to pass, as the angels were gone away from them into heaven, the shepherds said one to another, Let us now go even unto Bethlehem, and see this thing which is come to pass, which the Lord hath made known unto us.

16 And they came with haste, and found Mary, and Joseph, and the babe lying in a manger.

17 And when they had seen *it,* they made known abroad the saying which was told them concerning this child.

NOTES

The Birth of the Saviour

(Christmas)

Lesson Text: Luke 2:1-17

Related Scriptures: Psalm 96:1-13; Isaiah 9:6-7; Micah 5:2-4; Isaiah 60:1-4; Galatians 4:4-7

TIME: 6 or 5 B.C.   PLACES: Nazareth and Bethlehem

GOLDEN TEXT—"For unto you is born this day in the city of David a Saviour, which is Christ the Lord" (Luke 2:11).

Introduction

When you are telling a story that is foundational to the beliefs and hopes of a people, it is important to tell it well. Luke the historian had many sources at his disposal when, under inspiration, he wrote the story of Jesus' birth. In his day, many things were known about Jesus that have since been forgotten. All writers choose what they will include and how they will word the story.

One purpose of Luke's account of the birth of Jesus is to show the surprising ordinariness, even poverty, of the birth of the world's greatest king. The birth of Messiah is about the true Lord, whose majesty exceeds even Caesar's, though by appearance His birth had no majesty. Yet the glory does shine through in the events of Messiah's birth. The majesty of heaven shone through while the earthly circumstances seemed humble and ignoble.

LESSON OUTLINE

I. JOURNEY—Luke 2:1-5

II. BIRTH—Luke 2:6-7

III. ANGELS—Luke 2:8-14

IV. RUMORS—Luke 2:15-17

Exposition: Verse by Verse

JOURNEY

LUKE 2:1 And it came to pass in those days, that there went out a decree from Caesar Augustus, that all the world should be taxed.

2 (And this taxing was first made when Cyrenius was governor of Syria.)

3 And all went to be taxed, every one into his own city.

4 And Joseph also went up from Galilee, out of the city of Nazareth, into Judaea, unto the city of David, which is called Bethlehem; (because he was of the house and lineage of David:)

5 To be taxed with Mary his espoused wife, being great with child.

The decree of Augustus (Luke 2:1). Luke is widely thought to have been a non-Jewish disciple, one of Paul's circle. He was very much a part of the mission to the nations of the early Christian movement. Throughout the Gospel penned by him as inspired by the Spirit, Luke showed that the story of Jesus is the continuation of the story of Israel. One of the ways he informed his readers that Jesus' story is the next chapter after the Old Testament story is seen in his literary style. "And it came to pass" is used over three hundred times in the Old Testament as the beginning of an account. It is a Hebraic idiom for beginning a narrative of events.

Luke 2 brings the story of Jesus into the setting of the Roman Empire and the reign of Augustus, the first emperor and one revered as a god after his death. Paul, Luke's mentor and friend, taught in the congregations that Jesus is Lord. This is a way of saying that our Messiah is truly what Rome claimed its emperor to be: "Every tongue should confess that Jesus Christ is Lord, to the glory of God the Father" (Phil. 2:11).

{Luke's Roman readers could not have missed the irony that Jesus was born during the reign of Augustus and in Bethlehem because of a decree of Augustus. An Italian archaeological find called the Priene Inscription tells us something of how Augustus was revered by later generations: "The birthday of the god has marked the beginning of the good news for the world" (Brown, *The Birth of Messiah,* Doubleday). Yet Luke's readers would know about the real kingly birth. Augustus was nothing more than God's unwitting instrument.}[Q1]

The census of Quirinius (Luke 2:2-3). "Cyrenius" is a variant spelling of "Quirinius" (Publius Sulpicius Quirinius), the Roman governor of Syria. Historians have puzzled over Luke's statement about the census of Quirinius, since a very famous incident happened regarding a census of Quirinius in A.D. 6, when Jesus was approximately ten years old (Acts 5:37). It would not be the first time, however, that our incomplete records of the Jewish and Roman world were found to be filled in by additional information in the New Testament.

While history may not be able to verify Luke's statement, it is reasonable to believe that he was correct. {The main point is that Joseph and Mary had to go to Bethlehem because of a decree of Caesar regarding a census. This is important because it explains why a family from Nazareth gave birth far to the south in Bethlehem.}[Q2]

The journey of Joseph and Mary (Luke 2:4-5). Leaving Nazareth in the north to journey approximately eighty miles south to Bethlehem is described as going "up" because Judah is mountainous. From any direction, going to Jerusalem is going up. Bethlehem, five miles further south, is in the territory of Judah, called Judea.

Micah 5:2 says, "Thou, Bethlehem Ephratah, though thou be little among the thousands of Judah, yet out of thee shall he come forth unto me that is to be ruler in Israel; whose goings forth have been from of old, from everlasting." This city is apparently called Bethlehem Ephratah to distinguish it from Bethlehem of Zebulon (Josh. 19:15). The Messiah was to be born in the city of Messiah's precursor, King David.

When Joseph and Mary made this journey, the time for the birth was near. It is not necessary to believe that the birth happened within hours or even days of their arrival. Possibly they found no secure lodging for a while in the small town of Bethlehem. Pilgrims traveling in Israel were accustomed to living for extended periods in temporary lodgings.

BIRTH

6 And so it was, that, while they were there, the days were accomplished that she should be delivered.

7 And she brought forth her first-born son, and wrapped him in swaddling clothes, and laid him in a manger; because there was no room for them in the inn.

Days accomplished for birth (Luke 2:6). Again, readers with a keen eye for biblical storytelling will realize that Luke was using key words from the Old Testament. The idea of days being accomplished shows up in several earlier Scriptures. The Persian king Ahasuerus decreed a period of time for beauty treatments for selected women, including Esther. Esther waited until her days were "accomplished" (Esth. 2:12). Jeremiah told the leaders of Jerusalem that their days were "accomplished," meaning the heavenly King had decreed their end (Jer. 25:34).

{Does the idea of days being accomplished in Luke 2:6 mean simply that Mary's time of pregnancy was at an end? Or does it mean that Messiah was born at the time decreed by God? Both are true. Mary's term of pregnancy was indeed accomplished, but the words could be a hint of more. That Messiah was born through the normal period of human gestation is already a startling thought. That God brought history to just the right day for His birth is an even deeper thought.}Q3

Swaddling and a manger (Luke 2:7). These two details about how the infant would be found are repeated later in the account of the shepherds. The swaddling and manger both are mentioned by the angel in verse 12. The fact that when the shepherds came they saw Jesus in a manger is mentioned in verse 16.

When we read that there was no room at the inn, we should not picture a hotel or tavern with private rooms for single families. Bethlehem was a small town. Travelers might stay in homes, whether by invitation through hospitality or by paying a stranger. Lodging places for travelers are mentioned in the Old Testament (Jer. 14:8). {The added detail that there was no suitable lodging place for the birth of Jesus is necessary so that readers will understand why the infant Messiah was born in such a crude setting.}Q4

{Swaddling clothes are strips of cloth or blanket wrapped around an infant to keep him secure. They are a sign of parental care.}Q5 The custom is mentioned in Wisdom 7:4-5 (a Jewish writing found in the Apocrypha), where it says King Solomon was swaddled as an infant. Swaddling was not a sign of poverty but of loving care. What is unusual is that a baby who was cared for by good parents would be laid in a manger, an animal feeding trough. This would be the definitive sign to the shepherds that they had found the correct baby.

ANGELS

8 And there were in the same country shepherds abiding in the field, keeping watch over their flock by night.

9 And, lo, the angel of the Lord came upon them, and the glory of the Lord shone round about them: and they were sore afraid.

10 And the angel said unto them, Fear not: for, behold, I bring you good tidings of great joy, which shall be to all people.

11 For unto you is born this day in the city of David a Saviour, which is Christ the Lord.

12 And this shall be a sign unto you; Ye shall find the babe wrapped in swaddling clothes, lying in a manger.

13 And suddenly there was with the angel a multitude of the heavenly host praising God, and saying,

14 Glory to God in the highest, and on earth peace, good will toward men.

Shepherds in the field (Luke 2:8). The birth of Messiah happened in lowly circumstances. His first bed was a manger where animals were fed. His parents were traveling outsiders, living without the comforts usually associated with kings and courts.

Shepherds have always been rather low on the social order. Certainly the announcement to shepherds was God's way of showing the humbleness of Jesus' birth. {Yet there are specific reasons why shepherds were fitting witnesses of Messiah's birth. King David was a shepherd in Bethlehem. Ezekiel 34:23 promises Messiah would come as a shepherd. Jesus would use the shepherd illustration about Himself (John 10; cf. Matt. 26:31; Mark 6:34).}Q6

Perhaps there is one other reason shepherds made such an appropriate group of witnesses. Jesus Himself would be the Passover Lamb (John 1:29, 36; 19:33-37). He would be crucified on Passover. The shepherds of Bethlehem were the first witnesses to the birth of the Shepherd who was also the Lamb.

The angel with a message (Luke 2:9-10). Although "the angel of the Lord" appears a number of times in Scripture, this designation of a messenger is used only once to announce an accomplished birth: to shepherds concerning the birth of Jesus.

"Glory" in Scripture refers to the light of divine power, which the angelic beings bear as well, though it emanates from God. The same word can also be used for the glory of human kings. {The humble shepherds saw heavenly, majestic light. Their fear was normal, because they were seeing miraculous signs. Yet, more than this, the angelic messengers of God bear some of His holiness and splendor. Human beings are overwhelmed by even a small particle of God's glory.}Q7

{"Good tidings" is a term especially related to Messiah and the kingdom of God.}Q8 Isaiah 52:7 is the place where the idea of "good tidings" first develops as God's rule being established at a specific time through His Messiah. Our modern word "gospel" is derived from it. The four books about the life, death, and resurrection of Jesus have always been called Gospels. Paul said the gospel is the death, burial, and resurrection of Jesus (I Cor. 15:1-8). Jesus would tell the people the gospel of the coming kingdom (Luke 4:18; 7:22; 20:1). In Luke's second book, Acts, he many times showed the apostles proclaiming the good news.

{"Good tidings" also relates the birth of Messiah to the kinds of things said about Roman emperors, especially Augustus.}Q8 As mentioned previously, an ancient inscription found at Priene, Italy, calls the birthday of Augustus the "beginning of the good news for the world." Luke shows that the humble birth of Messiah, in contrast to the wealth of Augustus, was the true good tidings.

The Saviour and a sign (Luke 2:11-12). The angel of the Lord mentioned three titles for the infant: "Saviour," "Christ," and "Lord." Each of these titles had a different connotation.

The term "Saviour" was not only associated with dying on a cross. God is many times called Israel's Saviour. A savior could also be a human king sent to deliver in war (Isa. 19:20). This title suggested one who would save Israel from Roman oppression.

{"Christ" means the same thing as "Messiah": one anointed, as in the ancient custom of anointing a priest or king.}Q9 A major theme of the teaching of Jesus would be that the people did not yet understand the true mission of the Messiah.

Jesus was revealed to be more than a man and more than a human messiah figure. The word "Lord" used for Jesus in later contexts refers to His divinity. Yet the same word is also used of kings and high officials.

The shepherds of Bethlehem could hardly know that the infant in the manger was the Saviour from sin, the suffering Christ, and the one and only divine Lord. Yet Luke's readers know this.

The choir of angels (Luke 2:13-14). The multitude of God's host (for He is the Lord of Hosts, that is, the heavenly armies) went far beyond other appearances of angels in the history of Israel. Jacob saw a vision of a ladder (Gen. 28), but it was merely a vision. In no other place does there actually appear, in reality and not a vision, a host of angelic beings.

Scripture indicates that the meaning of Jesus' birth is good news. The true glory is not that of the Roman emperor, with his legions and taxes, but of the Child born in a small Israelite town into the most humble of circumstances.

RUMORS

15 And it came to pass, as the angels were gone away from them into heaven, the shepherds said one to another, Let us now go even unto Bethlehem, and see this thing which is come to pass, which the Lord hath made known unto us.

16 And they came with haste, and found Mary, and Joseph, and the babe lying in a manger.

17 And when they had seen it, they made known abroad the saying which was told them concerning this child.

The shepherds (Luke 2:15-16). The shepherds found the scene just as the angel of the Lord had said (vs. 12). The unusual sight of a beloved baby being cradled in a feeding trough was the sign by which they knew which child was Saviour, Christ, and Lord.

Spreading the news (Luke 2:17). {It was important for Luke's readers, living decades after Jesus, to know that the spreading of the good news of Jesus had been happening since the beginning.}^Q10 By their time, the tiny movement of Jesus followers in Jerusalem had spread all over the Roman Empire. The movement was still small, but no doubt all were amazed by how a small, originally Jewish, group with a message about a Saviour (strange to Roman ears) could appear and grow in so many places.

The simple truth is that what has been revealed in Jesus is too wonderful to hide. Just as the shepherds told their story to many, so all followers of Jesus in every age have an understanding that other people would be blessed to hear.

—*Derek Leman.*

QUESTIONS

1. Why was it important to Luke's first readers that Augustus decreed the census?

2. Why did God arrange for Jesus to be born in Bethlehem?

3. What two complementary meanings could "the days were accomplished" have in Luke 2:6?

4. Why is the mention that there was no lodging place for Joseph and Mary important?

5. What was the purpose of swaddling clothes?

6. Why were the shepherds fitting witnesses of Jesus' birth?

7. Why were the shepherds terrified by the angels?

8. What is important about the phrase "good tidings" (vs. 10)?

9. What is the meaning of the title "Christ," or "Messiah"?

10. Why did Luke write that shepherds spread the news about Jesus?

—*Derek Leman.*

Preparing to Teach the Lesson

Doctor Luke has given us an orderly record of the life of Christ, beginning with the events surrounding His birth, so that we might be certain of the reality of Christ and thus place faith and trust in Him. The previous lessons this quarter have laid the groundwork for what we look at next.

Birth predictions and rhapsodic responses have been the order of the day thus far. Unless a person's heart is unbelieving or cold, what transpires next should inspire him to join with the multitude of angels in praise of God. Mary and Zacharias have had their turns to burst forth in song. Now it is up to the reader to decide what he will do. Will he extol the mercy and grace of God because He has sent a Saviour who can save the most vile sinner? Or will he be untouched?

TODAY'S AIM

Facts: to set forth the mysterious way God worked to bring about His plan.

Principle: to see that it was not beneath God to take on humanity in order to redeem sinners.

Application: to show that Christmas is about God's gift to a world He loved.

INTRODUCING THE LESSON

Since the lesson is about the birth of Jesus, ask the class what they think God thinks about the way Christmas is celebrated today. Why do they suppose people, even the unsaved, give gifts to one another? What would God most like to see in those who accept His gift? What gifts are appropriate to give God?

DEVELOPING THE LESSON

We will examine this week's text under the following topics: the unseen hand of God, the birth of the Son of God, and the birth announcement.

1. The unseen hand of God (Luke 2:1-2). English poet William Cowper wrote, "God moves in a mysterious way His wonders to perform." The Prophet Micah had recorded centuries earlier that Messiah would be born in Bethlehem (Mic. 5:2); yet Joseph and Mary lived in Nazareth, some ninety miles north. If Scripture was to be fulfilled, the couple had to make a move.

God did not raise up a prophet to nudge Joseph to read Micah and consider what he should do. Rather, He used a pagan Gentile ruler to call for a census for taxation purposes.

Believers should be on the lookout for the unseen hand of God, because what people often call coincidence may actually be a divine appointment. God has a way of bringing people across the path of a faithful believer in order to accomplish something, perhaps even evangelization. We should think less in terms of happenstance and more of God's sovereign appointments.

2. The birth of the Son of God (Luke 2:3-7). The census required people to register in the place of their ancestral home. Since Joseph was of the line of David, he traveled to the city of David, Bethlehem. Going "up from Galilee" sounds strange, since Bethlehem was south of Galilee, but it has more to do with elevation than direction.

Mary was not required to go with Joseph, but we find her by his side. She is called his "espoused wife" (vs. 5), which indicates their betrothal had taken place, but we also know the marriage was not consummated until after the birth of Jesus (Matt. 1:25). We do not know just how close Mary was to delivering, but she was "great with child" (Luke 2:5), which means she was quite far along. While still in Bethlehem, Mary gave birth and, following tradition, wrapped the baby in strips of cloth. A nearby animal feeding trough was put to unusual use.

The word for "inn" (vs. 7) does not necessarily mean a hotel- or motel-like place, which has become nearly universal in the mind-set of many. It is the word for "guestchamber" and is found in 22:11 and Mark 14:14. A possible scenario is that Joseph and Mary were in a private home in which the guest room was already taken and thus they stayed in the family quarters, which were often joined under one roof with an area for animals.

3. The birth announcement (Luke 2:8-17). The first to know of the event were not the religious elite, but shepherds on nearby hills. Shepherds were an almost outcast group, and to these unassuming, God-fearing men the angel appeared.

What started as a frightening moment when the angel appeared turned into a joyous occasion as the announcement was given. A Saviour and Lord had come into the world, and the shepherds were personally invited to see Him. They did not have to wash up or dress up—just show up. After a large group of angels appeared, praising God, the shepherds made their way to where the child lay to see for themselves.

Just as Mary and Zacharias could not be quiet about what God was doing, so the shepherds could not be silent, either. They were not only the first witnesses but also the first missionaries.

Shepherds as a group were not on anyone's party list, but God exalted these above all that night. God identifies with shepherds by being one Himself (Ps. 23:1; Isa. 40:11; Ezek.

34:23). Jesus called Himself the "good shepherd" (John 10:11), and He identified with sinners when undergoing John's baptism.

ILLUSTRATING THE LESSON

God responded to humanity's lostness by providing a Saviour. He did not send a conquering king but a baby.

CONCLUDING THE LESSON

Our lesson is an illustration of what the Apostle Paul wrote to the believers at Corinth when he reminded them that God does not do things the way people do. Paul told them to consider their own calling. God does not call those who think they are somebody; Instead, He calls, in essence, nobodies and then makes them somebodies in Christ.

This Sunday is Christmas, and people are super busy. Cash registers have been ringing. But where people should go overboard is not in gifting but rather in glorifying God.

ANTICIPATING THE NEXT LESSON

Next week we will examine the blessing of reconciliation with God through Christ.

—Darrell W. McKay.

PRACTICAL POINTS

1. God acts in time with His eternal plan (Luke 2:1).
2. God uses even the acts of pagan leaders to fulfill His prophetic Word (vss. 2-3).
3. God uses obedient people to carry out His plan (vss. 4-6).
4. Christ's incarnation is a great miracle; God in the flesh identified with us (vs. 7).
5. God uses angels (messengers) to accomplish His eternal purposes on earth (Luke 2:8-14; cf. Heb. 1:13-14).
6. Our first response to God's calling should always be obedience (Luke 2:15-17).

—Paul R. Bawden.

RESEARCH AND DISCUSSION

1. How do you think Joseph and Mary felt when they found out that there was no room for them in the Bethlehem inn?
2. What is the relationship between Luke 2:1-6 and Micah 5:2? What does a prophecy like this being fulfilled some seven hundred years later tell us about the accuracy of God's Word?
3. In what ways was the birth of Christ different from other births?
4. Why did God use angels to announce the birth of Christ (Luke 2:8-14; cf. Heb. 1:14)?
5. How might seeing the Christ Child have changed the lives of the shepherds? How might this compare to how Christ has changed your life?

—Paul R. Bawden.

ILLUSTRATED HIGH POINTS

Ye shall find the babe wrapped in swaddling clothes (Luke 2:12)

The birth of Jesus that we celebrate during this joyous season of Christmas always brings our attention to the fact that God chose to give us the greatest gift in history through the humblest of circumstances and worked things out through the most insignificant of people.

Samuel Logan Brengle, who served in the Salvation Army, was once introduced as "the great Dr. Brengle." His immediate response was one of humility, and he reportedly concluded, "I am so concerned that He uses me and that it is not of me that the work is done. . . . O that I may never lose sight of this." This week we learn that Mary's humble attitude of total submission to the divine task that had just been given to her was one of total obedience to God's will.

A multitude of the heavenly host praising God (vs. 13)

George Whitefield, a well-known preacher in the 1700s, was once preaching on the matter of eternity when he suddenly declared to his congregation, "Hark! Methinks I hear [the saints] chanting their everlasting hallelujahs, and spending an eternal day in echoing forth triumphant sounds of joy. And do you not long, my brethren, to join this heavenly choir?"

Whitefield proclaimed to his hearers the significance of the saving message of the good news for the world.

In our lesson this week, God used the angels to proclaim the good news of Jesus to the world. We are challenged to recognize through the angels that Jesus is indeed our promised Messiah.

—A. Koshy Muthalaly.

World Missions

Jesus, wrapped up and given to the world, was the perfect gift.

There is no culture, no people group, no nation where He is not the most needed, most important gift that can be given. More than food for the hungry or deliverance from oppression, the good news of salvation is the best Christmas gift that can be given to the world. It is the only gift that lasts for all eternity, the one gift that gives people not only peace for today but also hope for tomorrow, lasting freedom, and eternal joy.

For many, that gift—the good news of salvation—does actually come wrapped up in bright, cheerful paper in the unassuming form of a shoe box—unassuming, like Jesus in a manger.

Children all over the world, many who have never received a gift in their lives, run cheering toward a volunteer who hands out a truckload of shoe boxes.

Eyes alight, each child opens his or her very own shoe box. The box is filled with small toys and practical items like toothbrushes and socks. Children grin as they hold up a brand-new coloring book, or a ball, or a set of tools.

Then, reaching down below the other things, the children pull out a book, their very own, that tells them about Jesus—God's gift to the world, God's gift to each child.

For many children, that shoe box becomes the carrier of God's greatest gift—salvation.

It is not just one missionary who provides these shoe boxes to a small, select few. Christians all over the world pack up shoe boxes and deliver them to centers where they are packaged and shipped to over 130 countries worldwide. Each person who helps is part of the gift.

Arthur, a schoolchild in Russia, received one of the millions of shoe boxes. In it he was given material gifts and the gift of the gospel. Arthur trusted Christ.

Enclosed in the shoe box was a response card. One morning, Arthur reminded his mother to mail the response card in. He wanted everyone to know about his decision.

His mother promised to mail it, then sent him off to school. Later that day, terrorists came into his school and held the schoolchildren hostage. Arthur was killed.

That shoe box did so much more than simply give a child a smile and a few toys. It carried the news of eternal life to a boy who is now in heaven because of it.

As we celebrate this Christmas this perfect gift, let us not just enjoy all the gifts we receive; rather, let us ask God what we can give Him and especially what we can do to tell of His gift of salvation to others.

Whatever it is, great or small, if it carries the message of salvation, it is the best Christmas gift you could ever give someone.

Instead of exchanging names for gifts or buying a huge pile of toys for your own children or grandchildren, why not consider (as a family or an office or a church group) giving the money you would have spent on gifts for one another to a ministry that gives the gift of Jesus? Why not have a family discussion and choose to make this Christmas more about giving something to Jesus than about receiving something yourselves?

What can you give to the One who has been your greatest gift?

—*Kimberly Rae.*

The Jewish Aspect

Christians regard Bethlehem as a special town, for that is where Jesus was born. What we often do not consider is that Bethlehem is also a special town for Jews, though for a completely different reason.

The Bible's first reference to Bethlehem occurs in Genesis 35:19. "And Rachel died, and was buried in the way to Ephrath, which is Bethlehem." Rachel died about 1900 B.C., so Bethlehem is an ancient town. Some Jews believe that Jacob buried Rachel in Bethlehem rather than in the patriarchal burying place at Hebron because "he foresaw that his descendants would pass this site during their exile into Babylon and that Rachel would pray for their safety and ultimate return" (Bedein, "Mother Rachel's Yahrtzeit," www.torah.org).

The story of Boaz and Ruth also occurred in Bethlehem (Ruth 1:1, 22). This became a crucial event in the town's history, since they were direct ancestors of David (4:21-22). David's father, Jesse, was called the Bethlehemite (I Sam. 16:1).

David watched the sheep near Bethlehem (I Sam. 16:11), and that was where Samuel anointed him king of Israel (vs. 13). Jews called Bethlehem "the city of David," as recognized in Luke 2:4.

Rehoboam fortified Bethlehem (II Chr. 11:5-6). The Prophet Micah identified Bethlehem as the place of Messiah's birth (Mic. 5:2), which the Jewish chief priests and scribes knew at the time of Jesus' birth (Matt. 2:3-6). After the Babylonian Captivity, 123 people who returned to Judea were exiles from Bethlehem (Ezra 2:21).

The town of Bethlehem is a sacred place for Jews. Rachel's tomb attracts Jews from all over the world. They revere it as a sacred prayer site. A Jewish midrash says that when Joseph was sold into Egypt by his brothers, the caravan passed her tomb. He escaped and ran to it, beseeching her to rescue him. After he heard his mother's voice telling him not to fear but to "go with them and may the L-rd be with you," he voluntarily went back to the caravan (Rossoff, "Tomb of Rahel," www.jewishmag. com). Of all the matriarchs of Judaism, Rachel is considered the most loving mother of her children.

Jews consider Jeremiah's words critical for their nation: "A voice was heard in Ramah, lamentation, and bitter weeping; Rahel weeping for her children refused to be comforted for her children, because they were not" (31:15). Rachel stands for the women of Israel, who are pictured as weeping over the Jews going into the Babylonian Captivity and the deaths of their children in that time.

Jews continue to regard the tomb of Rachel as critical to their religious life. "For millennia, Jews have made pilgrimages to Rachel's Tomb, considered the third holiest shrine in the Land of Israel. The site has absorbed countless tears of barren women beseeching G-d in the merit of Mother Rachel, who herself had been barren for many years. Jews have poured out their hearts there, praying for everything from world redemption to a suitable marriage-partner" (Bedein).

The critical element—which Jews have missed—is that Jeremiah's words were fulfilled at the time of Christ's birth. Matthew specifically connects the prophecy to Herod's slaughter of the children at Bethlehem (2:16-18). Neither the Babylonians nor Herod, however, could stop God's redemptive work through His Messiah.

—R. Larry Overstreet

Guiding the Superintendent

Unlike other stories, the Christmas story never grows old. People of all ages enjoy hearing it told over and over again. With Christmas falling directly upon this Sunday, it is very appropriate to review this story of the birth of Jesus.

The Bible actually tells the story twice. The lesson this week will review the story that is found in Luke's second chapter.

DEVOTIONAL OUTLINE

1. The birth of Jesus (Luke 2:1-7). Considering the greatness of who Jesus Christ is, it is always amazing how simple the story of His birth is.

The simple details are well-known. The government of the day required that Mary's husband journey to his ancestral home of Bethlehem to be registered for a census. It was while in Bethlehem that Mary gave birth to her first son.

Due to a shortage of accommodations that night, Joseph and Mary ended up in a local barn. As was the custom of the day, Mary wrapped her newborn in swaddling clothes and laid Him in a manger used to feed cattle.

How unlikely this would be if a king were born today! His mother would receive the greatest of medical care. The event would be covered by the world's news reporters. While the world might not have announced Jesus' birth, God did. It is only fitting that God would announce this great event to the world. What is more significant is to whom He made the announcement.

2. The shepherds' visit (Luke 2:8-17). It is significant that it was to shepherds that the good news of Jesus' birth was announced. They represented the uneducated, the poor—the common people of the age. It was not to the palaces that God sent His messenger but to these lowly shepherds.

The angel told these simple folks not to fear but to rejoice, for he brought the good news that in David's city "a Saviour, which is Christ the Lord" (vs. 11), had been born. In contrast to this great event is how they would recognize Him. He would not be surrounded by great pomp and ceremony or outward glory. He would be found in humility and obscurity, wrapped up and lying in a manger.

The lone divine messenger was now joined by a great company of angels, all giving glory to God and proclaiming peace on earth.

No sooner had the angels left than the shepherds obeyed and went looking for this new Saviour who had just been born. Their desire was rewarded, and they found the baby, just as they had been told. They became some of the first preachers to spread the good news of Jesus' birth.

CHILDREN'S CORNER

Since the Christmas season is so highly commercialized, it is important that children hear the real story of Christmas that this lesson describes. There are many children in our world today for whom Christmas is nothing more than Santa, elves, and a pile of presents under the tree. The children in your classes should have a better perspective than that, but it can be hard for them to focus on the celebration of the birth of Christ with all the commercial hoopla. Make sure it is emphasized that Christmas is all about Jesus. All the other elements of the season are merely extras.

—*Martin R. Dahlquist.*

SCRIPTURE LESSON TEXT

II COR. 5:11 Knowing therefore the terror of the Lord, we persuade men; but we are made manifest unto God; and I trust also are made manifest in your consciences.

12 For we commend not ourselves again unto you, but give you occasion to glory on our behalf, that ye may have somewhat to *answer* **them which glory in appearance, and not in heart.**

13 For whether we be beside ourselves, *it is* to God: or whether we be sober, *it is* for your cause.

14 For the love of Christ constraineth us; because we thus judge, that if one died for all, then were all dead:

15 And *that* he died for all, that they which live should not henceforth live unto themselves, but unto him which died for them, and rose again.

16 Wherefore henceforth know we no man after the flesh: yea, though we have known Christ af- ter the flesh, yet now henceforth know we *him* no more.

17 Therefore if any man *be* in Christ, *he is* a new creature: old things are passed away; behold, all things are become new.

18 And all things *are* **of God, who hath reconciled us to himself by Jesus Christ, and hath given to us the ministry of reconciliation;**

19 To wit, that God was in Christ, reconciling the world unto himself, not imputing their trespasses unto them; and hath committed unto us the word of reconciliation.

20 Now then we are ambassadors for Christ, as though God did beseech *you* **by us: we pray** *you* **in Christ's stead, be ye reconciled to God.**

21 For he hath made him *to be* sin for us, who knew no sin; that we might be made the righteousness of God in him.

NOTES

Blessing of Reconciliation

Lesson Text: II Corinthians 5:11-21

Related Scriptures: Romans 5:1-11; Colossians 1:18-23

TIME: probably A.D. 55   PLACE: from Macedonia

GOLDEN TEXT—"If any man be in Christ, he is a new creature: old things are passed away; behold, all things are become new" (II Corinthians 5:17).

Introduction

This week our focus shifts to the city of Corinth. The apostle Paul was addressing problems that plagued the church there. Some false teachers had wormed their way into the fellowship and were challenging Paul's authority and integrity.

Arriving in Macedonia from Ephesus, Paul was greatly relieved to learn from Titus that the situation in Corinth was more encouraging than he had previously thought (II Cor. 7:5-9). Nevertheless, Paul devoted a considerable portion of this letter to defending himself against his detractors. In doing so, the apostle revealed much personal information concerning both his struggles and his goals in ministry.

In the first part of chapter 5, Paul deals with the resurrection body, since some had been questioning its reality. Unlike the earthly tent in which we now reside, Paul longed for a "house not made with hands, eternal in the heavens" (vs. 1). Once we depart this earthly body, we will be "present with the Lord" (vs. 8) and "must all appear before the judgment seat of Christ" (vs. 10).

LESSON OUTLINE

I. CONSTRAINED BY THE LOVE OF CHRIST—II Cor. 5:11-15

II. CHANGED BY THE POWER OF CHRIST—II Cor. 5:16-17

III. CALLED TO SHARE THE MESSAGE OF CHRIST—II Cor. 5:18-21

Exposition: Verse by Verse

CONSTRAINED BY THE LOVE OF CHRIST

II COR. 5:11 Knowing therefore the terror of the Lord, we persuade men; but we are made manifest unto God; and I trust also are made manifest in your consciences.

12 For we commend not ourselves again unto you, but give you occasion to glory on our behalf, that ye may have somewhat to answer

them which glory in appearance, and not in heart.

13 For whether we be beside ourselves, it is to God: or whether we be sober, it is for your cause.

14 For the love of Christ constraineth us; because we thus judge, that if one died for all, then were all dead:

15 And that he died for all, that they which live should not henceforth live unto themselves, but unto him which died for them, and rose again.

Fear of the Lord (II Cor. 5:11). The word translated "terror" is the Greek word *phobos* and is usually rendered "fear" in the New Testament. {Having just spoken of one day standing before the judgment seat of Christ (vs. 10), Paul acknowledged that this prospect moved him to fear the Lord. A healthy fear of God is necessary to serve Him faithfully.}[Q1]

Believers will have to answer concerning the use of their talents and opportunities to serve God (I Cor. 3:13-15). This is a strong motivation to "persuade men" (II Cor. 5:11) to follow Christ.

Leading others to Christ involves persuading them to forsake sin and trust in Him; thus we must appeal to both head and heart when involved in the evangelistic task (cf. Acts 17:2; 18:4; 24:25; 26:28). Perhaps our greatest challenge is to get people to see their need for repentance, for many do not view themselves as lost in sin (II Pet. 3:9).

Although some might have thought that Paul had goals other than winning the lost, his heart was known by God— and should have been recognized by the Corinthians as well. Paul had no hidden agenda and was not "handling the word of God deceitfully"(II Cor. 4:2). Since he had planted the church in Corinth, these saints should have had no doubts concerning his motives.

Even so, they had become enamored of the false teachers, who were casting doubt on Paul's character.

Not commending ourselves (II Cor. 5:12-13). Paul was not commending himself, as might be supposed. Rather, Paul was giving the Corinthians an opportunity to be rightfully proud of his ministry, which had brought them the message of salvation.

{This, of course, was quite a contrast to the false teachers, who were prone to "glory in appearance, and not in heart" (vs. 12). While Paul's opponents might have been questioning his sincerity, he questioned the hearts of those who were concerned only with outward appearances. If, as some suggest, these teachers were Judaizers, we know that they were particularly concerned with outward ritual (cf. Acts 15:1; Col. 2:16).}[Q2]

"If we live only for the praise of men, we will not win the praise of God at the Judgment Seat of Christ. To live for man's praise is to exalt reputation over character, and it is character that will count when we see Christ" (Wiersbe, *Bible Exposition Commentary,* Victor).

To be beside oneself (II Cor. 5:13) was to be insane, apparently an accusation that some had leveled at the Apostle Paul. If in his zeal the apostle seemed to be out of his mind, it was for the glory of God. On the other hand, if Paul seemed too serious, it had the benefit of blessing the Corinthians. This would not be the last time Paul would be accused of being insane. When Paul was attempting to convert King Agrippa, Festus interrupted the sermon and said, "Paul, thou art beside thyself; much learning doth make thee mad" (Acts 26:24).

{Perhaps some accused Paul of having lost his mind because of his refusal to take financial support from the Corinthians (I Cor. 9:14-15; II Cor.

11:8). His choice to focus on Christ instead of relying on human wisdom may have caused some to conclude he was mad (I Cor. 2:1-4). Even his use of spiritual gifts might be involved (14:18). Some have suggested that his "thorn in the flesh" (II Cor. 12:7) was epilepsy, which could be confused with madness.}Q3

The love of Christ (II Cor. 5:14-15). {The real reason Paul served the Lord was the love of Christ.}Q4 The word for "constraineth" can be translated "controls" or "compels," thus indicating that Christ's love was the primary motivation for Paul's ministry. The construction can mean that Paul was talking about either Christ's love for him or his love for Christ (John 3:16; Rom. 5:8; I John 4:9). The former is more likely than the latter.

If Christ died for all—and He did— "then were all dead" (II Cor. 5:14; cf. Heb. 2:9). The idea is that all of us, because we are "dead in trespasses and sins" (Eph. 2:1), were represented on the cross, where Christ offered Himself as a substitute on our behalf (I Cor. 15:3; I Pet. 1:18-19; 3:18; I John 2:2). "In all his redemptive actions Christ was a representative of humanity, so that what was done by him for the race could be viewed as done by the race in him" (Allen, ed., *Broadman Bible Commentary,* Broadman).

As Paul said elsewhere, believers are crucified with Christ (Gal. 2:20), buried with Him (Col. 2:12), and raised to walk in newness of life (Rom. 6:4). "The proclamation of this message includes a call to believe the good news and be baptized, and so be united to him who died and rose for them. Then they will know in their own lives the power of his death for their sin and the power of his resurrection for their living" (Allen).

{Since Christ died to give us a new life, it behooves us to dedicate our lives to serving Him.}Q5 As Paul felt constrained to proclaim the message of redemption, so those who have responded to that message should commit their lives to serving Him. We have indeed been saved to serve!

CHANGED BY THE POWER OF CHRIST

16 Wherefore henceforth know we no man after the flesh: yea, though we have known Christ after the flesh, yet now henceforth know we him no more.

17 Therefore if any man be in Christ, he is a new creature: old things are passed away; behold, all things are become new.

Knowing Christ (II Cor. 5:16). To know someone "after the flesh" might indicate looking at someone purely from a worldly standpoint. As a Pharisee, Paul likely viewed both people and positions in such a manner (cf. Phil. 3:4-7). Having come to know the Lord, however, he gained a new perspective. He wanted to see people as Christ saw them. As Jesus was willing to divest Himself of great privilege to come to earth, so believers must share a similar attitude (2:5-11).

Paul's statement "We have known Christ after the flesh" (II Cor. 5:16) has led some to conclude that Paul had a personal knowledge of and acquaintance with Jesus of Nazareth while He was on earth. This, however, is doubtful. The fact that Paul made no reference to a personal knowledge of the life of Christ probably indicates that he was in the city of Tarsus during those years of Jesus' earthly ministry.

Paul probably arrived in Jerusalem shortly after the founding of the church on Pentecost and simply accepted the word of the religious leaders who had been responsible for the crucifixion.

These men, of course, believed Jesus to be a blasphemer and an impostor. Prior to his dramatic conversion on the road to Damascus, Saul (Paul) believed the same thing (Acts 26:9-11; I Tim. 1:13).

Now, however, things were different. Paul realized that Jesus of Nazareth is the eternal Son of God who gave His life on the cross to "save sinners; of whom I am chief" (I Tim. 1:15). Paul now viewed Christ quite differently from the way he had previously.

Since Paul came to view Christ differently as a result of his conversion, he could now view all people differently. "Paul affirms that the new man sees the world with new eyes, since this world is seen in the light of the world to come, and therefore, it is seen and understood more perfectly" (Allen).

A new creature (II Cor. 5:17). {The expression "in Christ" is a favorite of the Apostle Paul. It denotes our union with Christ and our incorporation into His spiritual body (I Cor. 12:13). To be *in Christ* is to be a Christian; it is to be changed by His power into a completely new person.}[Q6]

So great is the change that Christ makes that Paul could describe it as becoming a "new creature" (II Cor. 5:17), or new creation. The same concept was expressed by Christ when He said, "Ye must be born again" (John 3:7).

This new birth affects not only the inner person but also all things related to that person. "Adam was the head of the old creation, and Christ is the Head of the new creation. The old creation was plunged into sin and condemnation because of the disobedience of Adam. The new creation means righteousness and salvation because of the obedience of Jesus Christ. Because we are a part of the new creation, everything has become new" (Wiersbe).

Being new creatures in Christ, however, does not mean that we will no longer struggle with temptation and sin. If we yield to the power of the Spirit, we can find victory over the forces of evil (Rom. 7:24-25). The saints in Corinth certainly knew that the power of God could deliver them from sin. Prior to trusting in Christ, some of them had led very sordid lifestyles (I Cor. 6:9- 11). They knew that the battle with sin was not over, as the two Corinthian epistles certainly indicate.

CALLED TO SHARE THE MESSAGE OF CHRIST

18 And all things are of God, who hath reconciled us to himself by Jesus Christ, and hath given to us the ministry of reconciliation;

19 To wit, that God was in Christ, reconciling the world unto himself, not imputing their trespasses unto them; and hath committed unto us the word of reconciliation.

20 Now then we are ambassadors for Christ, as though God did beseech you by us: we pray you in Christ's stead, be ye reconciled to God.

21 For he hath made him to be sin for us, who knew no sin; that we might be made the righteousness of God in him.

Ministry of reconciliation (II Cor. 5:18-19). {Having been reconciled to Christ, Paul was given the ministry of reconciliation.}[Q7] The change from the old to the new was, in fact, the work of God. Salvation is of the Lord, from start to finish. This being so, we cannot boast as if we achieved salvation through our own efforts; it is the gift of God (Eph. 2:8-9).

The word "reconciled" (II Cor. 5:18) speaks of a change from enmity to friendship. "Just as sin involves man in a dual estrangement, from God and from his fellow man, so reconciliation is God's work in bringing man into proper relationship with himself and with his fellow man" (Stagg, *New Testament Theology,* Broadman). Now that we have been reconciled to God through Christ, we must carry on the "ministry of reconciliation" to others.

{"Not imputing their trespasses unto them" (vs. 19) means that God was not counting sins against those who come to Christ for salvation.}[Q8] However, if we refuse to receive Christ, we will die in our sins, thus facing the consequences of that dreadful choice (John 8:24).

The "word of reconciliation" (II Cor. 5:19) is the gospel Paul preached. It is still proclaimed today by faithful servants of God.

Ambassadors for Christ (II Cor. 5:20). An ambassador has a dual role: he is a messenger and a representative. In actuality, he has no authority of his own. His authority derives from the one who sent him. In this case, Paul viewed himself as an ambassador for Christ. This was particularly true with regard to his apostolic ministry (Gal. 1:11-12).

{All Christians, however, should view themselves as the Lord's ambassadors. There are not enough ministers and missionaries to reach everyone. All believers must take seriously the privilege of witnessing for Christ. We do not carry our own message but the reconciling message of the Lord Jesus.}[Q9]

"No graver issue can be set before man than for him to learn of the reconciliation achieved by Christ and the necessity for him to end his rebellion against God. The reason for this gravity is clear: the reconciliation between God and the individual is incomplete so long as the individual withholds repentance, maintains his resistance to God, and declines to acknowledge Christ as Saviour and Lord" (Allen).

Made sin for us (II Cor. 5:21). As the holy Son of God, Jesus Christ "knew no sin." This was in spite of the fact that He "was in all points tempted like

as we are" (Heb. 4:15). That He never succumbed to the allurements of the devil uniquely qualified Him to be our Saviour, the One who "was wounded for our transgressions, [and] bruised for our iniquities" (Isa. 53:5).

{That God "made him to be sin for us" (II Cor. 5:21) means that Christ became a sin offering on our behalf. This should not be taken to mean that Jesus became a real sinner; rather, He took the place of sinners on the cross. His substitutionary atonement made possible our righteousness and thus our right standing before God (cf. Rom. 5:17).}[Q10] This is not based on what we have done but on what He has done for us!

—John A. Owston.

QUESTIONS

1. What future event motivated Paul to persuade others to trust in Christ?
2. Why is it wrong to "glory in appearance" (II Cor. 5:12)?
3. What are some possible reasons some might have thought Paul was mad?
4. What was the primary motivation for Paul to serve Christ?
5. Because Christ "died for all" (vs. 15), how should we live?
6. What does being "in Christ" (vs. 17) mean for us?
7. What ministry was given to Paul?
8. What does "not imputing their trespasses" (vs. 19) mean?
9. How can we be "ambassadors for Christ" (vs. 20)?
10. How did Christ become "sin for us" (vs. 21)? What results because of His sacrifice?

—John A. Owston.

Preparing to Teach the Lesson

The first part of II Corinthians 5 reveals that those who belong to Christ need not be terrorized by thoughts of death. They should actually be yearning to move on to heaven and be with God in glorified bodies. The one sobering thought is that they will appear before the judgment seat of Christ to be rewarded for or disappointed by their works (II Cor. 5:1-10; cf. I Cor. 3:12-15). Unrepentant sinners, however, should rightfully fear the coming terror of the Lord, for not just their works but their eternal souls are in danger of hellfire.

TODAY'S AIM

Facts: to see what Paul wrote to the Corinthians about the tremendous changes that take place when sinners become new creatures in Christ.

Principle: to be aware that believers have an obligation to work for Christ in reconciling sinners to Him, even as God through Christ reconciled them to Himself.

Application: to urge Christians to include in their new way of life efforts to bring sinners to righteousness by faith in Christ.

INTRODUCING THE LESSON

Many idealistic people believe that individuals are inherently good. Some even say each person has a "spark of divinity" that just needs to be fanned into flame. Those who are realistic, however, soon learn that individuals are motivated by their sinful natures to think, say, and do many evil things.

There are psychologists, psychiatrists, counselors, criminologists, penologists, and liberal pastors who promote the idea that education and rehabilitation will radically change a person. But the Bible is very clear that the human heart must undergo the transforming power of God's grace in order for true change to take place.

DEVELOPING THE LESSON

1. Ministering men (II Cor. 5:11-13). Paul and his team of itinerant missionaries described themselves as ministers of the gospel, commissioned to do all they could to persuade sinners to avoid the terror of God's judgment.

Ask your students to study II Corinthians 5:11-13 to determine the motives of Paul and his colleagues, who stated that these were manifest to God and hopefully to the Corinthian believers. Be sure they touch on the following:

a. They did not commend themselves but called on the Corinthians to compare them with false teachers who gloried in appearance rather than in sincere heart attitudes.

b. They said that whether they seemed to act in an insane manner or in a sober manner, they worked on the Corinthians' behalf.

2. Ministering Saviour (II Cor. 5:14-16). Paul said that it was Christ's love for them that constrained the missionaries to work as ministers. They knew that all people are spiritually "dead in trespasses and sins" (Eph. 2:1). This had a tremendous impact on their thinking.

Paul went on to state that all who live, or have been quickened in Christ and raised up to sit in a heavenly position with Him, according to Ephesians 2:5-6, should be guided not by selfish motives but by motivation to serve Him (II Cor. 5:15).

Paul said that people should not be viewed according to human standards of reasoning. These men had once perceived Jesus as merely a man, but after conversion they saw

Him as the divine Son of God.

Paul's motivation to serve Christ was obviously intense. Turn the attention of your students to the list of things Paul suffered as a minister of the gospel (II Cor. 11:23-28). He saw people as sinners in need of the Saviour, not in idealistic terms of innocence.

3. Ministry of reconciliation (II Cor. 5:17-21). The biblical meaning of "reconciliation" involves a change of relationship between God and people made possible by the redemptive work of Christ at Calvary. Reconciliation thus provides the basis for fellowship with God. Have your class members note that this truth underlies verses 17-18. Paul expressed the idea as sinners being made new creatures in Christ, resulting in the passing away of the old life controlled by the sinful nature and the birth of the new righteous nature.

Now have your students see that the next logical step is for believers to take up their God-given ministry of reconciliation of sinners. This ministry involves telling sinners that God was in Christ bringing the world of mankind to Himself by providing for the forgiveness of their sins. Christians, therefore, can be described as ambassadors, or envoys, for God by representing Him as the source of salvation.

Take time to carefully explain the exact meaning of II Corinthians 5:21 so that your students understand it. Perhaps the following paraphrase will help some: "God made Christ to be a sin offering for us, even though He, Christ, was free from sin, so that we could be made righteous, like God, through our identification with Christ." Changed creatures can help others experience this change.

ILLUSTRATING THE LESSON

The ministry of reconciliation involves showing a sinner how to stop being an old creature dominated by a sinful nature and move on through and beyond the terror of divine judgment to become a new creature dominated by a righteous nature. Being such an ambassador is both a responsibility and a privilege.

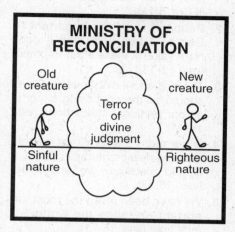

CONCLUDING THE LESSON

An unsaved young man once said to his Christian mother, "If I really believed that people were going to hell, I would be on my knees begging them to get saved." Statements like this should encourage us to spread the gospel message. Paul and his companions really believed in the terror of the Lord, and they spent their time trying to lead sinners to salvation.

It is important that all of us who are Christians be motivated by love in our attempts to spare sinners from eternal torment. New creatures should reproduce other new creatures.

ANTICIPATING THE NEXT LESSON

The next lesson describes how we have been blessed with forgiveness and new life in Christ. God is both just and the justifier of the ungodly through the atoning sacrifice of Christ. By His blood He only can forgive our sins, and He also cleanses us from all our unrighteousness.

—*Gordon Talbot.*

PRACTICAL POINTS

1. We should seek to live transparently before God and other people (II Cor. 5:11).
2. Decorum is not as important to God as a true heart, but it does have value in ministering to others (vss. 12-13).
3. The self-sacrificing love of Christ should be the controlling factor in all our personal interactions (vss. 14-15).
4. If we really believe that people become new creatures in Christ, it should affect how we treat others (vss. 16-17).
5. We have been given the most important message the world will ever hear (vss. 18-21).

—Kenneth A. Sponsler.

RESEARCH AND DISCUSSION

1. Under what circumstances or in what form is it ever appropriate to seem to be out of one's mind for God (II Cor. 5:13)?
2. How can it be said that all are dead (vs. 14)? What implications does this have for our daily conduct?
3. What does it mean to know "no man after the flesh" (vs. 16)? How well do we do this in our daily interactions?
4. Since we still have the flesh, with its sinful proclivities, exactly what has passed away when we became new creatures in Christ (vs. 17)?
5. How does being an ambassador for Christ (vs. 20) affect the choices you make regarding how you spend your time?

—Kenneth A. Sponsler.

ILLUSTRATED HIGH POINTS

All things . . . new (II Cor. 5:17)

While in the military and abroad, Larry had lived a fast-paced and worldly life, a life of partying and alcohol abuse.

The Lord sent people into Larry's life who witnessed to him and pointed him to Christ. One night while driving in his car, he met the Lord in a profound and dramatic way. This was the beginning of great changes in his life. He poured his alcohol down the drain and destroyed his ungodly magazines. He stopped using profanity. He started reading his Bible and going to church. He found new friends and adopted a whole new lifestyle. All things had become new in Larry's life.

Ministry of reconciliation (vs. 18)

After Larry became a Christian, the Lord gave him a great burden to share his faith with others. He began witnessing to his family, friends, and people at work. Some turned to Christ; others turned against Larry and ridiculed him, but he was not deterred. His intense, newfound love for souls motivated him to take every opportunity to spread the gospel.

Larry even began a visitation ministry, calling on people for the express purpose of winning them to Christ. He recruited others from his church to go with him. He got permission from his pastor to teach an evangelism class during the Sunday school hour. Larry had truly captured the vision for the ministry of reconciliation.

Not all Christians are able to employ Larry's aggressive style of personal evangelism. Methods may vary according to individual giftedness and opportunities available. All of us, however, share in the responsibility to be involved in the ministry of reconciliation.

—Bruce A. Tanner.

Golden Text Illuminated

"If any man be in Christ, he is a new creature: old things are passed away; behold, all things are become new" (II Corinthians 5:17).

Since the fall of Adam and Eve into sin, God has been in the business of reconciliation. God has not been content to just change the outward appearance of His creation, and He does not coerce obedience. Rather, God makes us new creatures. He changes our whole nature from one kind of being to another.

Most of the religions of the world aim to find a way to God. The unique thing about Christianity is that it involves God seeking man.

Most religions also give lists of things that must be done in order to gain God's approval. Again, Christianity is unique in that it involves God changing us into the people He wants us to be.

Paul used the phrase "in Christ" to refer to the believer's spiritual relationship with Christ and God the Father. When we are born again, we die to our former lives and are born into Christ's family, which is what being "in Christ" is about.

Being a new creature is less about trying to be like Christ and more about dying to self so that Christ can live through us. Paul may have understood this concept better than anyone. In Acts 9 we see that he went from being a persecutor of Christians to one who proclaimed the message of Christ. This change did not happen through Paul's efforts. It came about when he died to himself and began living for Christ.

Paul explained in Romans 4 that we are made righteous, or brought into a right relationship with God, not by our own efforts but by faith. This was not readily grasped by people then or now.

In Romans 6 Paul explained that when we are born again, we die to sin so that there is no longer any reason to live in it or to keep sinning. Verse 4 says that we were baptized into Christ's death so that we can live a new life. It is through identifying with the death and resurrection of Christ that we can overcome sin.

Romans 6:11 says we should "reckon" ourselves dead to sin but alive to God. The word translated "reckon" is from a Greek accounting term that means to add up a group of numbers to see what the total is. It is not feeling, pretending, hoping, or any such thing. Reckoning means to recognize truth as truth, as you would in math.

This is not as simple as just saying we are dead to sin and alive to God. This really does include our dying to sin and our old life and living by the Spirit. It involves giving up all claims to our lives, property, and future and putting it all into God's hands. We do this by faith. We do it by "reckoning" it to be so. It is already true whether we recognize it or not, but it can be realized in our lives only as we have faith in the truth.

In Galatians Paul talked about walking, or living, in the Spirit. He said in 5:24 that those who belong to Christ have crucified the flesh, or sinful nature.

Our sinful nature was crucified with Christ, but we sometimes lose touch with this truth, and we slip back into living according to the flesh. We have to keep crucifying our flesh daily in order for our new life in Christ to flourish.

—*James Jordan.*

Heart of the Lesson

When God created the world, He spoke and made everything come into being. God created everything through Christ, His Word. His purpose was for humans to have complete fellowship with their Creator.

The ugliness of sin, however, created a huge chasm between the loving Creator and His creation. After sin entered people's lives, they knew they were wrong and tried to hide from God.

In some ways, parents can understand what this meant to God. The ones He had created, His children, turned their backs on Him. Parents experience this type of a break with their own children. It can be as temporary as an argument or a small child's lack of obedience, or it can be a major break when a child is older and chooses to turn his back on his parents. How the saddened parents pray for reconciliation with their children! It is wonderful when a child does choose to return to the family. It is truly a new beginning.

In this week's text Paul talks about how God creates a new person.

1. Compelled by God (II Cor. 5:11-15). It is important for people to fear God, realizing that they are responsible to Him. False teachers try to persuade people to follow them. Their warped views may sound true until they are more closely investigated and reveal that they do not know God at all.

Paul told of himself and other men who traveled around, preaching Christ crucified. Their only motive was to tell of Christ. They were definitely not in it for any money or fame or popularity. It is a good thing too, for wherever Paul went, trouble followed. He had too many enemies to be able to have an easy life.

Paul and the others were compelled by God to present the message of Christ dying for all. They no longer lived for themselves but for Christ. This gave their lives a whole new perspective, away from being me-oriented and becoming Christ-oriented.

2. Newly created by God (II Cor. 5:16-17). Life before faith in Christ is lived according to the flesh. New life in Christ means a whole new view of the world too. What a person thought was important and vital—such as wealth and prestige—means nothing. There is a new life now with new meaning.

When a person becomes committed to Christ and united to Him, he takes on a whole new being. The things of the past are gone, and there is a whole new way of thinking and living.

Becoming a Christian is really a restoration and fulfillment of God's purposes in creation. The person becomes God's true child. Only God can do this.

3. Reconciled to God (II Cor. 5:18-21). Jesus is our mediator who reconciles us with God. He is our go-between who speaks up for us in God's presence.

We as believers are also to be reconcilers of others to God. We can tell them how He wants to wipe the slate clean from sin if they will repent and turn toward Him. In this way we can be ambassadors for God, His spokespeople, handpicked to make Christ's appeal to others.

Only because of Christ can we be reconciled to God. Jesus, totally righteous, with no sin, became sin for us. He took the load and endured the punishment we deserved. Through Him, we can receive His righteousness and be reconciled to God.

When we trust Jesus Christ as Saviour, there is a change in our status. We become a new creation.

— *Judy Carlsen.*

World Missions

Missions transforms societies one individual at a time. If you get enough saved people, the world becomes a different place. Christians have different life goals and motivations.

When a missionary gets to the area and people group where he is to minister, he usually finds a culture that is strange to him. Each of us grows up with certain basic beliefs, a dominant language, and a set of rules for living that define what is right and wrong, good and bad, acceptable and unacceptable.

Should Christians go to rodeos? Not in the Navajo community. There were too many false religious activities practiced at these events. Sometimes the Christians put on small rodeos for themselves, though. I went to one. It was a great time of horse riding and games, followed by gospel music and food.

A man came to me and asked whether I thought it was OK to eat the head of a sheep and make a pudding out of the blood. What would you have said? Missionaries face these types of questions all the time. They have to study the culture and consult with native Christians.

More mature native Christian leaders and churches can decide these things for themselves. This is part of being a new creature in Christ, for God gives us a will to find and do His will. He does not program us with a set of behaviors. We have to choose daily, even moment by moment, to follow the leading of the Holy Spirit and the illumination of the Bible.

Is chewing betel nuts a sin? In Southeast Asia, one-tenth of the world's population uses it. It is addictive, like tobacco. Is using tobacco a sin? The Yanomamo tribe uses it to keep their digestive tracts free of worms.

I heard a missionary describe the way an African church had forbidden its members to show grief at funerals on pain of excommunication. That seems harsh to me; but I am here, not there.

What do polygamists do with their multiple wives when they get saved? Do we have to force Christian converts to also believe our understanding of the role of germs in infection?

What exactly becomes new for a Christian? Certainly his moral standards do, and probably his music and no doubt his speech. He might put away alcoholic beverages, although in Europe, I have been told, Christians drink wine or beer socially. A believer's entertainment is different. Is dancing permissible? His spare time is spent differently. He attends church services and functions.

I saw a movie taken by the first missionaries to reach the Balim Valley in Irian Jaya. The men were fighting with long spears, wearing gourds, and coating their bodies with pig grease. Women who were grieving for dead relatives hacked off their fingers with stone axes. What do you think changed when they got saved?

For new believers in cultures where there have never been Christians before, the missionary and his family are the standard. They observe what he does and copy it.

The principle that we can teach new believers is to get to know the Word of God and allow the Spirit to convict their hearts. Try to witness and win souls, and be willing to adopt or divest yourself of whatever would hinder that effort. Be slow to judge others and quick to evaluate yourself.

We have to maintain our liberty in Christ and not make a legalistic system that is rigid and unyielding. Living freely and yet faithfully by God's Word requires much prayer.

—Philip J. Lesko.

The Jewish Aspect

Paul's father was a Pharisee, and Paul became a Pharisee (Acts 23:6). Growing up in that environment, he would have developed certain attitudes toward Gentiles.

Alfred Edersheim (*The Life and Times of Jesus the Messiah*, Eerdmans) detailed these attitudes. A Gentile child was regarded unclean from birth. A Gentile mother giving birth was not to be given aid, and her baby was not to be given food. A Gentile going into danger was not to be warned. A Gentile house was unclean. A Jew was not to seek medical aid from a Gentile, even if it cost him his life. Jews were not to rent houses or land to Gentiles and were not to sell them cattle.

The gulf between Jew and Gentile did not exist in this life alone. It was believed that Gentiles would suffer the eternal torments of Gehenna's hellfire. Righteous Jews, on the other hand, were completely delivered from torment. Less than righteous Jews would suffer for a while, but would ultimately be delivered by Abraham or the Messiah.

The only way a Gentile could avoid the animosity of Jews, and gain hope of eternal peace, was to become a proselyte. If a Gentile adopted Judaism as his faith, he was regarded as a child of Abraham.

Modern Judaism has greatly broadened its relationships with Gentiles. While modern Jews still welcome the conversion of non-Jews to their religion, "no one has to do so in order to be saved, whether in this world or the next" (Steinberg, *Basic Judaism*, Harcourt Brace Jovanovich). Indeed, modern Judaism teaches that "the righteous of all people have their share in the world to come."

When Paul wrote II Corinthians, his background would have given him a dislike for Gentiles. God, however, had saved Paul from his former life. He had changed him and commissioned him to become "the apostle of the Gentiles" (Rom. 11:13).

These ideas are crucial to understanding Paul's words in II Corinthians 5. He asserted, "Henceforth know we no man after the flesh" (vs. 16). Paul meant that he no longer evaluated people by their nationalities. "It was now his custom to view men, not primarily in terms of nationality but in terms of spiritual status. The Jew-Gentile division was less important for him than the Christian-unbeliever distinction" (Gaebelein, ed., *The Expositor's Bible Commentary*, Zondervan). Paul's formerly limited Jewish viewpoint changed radically because of God's work in reconciling people to Himself (vss. 18-19), resulting in a new creation (vs. 17).

Paul's use of the word reconciliation differed from its use in ancient Jewish literature. In the apocrypha, for example, God is the one who is reconciled to the Jews as a result of their prayers. In contrast, Paul asserted that it is man who needs to be reconciled to God. The problem is that no man can reconcile himself to God by his own efforts. No man can eliminate the guilt and stain of sin from his own life. No man can make himself a part of God's new spiritual creation.

To solve this sin problem, God "hath reconciled us to himself by Jesus Christ" (II Cor. 5:18). Christ's work on the cross made it possible for man to be His friend. That is the message we must share with others as "ambassadors for Christ" (5:20).

— *R. Larry Overstreet*

Guiding the Superintendent

As a young pastor, I had dreams of one day leading a large, contemporary church that was on the cutting edge of Christian ministry. As a part of this dream, I became enamored of attending seminars and conferences on church growth that emphasized the latest innovative approach to ministry.

Although I never fulfilled my dream, I did attend a church whose philosophy of ministry was based on contemporary innovation. What I began to discover after fifteen years of attending that church actually startled me. After all those years, I found myself strangely attracted to a more conservative approach to ministry. I longed for the older hymns of the faith and welcomed preaching that emphasized the foundational message of salvation by grace through faith.

In this week's text, Paul taught his readers about a foundational spiritual principle: "If any man be in Christ, he is a new creature: old things are passed away; behold, all things are become new" (II Cor. 5:17). Now that moves me!

DEVOTIONAL OUTLINE

1. To persuade men (II Cor. 5:11-15). Paul strove to convince men of the truth of the gospel message and of his own ministry credentials. He also wanted everyone to know that based on Christ's ultimate example of self-sacrifice for all, his desire was to selflessly glorify God in all he did.

2. To be a new creation (II Cor. 5:16-19). Paul stated that his life had been impacted by Christ's death in two distinct ways. First, he evaluated other people according to their spiritual relationship to Jesus Christ. Second, he was convinced that belief in Jesus Christ caused the person who believed to become a new person in Him.

How are we made new? We are given a new heart, a new spirit, by the working of the Spirit of Christ, who comes to indwell us when He brings us to faith. Most important, God "hath reconciled us to himself by Jesus Christ" (vs. 18). We are no longer enemies of God living in hostility to Him but have been cleansed and brought into close relationship with our loving Father.

3. To be an ambassador (II Cor. 5:20-21). Paul lived under the realization that believers are to act as Christ's appointed messengers. He strongly implored his unsaved readers to accept Christ's invitation of salvation. This appeal was based on the reality that Christ took the place of sinful man on the cross so that sinful man could receive God's righteousness.

CHILDREN'S CORNER

Encourage your teachers to boldly proclaim the gospel message of salvation by grace through faith to their young children. Challenge them, however, concerning the simplicity of their appeal (cf. II Cor. 11:3). The young and receptive hearts of children must be respected; therefore, teachers should concentrate on the basic truths of God's love and the forgiveness of sin.

Children will respond to the invitation of an ambassador of Christ when the appeal is made in loving sincerity and explained in simple terms, using Scripture verses to make the gospel clear to them. Never think the message is "above" them. Remember what Jesus said about the faith of children and how we must emulate that faith ourselves (Matt. 18:3).

—*Thomas R. Chmura.*

SCRIPTURE LESSON TEXT

I JOHN 1:1 That which was from the beginning, which we have heard, which we have seen with our eyes, which we have looked upon, and our hands have handled, of the Word of life;

2 (For the life was manifested, and we have seen *it,* and bear witness, and shew unto you that eternal life, which was with the Father, and was manifested unto us;)

3 That which we have seen and heard declare we unto you, that ye also may have fellowship with us: and truly our fellowship *is* with the Father, and with his Son Jesus Christ.

4 And these things write we unto you, that your joy may be full.

5 This then is the message which we have heard of him, and declare unto you, that God is light, and in him is no darkness at all.

6 If we say that we have fellowship with him, and walk in darkness, we lie, and do not the truth:

7 But if we walk in the light, as he is in the light, we have fellowship one with another, and the blood of Jesus Christ his Son cleanseth us from all sin.

8 If we say that we have no sin, we deceive ourselves, and the truth is not in us.

9 If we confess our sins, he is faithful and just to forgive us *our* sins, and to cleanse us from all unrighteousness.

10 If we say that we have not sinned, we make him a liar, and his word is not in us.

2:1 My little children, these things write I unto you, that ye sin not. And if any man sin, we have an advocate with the Father, Jesus Christ the righteous:

2 And he is the propitiation for our sins: and not for ours only, but also for *the sins of* the whole world.

3 And hereby we do know that we know him, if we keep his commandments.

4 He that saith, I know him, and keepeth not his commandments, is a liar, and the truth is not in him.

5 But whoso keepeth his word, in him verily is the love of God perfected: hereby know we that we are in him.

NOTES

Blessing of Forgiveness and New Life

Lesson Text: I John 1:1—2:5

Related Scriptures: Psalms 51:1-17; 130:1-8; Matthew 6:12-15

TIME: about A.D. 90-95

PLACE: probably from Ephesus

GOLDEN TEXT—"If we confess our sins, he is faithful and just to forgive us our sins, and to cleanse us from all unrighteousness" (I John 1:9).

Introduction

The captain of the ship looked into the dark night and saw faint lights in the distance. Immediately he told his signalman to send a message: "Alter your course 10 degrees south." Promptly a return message was received: "Alter your course 10 degrees north." The captain was angered; his command had been ignored. So he sent a second message: "Alter your course 10 degrees south—I am the captain!" Soon another message was received: "Alter your course 10 degrees north—I am a seaman third class."

Immediately the captain sent a third message, knowing the fear it would evoke: "Alter your course 10 degrees south—I am a battleship." Then the reply came: "Alter your course 10 degrees north—I am a lighthouse." Oh, the importance of paying attention to the light!

Only the light of Christ brings the blessing of forgiveness and new life.

LESSON OUTLINE

I. THE MANIFESTATION OF THE WORD—I John 1:1-4

II. THE PRACTICE OF WALKING IN THE LIGHT—I John 1:5-10

III. THE TEST OF KNOWING THE CHRIST—I John 2:1-5

Exposition: Verse by Verse

THE MANIFESTATION OF THE WORD

I JOHN 1:1 That which was from the beginning, which we have heard, which we have seen with our eyes, which we have looked upon, and our hands have handled, of the Word of life;

2 (For the life was manifested, and we have seen it, and bear witness, and shew unto you that eternal life, which was with the Father,

and was manifested unto us;)

3 That which we have seen and heard declare we unto you, that ye also may have fellowship with us: and truly our fellowship is with the Father, and with his Son Jesus Christ.

4 And these things write we unto you, that your joy may be full.

Declaring what was manifested (I John 1:1-2). This letter was written by the Apostle John and can possibly be dated somewhere between A.D. 90 and 95, probably making it prior to his exile on Patmos, where he wrote Revelation. As one of the twelve apostles and one of the three in the "inner circle" of the Lord, he had known Jesus intimately. He had been with Him from the beginning of His ministry and stayed with Him through the end. As mentioned in verse 1, he had seen Him, heard Him, and touched Him, for Jesus was a man in human flesh.

{John emphasized the humanity of Jesus because of false teaching that was infecting the churches.}[Q1] In the second century, Gnosticism became prominent, teaching that matter was inherently evil and only that which was spiritual was good. Therefore, a holy God could not take on human flesh, leading to the conclusion that Christ could not have become incarnate. Many Gnostics thus made a distinction between the human Jesus and the spiritual Christ, who came upon Him at His baptism. John was hearing the beginnings of this heretical teaching.

{John stated that the eternal Word of life had come directly from the Father and was manifested among them ("we" and "us" probably refer to the apostles). They, in turn, declared exactly what they had witnessed, and there was no doubt in their minds that He was the eternal Son of God manifested in human flesh.}[Q2] John was well qualified to teach about Him, for he had been one of those eyewitnesses to everything Jesus did throughout His ministry. John's readers had not seen Jesus personally, but they could rely on the apostle's testimony.

Looking for fellowship and joy (I John 1:3-4). {John had a purpose for writing what he knew about Jesus. He wanted his readers to have fellowship with the apostles, whose own fellowship was with both the Father and the Son.}[Q3] Chapter 2 indicates that his readers were genuine believers (vss. 12-14). What John was talking about here is the genuine fellowship that true believers experience. The word translated "fellowship" in the New Testament is *koinōnia*, which refers to sharing in a mutual relationship. Fellowship is a companionship based on similar interests.

It is important that all believers understand and accept the true humanity as well as the deity of Christ. Salvation had been made available through the God-Man, Jesus Christ. To believe anything less was to render the whole truth of salvation uncertain. As the believers John wrote to understood all about Jesus, they were sharing with the apostles in the truth. Since the apostles were in fellowship with God the Father and His Son, those believers would then also be in fellowship with both.

This understanding about Christ was the source of true joy. Regarding verse 4, the *Holman New Testament Commentary* states, "The prologue concludes by linking John's own joy with the spiritual welfare of his readers. He reaffirmed these truths so that their joy could be made complete. John was so concerned about their welfare that he could not experience complete joy himself as long as they were struggling with doubt created by these false teachers" (Anders, ed., Broadman & Holman).

THE PRACTICE OF WALKING IN THE LIGHT

5 This then is the message which we have heard of him, and declare

unto you, that God is light, and in him is no darkness at all.

6 If we say that we have fellowship with him, and walk in darkness, we lie, and do not the truth:

7 But if we walk in the light, as he is in the light, we have fellowship one with another, and the blood of Jesus Christ his Son cleanseth us from all sin.

8 If we say that we have no sin, we deceive ourselves, and the truth is not in us.

9 If we confess our sins, he is faithful and just to forgive us our sins, and to cleanse us from all unrighteousness.

10 If we say that we have not sinned, we make him a liar, and his word is not in us.

God is light (I John 1:5-6). {John had already mentioned that he and the other apostles had heard Christ. Now he specified what the message was that came from Him. It was simply that God is light; there is no darkness in Him.}Q4 Light and darkness represent two extremes. Light stands for what is good, pure, holy, and righteous. Darkness stands for what is sinful, evil, and false. Light shines and reveals, while darkness hides and covers. In His very nature and moral character, God is completely light. Darkness cannot touch Him.

This statement about God is powerful. He is not *a* light or *like* light. {He *is* light, meaning pure, glorious truth—holiness in His very nature.}Q5 The opposite of all this has never been and will never be a part of God. The truth is that because God is light, He exposes all that is sinful and evil. Those of us who are in God's family, then, walk in the presence of light.

{Walking in darkness should be completely foreign to us. John wrote that if we claim to be in fellowship with God but walk in darkness, we are lying.}Q6

{Walking in darkness indicates the presence of continual sin in our lives.}Q7 We who are God's children must recognize that we cannot enjoy fellowship with God in the way He intends as long as we allow sin in our lives.

We walk in the light (I John 1:7-8). {John next wrote about what happens when we walk in the light, that is, when we live consistently obedient, pure lives before God.}Q7 When we live that way, we are living the way God's Son, Jesus Christ, is living! Since Jesus is truly God, it is just as true of Him as it is of the Father that there is no darkness in Him. He is entirely pure and holy and cannot be morally affected by sin and evil. When we walk in the light, we are compared to Jesus, who is in the light constantly.

It is then that "we have fellowship one with another" (vs. 7). The grammatical context here indicates that we and God are the two parties being referred to. The conclusion is that when we walk in the light as Jesus is in the light, we and God have fellowship with one another. This is even more meaningful than walking in fellowship with other believers, as wonderful as that is. When we live consistently in the light provided to us through God's Word, we experience a constant fellowship with our heavenly Father!

Nominal Christians are a tragedy. Their claims and the realities of their lives are inconsistent. Total obedience to God should not be an option we entertain but the choice we make because we love Him. We do need to recognize that because we are human, we cannot be perfect. To claim perfect holiness would be to live a lie. The cleansing blood of Christ, however, is available to cover every sin we confess to Him.

We can be clean (I John 1:9-10). John wanted his readers to know that even though people sin and cannot help doing so because of their fallen nature, God has provided a means by which they can be in fellowship with

Him. It comes through confession, which means to acknowledge or assent to something. God wants to forgive us our sins; that is why He sent His only Son to die for us. We still struggle with sin, and when we commit sin He wants us to agree with Him that what we have done is wrong. We know this by conviction from His Spirit.

{John also said that when we confess our sins, God cleanses us of all unrighteousness.}[Q8] He does this because He is faithful to all the promises He has made about His willingness to do so (cf. Col. 2:13). Furthermore, all the promises are legitimate because He is a just God. That is, He does everything in accordance with what is right, or righteous. The death of Jesus Christ has provided the moral grounds upon which God can forgive all who receive Him. He does not become unjust when He forgives us.

Although we become new creatures upon being saved (II Cor. 5:17) and possess a new nature, we still live in not yet redeemed bodies of flesh. That is why we sometimes sin as Christians. By repeating the warning that we cannot claim to be without sin, John was reminding us of the presence of sin. To deny this is to call God a liar, for He has clearly told us we are simply sinners saved by His grace. Read Romans 7:14-25 for an explanation by Paul of the continued presence of our unredeemed flesh.

THE TEST OF KNOWING THE CHRIST

2:1 My little children, these things write I unto you, that ye sin not. And if any man sin, we have an advocate with the Father, Jesus Christ the righteous:

2 And he is the propitiation for our sins: and not for ours only, but also for the sins of the whole world.

3 And hereby we do know that we know him, if we keep his commandments.

4 He that saith, I know him, and keepeth not his commandments, is a liar, and the truth is not in him.

5 But whoso keepeth his word, in him verily is the love of God perfected: hereby know we that we are in him.

Having an advocate (I John 2:1-2). The first two verses of this chapter seem to be the final thoughts on the subject of the previous chapter. It is important to recognize that while we do not need to feel guilty once we have confessed our sins, we also should not assume that we have the freedom to sin whenever we feel like it. There is an important balance here: when we confess our sins, God is faithful and just to forgive and cleanse us, but we do not have the right to commit sin just because we know we can confess and be forgiven.

John wrote that he was explaining these truths so that his readers would do their best not to sin. John was very old when he wrote this letter, and he thought of his readers as his children in the Lord. He was concerned that they understand that sin was a constant threat to them (just as any parent would be concerned about dangers threatening his children). He also wanted them to know that since we will not be sinless while in these present bodies, God has provided an Advocate to give us the help we so desperately need.

An advocate is someone who comes alongside to speak in defense of one in need. Jesus intercedes for us when we sin, for He has already paid for those sins. As the Father recognizes this truth, He is completely satisfied by the arrangement. The word "propitiation" (vs. 2) means that Jesus' sacrifice on the cross satisfies the demands of God's holiness to punish sin.

Keeping His commands (I John 2:3-4). {One of the ways we can be assured that we are truly saved is that we have a desire to obey God and His Word.}[Q9]

This particular test is easy to take, because either we have that desire or we do not. The person who claims to be a Christian but has no concern whatever about obeying God is lying, according to John. In fact, the truth is not in him at all. When a person receives Jesus Christ as personal Saviour, major changes take place in his heart. Worldly desires do not control him.

The key word here is "keep" (vs. 3), and the Greek word means "to guard." The idea is that we observe something and then we guard it by holding it fast in our memory. How often teachers in front of a classroom of students will say, "Now you must keep this information in mind, because I will be asking about it on the exam." In the Christian life we must keep in mind God's commands and then live by them. Ignoring them indicates we let them slip out of our minds. Then we act according to sinful desires.

Verse 4 says the same thing in reverse. Those who do not practice obeying God's Word give evidence that they have never received Jesus Christ as their personal Saviour. They are living in accordance with Satan's desires. Satan has no truth in him and is nothing but a murderer and a liar (John 8:44). Do you really want to obey God? If you do, even though you often fail, you are His child. If you listen carefully to the Holy Spirit and follow His leading, you can become a victorious Christian.

Growing to maturity (I John 2:5). {The ability to obey God comes as one loves God more deeply.}^{Q10} Notice Jesus' words in a conversation with His disciples. "He that hath my commandments, and keepeth them, he it is that loveth me" (John 14:21).

There is much disagreement as to what "in him verily is the love of God perfected" means (I John 2:5). Some think this is a reference to God's love for us rather than our love for Him, and it is possible to interpret it that way. What is not taught here is that our love becomes so perfect that we never fail in our efforts to defeat sin. But our love should mature as we grow in our understanding of God and His ways, but we will never achieve the total absence of sin as long as we live in our fleshly bodies.

We should, however, find ourselves becoming more sensitive to God's will and more responsive to the need to confess our sins. Maturing in Christ will lead to that sensitivity and enable us to maintain a closer fellowship with God. As we live according to the spiritual light given to us, our joy in Him will increase.
—*Keith E. Eggert.*

QUESTIONS

1. Why did the Apostle John emphasize the humanity of Jesus?
2. What did John offer as proof for his teaching that Jesus was truly God in the flesh?
3. What important result did John say would come from a correct understanding of who Jesus is?
4. What specific message did John say the Son had given him and the other apostles?
5. What does it mean to say that God is light?
6. What did John say about those who claim to know Christ but do not live according to His Word?
7. What does walking in light or walking in darkness mean?
8. By what means can believers be clean even though sinful?
9. What is the test that reveals whether someone truly knows God?
10. What should happen as we mature?
—*Keith E. Eggert.*

Preparing to Teach the Lesson

Fellowship with God is possible through Christ. This lesson will help us understand how to have fellowship with God the Father and God the Son.

TODAY'S AIM

Facts: to examine a passage from I John that deals with our fellowship with God.

Principle: to affirm that true fellowship with the God of light is possible through Christ.

Application: to encourage Christians to appreciate and cultivate their relationship with God by walking in the light.

INTRODUCING THE LESSON

For people to enjoy fellowship, they need to have things in common. The very word "fellowship" means "to have in common."

God is holy. We are sinners. God is infinite. We are finite. God is eternal. We are temporal. What could we possibly have in common with this transcendent God? How could fellowship with Him ever be possible?

This week's lesson explores issues relating to our fellowship with the God of indescribable light and righteousness.

DEVELOPING THE LESSON

1. Basis for fellowship (I John 1:1-2). It is obvious that the same person who wrote I John also wrote the Gospel of John. Focus initially on "that which was from the beginning." Refer the class to John 1:1 and Genesis 1:1. In the first verse of the lesson text, John referred to the eternal Word, who is coexistent and coeternal with the Father.

This same God who was "from the beginning" had actually been touched by human hands. Remind the class that John and the other apostles had physical contact with Jesus. The whole concept of the God-Man is an awesome paradox! John must have marveled that his own human hands had touched God. Discuss the significance of the phrase "Word of life" in describing Christ Jesus. Words communicate. God communicated Himself through Jesus Christ.

2. Breadth of fellowship (I John 1:3-4). Identify the "we" of verse 3. John and the other apostles were witnesses (cf. Acts 1:8) for Jesus. The word translated "fellowship" (*koinōnia*) means "something held in common." The declaration that John and the others made would allow fellowship to occur between the apostles and those who accepted their message. Discuss what Christians have in common with each other.

The fellowship potential created by the gospel is not restricted to other believers but also enables fellowship with the Father and the Son. This is an incredible concept! Discuss why it is so incredible. Considering human limitations and divine perfection, sharing with God is simply amazing. Read Isaiah 55:8. Do we appreciate having a fellowship relationship with God Himself?

3. Conditions of fellowship (I John 1:5-10). What does the text mean when it declares that "God is light"? Any form of sin is absolutely incompatible with God's holy nature. What does it mean to "walk in darkness" (cf. Isa. 9:2)? Professing does not always mean possessing. Refer to Matthew 7:22-23. A life of sin does not offer assurance of salvation.

Note that it is the blood of Christ, not a person's attempt to live a righteous life, that cleanses from all sin (I John 1:7). Discuss what it means to walk in the light. Christians who walk in the light have light in common with God.

When considering verse 8, remind the class that "have no sin" is present tense. Even as Christians, we are not without sin. Refer to Romans 7:15-19.

What does it mean to "confess our sins" (I John 1:9)? It means we agree with God's assessment of sin. Failure to confess sin does not result is one's loss of position in Christ (Rom. 8:1). Why, then, should a Christian confess sin?

4. Durability of fellowship (I John 2:1-2). Christians should make every effort not to sin. However, when they do, God has made provision for forgiveness. Define "advocate" as one who is called alongside, as a defense attorney would be. Jesus Christ Himself represents us if we should sin.

Explain that "propitiation" means "atoning sacrifice." Jesus represents and defends sinning Christians on the basis of the blood sacrifice that He has made for them. Discuss the significance of all this. Jesus' blood continues to divert God's wrath from sinning believers.

5. Results of fellowship (I John 2:3-5). Emphasize that knowing God is not the result of keeping His commandments. Rather, keeping His commandments is the result of truly knowing Him (cf. Gal. 2:8-9). Read also Matthew 7:16.

John has written that "whoso keepeth his word, in him verily is the love of God perfected" (I John 2:5). This can be interpreted as either love from God or love for God. Certainly, our love for God is expressed in our love for others. Love is the primary indicator of true, saving faith (cf. 2:9-11; 3:14). Discuss the meaning of the word "perfected" in the context of 2:3-5. Love originating

from God is perfect to begin with. The perfecting of God's love would seem to relate to a more complete experiencing of God's love as we allow it to flow through us to others.

ILLUSTRATING THE LESSON

The Christian walks in light. That is, the Christian is to be in fellowship with God.

WALK IN THE LIGHT

GOD

GOD IS LIGHT

CONCLUDING THE LESSON

The lesson begins with an introductory statement regarding the incarnate Word. The following verses develop the concept of fellowship with God. God is light. Walking in the light demonstrates our unity with God. Those who do not share in this illuminated life are self-deluded if they claim to be Christians.

When the Christian sins and deviates from the path of light, Christ advocates for him on the basis of His atoning sacrifice. Christians, in the fellowship of light, are the objects of God's love and the reflectors of God's divine love.

ANTICIPATING THE NEXT LESSON

Read Hebrews 4:14—5:10 as you anticipate a lesson on Christ's intercession.

—*Bruce A. Tanner.*

PRACTICAL POINTS

1. Jesus identifies with our problems because He is human; He can help us with our problems because He is God (I John 1:1-2).
2. Just as John witnessed about the Christ he knew, so too we must witness about the Christ we know (vss. 3-5).
3. We must have fellowship with God before we can have fellowship with other Christians (vss. 6-7).
4. The most foolish lie we can tell is the lie we tell ourselves (vss. 8-10).
5. After God has forgiven us, He can help us stop sinning (2:1).
6. Keeping God's commands cannot save us from our sins, but it shows that we have been saved (vss. 2-5).

—Ralph Woodworth.

RESEARCH AND DISCUSSION

1. What qualifications do you have to be a witness for God (I John 1:1-3; cf. Isa. 44:8; Acts 1:8)?
2. Do you believe that depression is sin for a Christian? Why or why not (I John. 1:4; cf. Ex. 14:13; Isa. 41:13; Matt. 9:2)?
3. What relationship do you see between a Christian's joy and his not sinning (I John 1:4; 2:1)?
4. In what ways is God "light" (1:5)? What is "darkness" (vs. 6)?
5. In verse 9, it seems that John is saying that confession is the only thing required of a person in order to be forgiven. Is it ever appropriate for us to add other conditions before we forgive others? Why or why not?

—Ralph Woodworth.

ILLUSTRATED HIGH POINTS

God is light (I John 1:5)

God alone is light and life. All else is darkness and death because of sin. How can He recognize and bless the works of darkness? It would be against His nature. He must somehow introduce light and life first. This He did through His Son, Jesus Christ. Anyone who believes in Jesus is immediately taken from the kingdom of darkness and brought into the kingdom of light.

We often underestimate this great deliverance and, through habit, fall back into old ways of thinking. The Scriptures remind us again and again that light has no communion with darkness (II Cor. 6:14).

Which is more amazing: the power of light to penetrate and destroy darkness or the willingness of the Saviour to come and live in our midst in order to save us?

The propitiation for our sins (2:2)

In December 1952, a toxic mix of dense fog and sooty black coal smoke killed thousands of people in London. As smoke coming out of chimneys mixed with the natural fog, the air turned colder. Londoners heaped more coal on their fires, making more smoke.

Roads were littered with abandoned cars. Midday concerts were canceled. Visibility fell to one foot. Archivists at the British Museum found smog in the bookstacks.

Cattle in the city's Smithfield market were killed and disposed of before the meat could be sold. The lungs of the animals were black. London's killer fog is a metaphor of the spiritual world into which Jesus came. The sinister and deadly darkness of sin covered the world when the Lord Jesus made His dwelling among us.

—Ted Simonson.

Golden Text Illuminated

"If we confess our sins, he is faithful and just to forgive us our sins, and to cleanse us from all unrighteousness" (I John 1:9).

We humans have an astonishing capacity to reframe our thoughts and actions so as to appear virtuous. As the culture around us continues to decline morally, the concept of sin becomes harder to nail down. As John Stonestreet, President of the Colson Center for Worldview, likes to say, "What used to be unthinkable is now unquestionable."

However, those who choose to follow God's ways instead of the world's ways will find a plumbline that never changes. The standard that God requires is constant—holiness (I Pet. 1:15-16; cf. Lev. 11:44). Unfortunately, our sinfulness also is constant (Ps. 14:3). Even after one has come to trust in Jesus for salvation, the battle against the tendency to sin continues (Rom. 7:13-25).

It can seem impossible to be the holy ones that God wants us to be. But God, in His mercy, "hath not dealt with us after our sins; nor rewarded us according to our iniquities. For as the heaven is high above the earth, so great is his mercy toward them that fear him" (Ps. 103:10-11). "Like as a father pitieth his children, so the Lord pitieth them that fear him. For he knoweth our frame; he remembereth that we are dust" (vss. 13-14).

In this week's golden text, John gives us a tremendous depiction of God's mercy when we follow His simple plan to restore fellowship with Him after we sin. Yet the one thing we are asked to do can be the hardest of all—confess our sins.

Confession of sin is not a new or revolutionary concept in John's let-ter. God included confession in the sacrificial system of the law (Lev. 5:5; 16:21; Num. 5:7). David proclaimed, "I acknowledged my sin unto thee, and mine iniquity have I not hid. I said, I will confess my transgressions unto the Lord" (Ps. 32:5).

In its simplest form, the word for confession that John uses here means "to say the same thing" or "to agree." In other forms, it refers to a public agreement or confession (for example, confessing that Christ is Lord).

Are we willing to call our unholy actions, thoughts, or attitudes the same thing God calls them? That is what God asks of us. Taking that step toward God brings freedom from guilt and the amazing blessing of restored fellowship with God (cf. Prov. 28:13).

But wait! It does not end there. Because we take the step to obey and agree that we missed God's target of holiness, He, who delights to show mercy (Mic. 7:18), goes above and beyond in His pardon. How? He not only forgives the sin we confess but searches us inside and out and cleanses us from all unrighteousness—things we did not even know to confess!

In God's goodness, He makes us "whiter than snow" and creates a "clean heart" and puts a "right spirit" within us (Ps. 51:7, 10). He can do this because Jesus has already paid the penalty for our sin at the cross (cf. Rom. 5:8-11).

I encourage you to freely enter into God's presence (Heb. 10:19-22) and frequently confess your sin so that you can walk in the blessing of forgiveness.

—*K. Hawver.*

Heart of the Lesson

This week's lesson deals with the first epistle of John. This epistle was probably written by the Apostle John when he was an older man. John wrote this letter to encourage Christian fellowship and to refute false teachings. True Christian fellowship can flourish only if believers understand the true nature of God, according to Scripture.

In John's day there were many heretics who made false claims about Jesus. False teachings can lead believers away from following Jesus. There are people today who do not believe that Jesus is God Incarnate. Those of us who believe the gospel of Jesus Christ must be careful not to be deceived by such false teachings.

The Apostle John was an eyewitness to Jesus' earthly ministry. He himself had heard, seen, and even touched the Lord Jesus Christ (1:1). John's epistle presents the Saviour as light, love, and life. Jesus is the Light of the world. Light drives away darkness. Light helps us see. Darkness is used to signify sin and evil. Jesus brought us out of darkness into His marvelous light.

Jesus is love. He offers unconditional love. Jesus loved us enough to lay down His life for us. There is no greater love than that.

Jesus is life. John's Gospel presents Him as the Bread of life. Eternal life is offered through Jesus Christ. He came so that we can have abundant life. The Lord Jesus Christ is the Way, the Truth, and the Life.

1. Having Christian fellowship (I John 1:1-10).
Fellowship denotes relating and interacting with others. Christians are blessed to have the opportunity to have fellowship with the Lord and with each other. We have fellowship with the Lord through a saving relationship with Him. Fellowship occurs as we relate to Him in prayer and when we worship Him and walk in His light. A relationship with the Lord is also developed when we acknowledge our trust in Him.

John encouraged his reading audience to have fellowship with himself and other believers. Their fellowship was with the Father and with His Son, Jesus Christ.

Imagine John as an older man who had walked with Jesus. He had witnessed what Jesus, the Saviour, had done. John saw the miracles He performed. Jesus' godly lifestyle was witnessed by John. He was a witness that Jesus is the Son of God. The apostles rejoiced at having fellowship with the Saviour. Therefore, John invited his readers to have the same joy—to walk in His light. Full joy comes from having fellowship with the Lord and with His people.

2. Maintaining Christian fellowship (I John 2:1-5).
Christians are called to fellowship with Jesus Christ (I Cor. 1:9). Maintaining fellowship with the Lord and with one another is an essential part of a Christian's lifestyle. Fellowship with the Lord is maintained through a consistent prayer life and a desire to live free from sin. Fellowship does not exist between the Lord and unbelievers. If a person does not know the Lord, he cannot have fellowship with Him.

Christians of like precious faith maintain harmonious fellowship when they regularly gather together. Developing a strong bond among ourselves will aid in maintaining fellowship. Sharing God's blessings with one another and having love and unity are also essential to maintaining Christian fellowship.

—*Arletta Merritts.*

World Missions

The idea that the heathen are in darkness may be ridiculed these days, but it is nevertheless true. People—civilized or not, affluent or otherwise—are in darkness without the illumination of the gospel of Jesus Christ.

This darkness extends from the question of origins to the prophecies of the end of the world. Jesus Christ is the Creator God. The lost of our educated elite postulate the evolution of the material universe from an ancient explosion. They go from there to the origin of life, theorizing that various amino acids combined randomly to make a primordial soup in which life came to be. Finally they seek to proclaim as fact the evolution of life from amoeba or algae to vertebrates and at last to humans.

This is darkness indeed! Nothing in the long series of postulations checks out with scientific fact. The Big Bang requires fudge factors. The atmosphere would destroy the life it is supposed to create, and the fossils do not support evolution.

In many places a missionary goes in the world, educated men and women will have been taught these fallacies. I know a missionary to the Philippines whose ministry is specifically combating evolution and promoting creation.

In the jungles of Africa there is a different darkness. It consists of animism, fetishes, and appeasement of demons. The people live in fear of curses and retaliation by spirits who have been offended. They fear the dead, whose souls wander the countryside. They offer animals as sacrifices and set out food to gain small favors.

The Bible teaches that the dead do not roam the earth and that God loves us and protects us. Disease is not the result of a witch doctor's curse. The light of the gospel brings deliverance to those held in such bondage. There is a Saviour from such fear: Jesus, the Word of life.

Hindus believe they are held in an endless cycle of life and reincarnation. They strive to rid themselves of their present sins and the sins of their past lives. How awful! This view of life gives a double and a triple load of sins.

Missionaries bring good news to such people, but the leaders of the religion resist the gospel. It does seem to disrupt society, but a social order based on fear and oppression is not good.

Such a society is found in nations ruled by Islam. We find no peace, no freedom, no escape. My son lived and worked in one such country and described it as such. Lying and deceit are a way of life. As you might expect, there is no freedom to proclaim the gospel message. It is kept out by violence. I just received a newsletter describing how a native preacher in a Muslim country was cut down by gunfire and paralyzed from the chest down.

We pray that the Lord will raise up many in his place. The Light was shining and drew attention. Darkness seems to be winning, but just as the Light conquered the Roman Empire of ancient days, so it can gain entrance to lands where imams put up barriers to keep it out. Nothing can keep out the Light.

Communism seeks to stamp out the message of salvation by grace through faith in Jesus Christ, which opposes Marxist thought. Nevertheless, the Chinese church is larger than ever. Missionaries are once again working in Russia. Are we praying for North Korea? How about Cuba?

Amid all the political upheaval around the world, our interest is in the progress of the gospel light as it shines into one heart at a time.

—*Philip J. Lesko.*

The Jewish Aspect

The Essenes, some of whom lived in desert communities such as Qumran, where the Dead Sea Scrolls were written, called themselves the sons of light. The rest of Israel, not enlightened by the unique teachings of the group, were called sons of darkness.

The Sadducees and the chief priests who ran the temple would have liked all Israel to be united. They would have liked all Israel to unite around the temple and the temple leadership.

The Essenes called for a higher level of purity—one that went by their interpretations. They found the temple and the leadership to be so corrupt that they moved out to the desert and lived outside the system. These Essenes, and other groups as well, emphasized that God is pure and unblemished by sin. Meanwhile, the Sadducees seemed to view God as somewhat lax, overlooking compromise and corruption as long as the temple worship continued.

Among the Dead Sea Scrolls, one of the most important writings is called the Rule of the Community. One of the purposes of this document is to help members learn "to love all the sons of light, each one according to his lot in God's plan, and to detest all the sons of darkness, each one in accordance with his blame in God's vindication" (Martinez, *The Dead Sea Scrolls Translated,* Eerdmans).

Some people in Israel thought that basically all Jews were right with God just by being born Jewish. The Essenes taught that most of Israel would be lost; only the ones who followed their teachings would be saved.

Although they obviously were wrong in many of their beliefs, the Essenes still have something in common with the New Testament. They believed that being born a certain way is not enough to make a person right with God.

The Essenes spoke of cursed deeds—sins that separate people from God. They used the image of darkness to describe such deeds: "accursed, without mercy, for the darkness of your deeds and sentenced to the gloom of everlasting fire" (Martinez). By contrast, those who followed the way of the Essenes could look forward to "everlasting blessings, eternal enjoyment with endless life, and a crown of glory with majestic raiment in eternal light."

Light and darkness are perfect images to describe good and evil. Darkness has no true form; it is not a substance. It is only the absence of light. Similarly, evil is nothing but a corruption of good. God did not make evil. Evil occurs when good things are misused or when good is absent.

John wrote his epistle to counter false teachers who denied that Jesus was God in the flesh. These false teachers made light of sin. Consciously or not, John wrote in a manner a bit like that of the Essenes. God is pure and uncorrupted by evil. Men who taught laxity in morals could not possibly be from God. As the Essenes opposed corruption in Israel, so John opposed it in the church.

John was unlike the Essenes in critical ways, though. He valued the Gentiles, whereas the Essenes did not believe Gentiles could be right with God unless they converted to Judaism. Also, whereas the Essenes promoted hatred for the sons of darkness, John spoke of love: "He that loveth not knoweth not God; for God is love" (I John 4:8). Above all, John knew by revelation the truth about Christ. He is light, but He is also love. The way of God is kindness and compassion as well as purity and truth.

—*Derek Leman.*

Guiding the Superintendent

One of the key mental pictures that Scripture uses to describe the difference between God and the devil is that of light and darkness. As we continue our study of Christ as the image of God, we turn this week to the Apostle John's first epistle. It is in this letter that the author used the idea of light to describe Jesus Christ.

The idea behind the imagery is one of clarity and precision. If someone wants to see something more clearly, he will turn on a light. Darkness, on the other hand, makes it difficult or impossible for one to see. It is in Jesus Christ, the divine Light, that we get a correct outlook on how we should live our lives.

DEVOTIONAL OUTLINE

1. Who is Christ (I John 1:1-5)? The apostle wrote that God is light and that this light can be seen in Jesus Christ Himself. We know that Christ is the light and image of God for several reasons. First, He was there in the beginning (vs. 1). That is, He has existed forever.

Not only is Christ God, but He is also totally human. John was very clear. God became human. John had heard Him, seen Him, and touched Him.

This combination of total divinity and total humanity helps reassure us that Jesus Christ can give us life and joy. That is, as the divine Light, Jesus Christ reveals for us what the worthwhile things of life are.

How should we respond to the light? It is rather obvious that in order to enjoy the benefits of light, one must come into the light. How does a believer come toward the light?

2. We are to conform to the light (I John 1:6-7). Light does us no good if we block it out. We must expose every area of our lives to Jesus Christ and His Word. Only then will we see the corruption and want to change.

3. We are to confess our sins (I John 1:8-10). When God's Word exposes sin in our lives, confession should follow. Just as a person who is walking through a dark forest must use a flashlight to find his way, so we are to study and apply God's Word as we walk through the darkness of the world around us.

4. We are to depend on Jesus Christ, the Word (I John 2:1-5). Our text refers to Jesus Christ as "the propitiation for our sins" (vs. 2). There is only one way a sinner can stay in God's light—he must have divine enablement. This is promised to us as we continue to focus on Jesus Christ and not on ourselves.

How will all this happen? John said it happens when we purposefully focus on obeying God's Word.

It all makes good sense. Jesus Christ is the divine Light. We should stay in the light. We stay in the light by obeying God's Word.

CHILDREN'S CORNER

Children learn best through images rather than abstract ideas. Our lesson this week focuses on Christ as the light that conquers. Have the children consider how light can conquer darkness.

If their classrooms can be darkened sufficiently, have teachers turn out the lights, allow the children's eyes to adjust to the dark, and then light a small light (such as a keychain flashlight or phone light). Have them make the point that Jesus is a light that shines brighter than any flashlight, candle, or lightbulb. When we put our trust in Him, He drives away the darkness in our hearts.

—*Martin R. Dahlquist.*

SCRIPTURE LESSON TEXT

HEB. 4:14 Seeing then that we have a great high priest, that is passed into the heavens, Jesus the Son of God, let us hold fast *our* profession.

15 For we have not an high priest which cannot be touched with the feeling of our infirmities; but was in all points tempted like as *we are, yet* without sin.

16 Let us therefore come boldly unto the throne of grace, that we may obtain mercy, and find grace to help in time of need.

5:1 For every high priest taken from among men is ordained for men in things *pertaining* to God, that he may offer both gifts and sacrifices for sins:

2 Who can have compassion on the ignorant, and on them that are out of the way; for that he himself also is compassed with infirmity.

3 And by reason hereof he ought, as for the people, so also for himself, to offer for sins.

4 And no man taketh this honour unto himself, but he that is called of God, as *was* Aaron.

5 So also Christ glorified not himself to be made an high priest; but he that said unto him, Thou art my Son, to day have I begotten thee.

6 As he saith also in another *place,* Thou *art* a priest for ever after the order of Melchisedec.

7 Who in the days of his flesh, when he had offered up prayers and supplications with strong crying and tears unto him that was able to save him from death, and was heard in that he feared;

8 Though he were a Son, yet learned he obedience by the things which he suffered;

9 And being made perfect, he became the author of eternal salvation unto all them that obey him;

10 Called of God an high priest after the order of Melchisedec.

NOTES

88

Blessing of Intercession

Lesson Text: Hebrews 4:14—5:10

Related Scriptures: Matthew 26:36-46; Luke 22:39-46;
John 11:32-45; 17:9-16, 20-24

TIME: about A.D. 67

PLACE: unknown

GOLDEN TEXT—"Seeing then that we have a great high priest, that is passed into the heavens, Jesus the Son of God, let us hold fast our profession" (Hebrews 4:14).

Introduction

Priesthood is an institution in almost all the religions of the world. Though the functions of priests have varied from one religion to another, they all attempt to bridge the gap between humans and deities they represent. This involves some form of mediation between weak, sinful mankind and the deity.

Priesthood was thus a feature of not only ancient Israel but also its surrounding neighbors. In Egypt the pharaoh was considered the high priest of every god, but he was assisted by a powerful priesthood. The Mesopotamian civilizations—Assyria, Babylon, and Persia—all had their priestly castes.

God instituted a priesthood in Israel—a priesthood that began with Aaron and was ordained by God to mediate for Israel and offer sacrifices for sins. And this was but a foreshadowing of the ministry of the Great High Priest, Jesus Christ.

LESSON OUTLINE

I. ENCOURAGEMENT FROM CHRIST'S HIGH PRIESTHOOD— Heb. 4:14-16

II. QUALIFICATIONS OF HIGH PRIESTS—Heb. 5:1-4

III. HIGH PRIESTLY QUALIFICATIONS OF CHRIST— Heb. 5:5-10

Exposition: Verse by Verse

ENCOURAGEMENT FROM CHRIST'S HIGH PRIESTHOOD

HEB. 4:14 Seeing then that we have a great high priest, that is passed into the heavens, Jesus the Son of God, let us hold fast our profession.

15 For we have not an high priest which cannot be touched with the feeling of our infirmities; but was in all points tempted like as we are, yet without sin.

16 Let us therefore come boldly unto the throne of grace, that we may obtain mercy, and find grace to help in time of need.

His identification with us (Heb. 4:14-15). The author of Hebrews had previously alluded to the high priesthood of Christ (2:17—3:1). But he had turned from this theme to give a warning, lest his readers fail to enter the spiritual rest God intended for them (3:7-12). Now with the words "seeing then" (4:14) he returned to it and began to expound Christ's priesthood more thoroughly. He affirmed that Christian believers "have a great high priest."

The fact that Jesus is a Great High Priest sets Him apart as superior to all other priests, particularly those of Aaron's order, a theme taken up in detail later. In addition, Jesus has passed through the heavens. Levitical high priests passed beyond the veil in the temple once a year to make atonement (Heb. 9:3, 7), but Christ passed into the highest heaven and God's presence when His work was completed (6:19-20; 8:1; 9:24).

{This Great High Priest is both human and divine—"Jesus the Son of God" (Heb. 4:14). His humanity is essential to His identification with those He is representing (2:17), and His deity is essential for Him to exercise His power and impart His righteousness for their forgiveness.}[Q1] Chapter 1 emphasizes His deity, and chapter 2 His humanity. Now they are brought together in unity.

These truths about Jesus Christ are the basis for the exhortation to hold firmly to our profession (or confession) of faith. This idea is a key thought in Hebrews (cf. 3:1; 10:23) because the readers were wavering in their faith. Because of who Jesus Christ is and what He has done, they were to hold their confession of Him tenaciously.

To encourage them further in this, the writer assured them that Christ was aware of their struggles and temptations. It is a constant blessing that He is "touched with the feeling of our infirmities" (4:15), able to sympathize with our weaknesses. The writer used a double negative to stress this positive point because the readers were apt to think a divine Person could not really understand their condition. That, our text affirms, is simply untrue.

{Jesus can identify with us in our weaknesses because in every way He was tempted just as we are yet remained without sin. Although God cannot be tempted by evil (Jas. 1:13), Jesus could be tempted because He also is human. The fact that He was tempted in every respect does not mean He experienced every single temptation of every person but that He faced every *kind* of temptation.}[Q2] Solicitation to evil dogged Him His whole life, not just at the time of Satan's recorded temptations.

The assurance that Jesus remained without sin includes the truth that He did not yield to temptation. But it goes further. As God, He was without the ability to sin. The temptations were real, but they found in Him no trigger to produce sin (cf. II Cor. 5:21). Does this make Him less able to understand our temptations? By no means, for One who is sinless would feel its keenness in a way a fallen being could never appreciate. In resisting to the end, He no doubt felt the full force of temptation.

Our bold access through Him (Heb. 4:16). {Because our High Priest can so completely identify with us, we are urged to "come boldly unto the throne of grace." "Come" speaks concisely of moving into close proximity. This is an important theme of this book—open access to God (cf. 7:19, 25; 10:19-22). Christ's priestly work opens the way to God's presence. We are encouraged to follow Him there boldly, with freedom to commune with God.}[Q3]

God's presence is called "the throne of grace" (4:16), which speaks of two things: God's sovereignty and His freedom to dispense His favor. When we pray, we should keep both of these in mind, knowing that a sovereign God bestows His grace through Christ's finished work (cf. 1:3). When we approach Him, we will receive God's mercy and compassion along with His grace to help us in our time of need. He is always ready to dispense whatever help is needed.

QUALIFICATIONS OF HIGH PRIESTS

5:1 For every high priest taken from among men is ordained for men in things pertaining to God, that he may offer both gifts and sacrifices for sins:

2 Who can have compassion on the ignorant, and on them that are out of the way; for that he himself also is compassed with infirmity.

3 And by reason hereof he ought, as for the people, so also for himself, to offer for sins.

4 And no man taketh this honour unto himself, but he that is called of God, as was Aaron.

Identified with humanity (Heb. 5:1-3). The author intended to deal in depth with the superiority of Christ's priesthood over Aaron's. But to do this he had to first set forth high priestly qualifications. The first of these was that a high priest was "taken from among men." Only a human being could represent other humans "in things pertaining to God." Specifically, he offered "both gifts and sacrifices for sins." He oversaw the ministry of expiating sin before a holy God.

His shared human experience enabled him to "have compassion on the ignorant, and on them that are out of the way" (vs. 2). "Have compassion on" is a verb referring to the appropriate use of our human sympathies. {The high priest had to steer a middle course in dealing with human weakness, being neither too lenient nor too harsh. He could do this because he saw the same weaknesses in himself.}Q4

The high priest had to deal with people who were ignorant and going astray. The Old Testament Law made abundant provision of atoning sacrifices for sins committed in ignorance and waywardness (Num. 15:24-29), but it made no provision for the defiant sinner (vss. 30-31). The compassionate high priest would be able to discern the difference and empathize with the repentant, because he himself was subject to weakness.

Indeed, the high priest, being human, was susceptible to sin himself, and therefore had to offer sacrifices for his own sins as well as the sins of others. The Law made this requirement clear. Aaron and his sons had to make atonement for themselves before they could do so for the people (Lev. 9:7), and every high priest on the annual Day of Atonement had to do the same (Lev. 16:6; Heb. 9:7). Thus, every high priest fully identified with the people. {Though Jesus too identified with humans in their weakness (cf. Heb. 2:17-18; 4:15), His weakness did not entail moral frailty. He did not sin and therefore did not have to offer a sacrifice for Himself, a fact that the author emphasized later (7:26-28). In fact, Jesus would be able to give His own body and blood as an atonement for the sins of others (9:12; 10:10).}Q5

Called by God (Heb. 5:4). A high priest had to be human, but he was not humanly appointed: "No man taketh this honour unto himself." No one could arbitrarily decide to become a high priest. Old Testament history records that disaster fell on those who independently tried to take on priestly duties (cf. Num. 16; II Chr. 26:16-21). Nor were high priests chosen by election or royal appointment.

{A high priest had to be called by God, just as Aaron was. This divine appointment was not only a personal one but also included Aaron's descendants}Q6 (Ex. 28:1; I Chr. 23:13). Having been appointed by God, Jewish high priests were expected to carry out His revealed will. Deviation was bound to bring judgment (cf. I Sam. 2:27-36).

By the time Hebrews was written, succession to the high priesthood had become irregular and politically motivated. No longer were all high priests descendants of Aaron. Besides, corruption of all kinds permeated the office. Readers of Hebrews would have been aware of that. So the author focused on God's ideal.

HIGH PRIESTLY QUALIFICATIONS OF CHRIST

5 So also Christ glorified not himself to be made an high priest; but he that said unto him, Thou art my Son, to day have I begotten thee.

6 As he saith also in another place, Thou art a priest for ever after the order of Melchisedec.

7 Who in the days of his flesh, when he had offered up prayers and supplications with strong crying and tears unto him that was able to save him from death, and was heard in that he feared;

8 Though he were a Son, yet learned he obedience by the things which he suffered;

9 And being made perfect, he became the author of eternal salvation unto all them that obey him;

10 Called of God an high priest after the order of Melchisedec.

Ordained by the Father (Heb. 5:5-6). From examining high priestly qualifications in general, the author began to show how Jesus Christ fulfilled them, declaring first His divine appointment: "So also Christ glorified not himself to be made an high priest; but he that said unto him, Thou art my Son, to day have I begotten thee." {Though He was the Messiah and the Son of God, Jesus did not appropriate to Himself the position of high priest. He awaited the appoint-

ment of His Father.}[Q7]

A quotation from Psalm 2:7 establishes Christ's divine sonship. We have seen this used once already in Hebrews to show His superiority over angels (1:5), and now it affirms His superiority over earthly priesthoods. Jesus has entered a heavenly sanctuary, where His sacrifice is pleasing to His Father (cf. 9:24).

A second quotation, from Psalm 110:4, further establishes the nature of Christ's priesthood (Heb. 5:6). "As he saith" refers to God's own witness when He declared, "Thou art a priest for ever after the order of Melchisedec." This messianic psalm first declares the Messiah's deity (vss. 1-3), then His priesthood (vs. 4), and finally His conquests (vss. 5-7). Thus, the offices of king and priest reside in the same Person.

{This quotation tells us two characteristics of Christ's priesthood. First, it is forever. It is eternal because the Priest Himself is eternal, never to be succeeded by another (Heb. 7:28). Second, it is based on the order of Melchizedek. The idea of an "order" is best understood as a precedent or pattern, for Melchizedek never established an order of priests. A king-priest of Abraham's day (Gen. 14), he was one of a kind, and thus a fitting picture of Christ.}[Q8]

Confirmed by human suffering (Heb. 5:7-9). The similarities of Melchizedek and Christ are dealt with in detail later. {But the author of Hebrews preferred at this point to examine the other major qualification of our High Priest—His identification with humans in their sufferings.}[Q9] "In the days of his flesh" calls attention to His earthly life and the weakness it entailed. Jesus' experience described here is most likely His agony in Gethsemane, though it could refer to the cross.

Hebrews 5:7 further tells us that Jesus offered up to God "prayers and supplications." The first of these terms is the general word for entreaties, or requests. The second term is more intensive and used only here in the New Testament. It portrays the extending of an olive branch by one making supplication. Jesus accompanied His prayers with loud cries and tears.

Jesus' prayers were offered to One who was able to save Him from death, and the writer of Hebrews argued that He was heard because He showed godly reverence. We might be tempted to argue that He was not heard, since He had to die. But that prayer was answered in His resurrection (cf. Acts 2:27-31).

{Thus, Jesus' human struggles completed His preparation for the high priesthood: "Though he were a Son, yet learned he obedience by the things which he suffered" (Heb. 5:8). His sonship may lead us to assume that He would not have to suffer, but suffering enabled Him to learn in human experience what it meant to obey God (cf. Matt. 26:39, 42; Phil. 2:6-8).}^Q10 As a Son, He had always been obedient; as a man, He confirmed by obedience—even unto death—His fitness to be the High Priest for mankind.

It is in this sense also that we should interpret "and being made perfect" (Heb. 5:9; cf. 2:10). The author was not implying any previous moral imperfection in Christ but rather was speaking of His complete fitness for His high priestly ministry as a result of His human suffering.

At this point Jesus became the source of eternal salvation for all who obey Him. He is the means of divine deliverance at every level. The key qualifier is that this is for all who obey Him, that is, respond in faith to His finished work as God has commanded (cf. Rom. 6:17; 10:16; II Thess. 1:8).

Called to a unique priesthood (Heb. 5:10). The author concluded the discussion of Christ's high priestly qualifications with a summary state-ment that He is "called of God an high priest after the order of Melchisedec." God the Father formally proclaimed His Son to have a unique high priesthood.

Being named a high priest in the order, or pattern, of Melchizedek carries connotations that we will not cover in this lesson. But what the author of Hebrews wanted to emphasize at this point is that we have a Great High Priest who has fulfilled all the qualifications expected of a priest. But He has also exceeded those qualifications and, for our sakes, has inaugurated a high priesthood that is unique.

—Robert E. Wenger.

QUESTIONS

1. Why is it essential that our Great High Priest be both human and divine?

2. How did Jesus' temptations compare with those we face?

3. How can we as sinners have access to God's throne of grace?

4. What course did a priest have to follow in dealing with human weaknesses?

5. How does Jesus' identification with humans differ from that of purely human priests?

6. From what ancestry did Jewish priests have to come? Why?

7. Did Jesus seek out the high priestly office? Explain.

8. How does Christ's priesthood differ from that of Jewish priests?

9. How did Christ identify with human beings?

10. In what sense did Christ learn obedience?

—Robert E. Wenger.

Preparing to Teach the Lesson

This week's passage focuses on the important truth that Jesus Christ "was in all points tempted like as we are, yet without sin" (Heb. 4:15). Use this lesson to affirm the sinlessness of Christ. It is not that Christ could have sinned but did not. Rather, Christ could not have sinned because He was holy—sinless in His essential nature. Theologians call this the impeccability of Christ. We are thankful for this truth, for if Christ had sinned, He would not have qualified to bear our sin.

TODAY'S AIM

Facts: to understand Jesus' role as the Great High Priest who can help all believers.

Principle: to recognize how Jesus as the Great High Priest is superior to human high priests.

Application: to come to Jesus Christ, the Great High Priest, in times of difficulty.

INTRODUCING THE LESSON

Our legal system today gives great prominence to the role of an attorney or a public advocate. These people represent us or come to our aid when we have a need or face a difficulty. (If you have an attorney or a government advocate in your class, let him or her share about a typical workday.)

Have you had occasion to use the services of an attorney or an advocate? How did that person help you? (Allow your students to share the situation they faced and how this person helped them.)

Understanding the role of an attorney or advocate helps us better understand the role of Jesus Christ as our Great High Priest who can handle our needs. Christ's high priestly role also shows His sovereignty, for He alone qualifies for this position.

DEVELOPING THE LESSON

1. The position of our Great High Priest (Heb. 4:14). The book of Hebrews was written to first-century believers who came out of Judaism. These believers faced persecution and perhaps wanted to return to their old beliefs, which offered a visible high priest who might in some way be of help to them. The writer of Hebrews urged his readers to hold fast their confession of Christ and not go back, for they already had their Great High Priest—"Jesus the Son of God," who had "passed into the heavens." Though they could not see Him, He was in heaven actively serving as their Mediator and Advocate.

2. The nature of our Great High Priest (Heb. 4:15). Since Jesus Christ was in heaven, the believers may have wondered how He could really know their needs and help them. The writer of Hebrews responded by saying, "We have not an high priest which cannot be touched with the feeling of our infirmities." Here he used a double negative to emphasize the fact that our Great High Priest does sympathize with our weaknesses. Though He is in heaven, He knows what we are facing because He "was in all points tempted like as we are." During His earthly years, Christ knew what it was like to experience the frailty of the flesh (cf. Matt. 4:1-11). So, like the Jewish high priests, Christ knows what we experience.

The major difference between Christ and the Jewish high priests was that Christ was without sin. Our Saviour experienced the full force of temptation but did not yield to those temptations. In contrast to our condition, His fleshly nature was uncorrupted by sin. This corruption affected all ordinary human priests, who were sinful and therefore had to offer sacrifices for themselves (Heb. 5:3).

So why did Christ experience such temptations? He did so not to find out whether He could resist them but to demonstrate His total victory over all sin. The temptations cast a focused light on Jesus' sinlessness.

3. The invitation of our Great High Priest (Heb. 4:16). Because Jesus, our High Priest, is the Son of God, and because He knows our needs, He invites us to "come boldly unto the throne of grace, that we may obtain mercy, and find grace to help in time of need." When we come, we can be sure He will give us the help we need. The role of Jesus Christ as our sinless Great High Priest demonstrates His sovereignty and superiority over all other priests.

4. The qualifications of our Great High Priest (Heb. 5:1-10). Lest some people wonder about Jesus' qualifications as a high priest, the writer set forth His credentials. First, He was qualified by appointment. Human priests were appointed by God. "No man taketh this honour unto himself, but he that is called of God, as was Aaron." Jesus Christ was appointed by God the Father. "So also Christ glorified not himself to be made an high priest" but was appointed "a priest for ever after the order of Melchisedec."

Second, He was qualified by training. Christ presented His offerings of prayers and petitions with loud cries and tears. He also learned obedience from the things He suffered. The result is that He was made perfect, or complete, and thus became the source of eternal salvation for all those who trust in Him.

ILLUSTRATING THE LESSON

We can come at any time to our Great High Priest.

OUR GREAT HIGH PRIEST

ALWAYS WELCOMING

CONCLUDING THE LESSON

Because Jesus Christ is our Great High Priest, we can come boldly before God's throne. He will not turn us away. For us, His throne is not a throne of judgment and condemnation (cf. Rom. 8:1; Rev. 20:11) but rather a place to find grace, mercy, and help. As we close our session today, let us spend some time before the throne of grace.

(Ask your students to gather in groups of two or three for a short time of prayer—men with men and women with women. Encourage each of them to share at least one special need he or she is experiencing and have the other person(s) pray for that need. Urge your students to share personal matters to the extent they are willing to do so, and remind everyone of the importance of confidentiality.)

ANTICIPATING THE NEXT LESSON

Next week we will study Galatians 5:1-17 and the blessing of our liberty in Christ.

—Don Anderson.

PRACTICAL POINTS

1. We know our High Priest can enter God's holy presence, for He is God (Heb. 4:14).
2. Our High Priest is able to relate to us because He has been tempted as we have (vs. 15).
3. Because of our High Priest, we can be confident that God will give us mercy and grace (vs. 16).
4. All other high priests in history have had to offer sacrifices for their own sins (5:1-3).
5. Jesus was appointed by God to be our High Priest forever in the order of Melchizedek (vss. 4-6).
6. Jesus was heard because of His reverence and obedience to the Father (vss. 7-10).

—Stuart Olley.

RESEARCH AND DISCUSSION

1. What does it mean that Jesus "is passed into the heavens" (Heb. 4:14; cf. Lev. 16)?
2. How has Jesus faced temptations as we have and overcome them (Heb. 4:15; cf. Matt. 4:1-11)?
3. Why can we approach the throne of grace with confidence (Heb. 4:15-16)? How do we know that Jesus relates to God perfectly?
4. Why were former high priests able to deal gently with the ignorant and the wayward (5:1-3)? How encouraging is it to know Jesus deals gently with us?
5. What does it mean for Jesus to be in the order of Melchizedek (Heb. 5:4-6, 10; cf. Gen. 14:18-20)?

—Stuart Olley.

ILLUSTRATED HIGH POINTS

Touched with . . . our infirmities (Heb. 4:15)

Sympathy was an expected trait of the Old Testament priest. If sympathy is carried to an extreme, however, it can make a person over-indulgent. Thus one also needs a high degree of objectivity and self-discipline. But people in caring professions often score low in sympathy because they try to protect themselves from too much emotional involvement. We all need balance.

Compassion for the ignorant (5:2)

I drove a friend to take the road test for his driver's license. We noticed that one inspector looked quite genial. The other looked like a sour lemon.

Sure enough, my friend drew Attila the Hun. They drove off but were back in minutes. My friend had failed to come to a complete stop at the first intersection—an automatic failure. We could not fault the inspector. He was doing his job.

Under the law, we get no breaks. But since Jesus fulfilled the law for us, we get His compassion.

Unto himself (vs. 4)

God chose Aaron and his descendants to be Israel's priests. It was an honor to serve, but it was also hard work. Priests had to sacrifice animals from pigeons to bulls. They had to remember a multitude of details pertaining to the offerings as well as become expert at diagnosing physical maladies, such as leprosy.

Priests probably found it especially difficult when they had to deal with spiritual needs. They had to be gentle with those who confessed their sins— not too harsh and not too lenient.

Christ ministers perfectly as the Son of Man.

—David A. Hamburg.

Golden Text Illuminated

"Seeing then that we have a great high priest, that is passed into the heavens, Jesus the Son of God, let us hold fast our profession" (Hebrews 4:14).

Having concluded his discussion of Christ's superiority over Moses, the author of Hebrews here introduces another section of his epistle. Broadly, the section that begins with our golden text shows that Christ is greater than Aaron, Israel's first high priest.

In Hebrews 2:17 and 3:1 Jesus is called a high priest. "Here the adjective 'great' is added. . . . by way of contrast with the Jewish high priest" (Erdman, *The Epistle to the Hebrews,* Westminster John Knox). Like the Jewish people, Christians also have a high priest, but He is a great one. Unlike Aaron and the high priests of Israel who followed him, our Great High Priest has "not passed beyond any mere material veil into 'a holy place made with hands,' but he has penetrated to the very throne of God, and occupies a place of supreme power" (Erdman).

Hebrews goes on to explain in detail the greatness of our High Priest and His unique priestly ministry in heaven. In introducing this subject, the author simply declared the greatness of the One who "passed into the heavens." His greatness is emphasized by His title, "Jesus the Son of God."

"Jesus" is the personal name of our Saviour, given to Him at birth according to the command of God (Matt. 1:21, 25; Luke 1:31). Throughout His earthly life, He was known by this name, which emphasized His humanity. Jesus is fully man, just as every high priest who served the nation of Israel was a man. And as one who is fully human and had faced temptation, hardship, and sorrow, Jesus could sympathize with us (Heb. 4:15).

However, Jesus is also "the Son of God." This is His divine title. "The term *son of God* denotes equality and identity of essence, which means . . . He is God" (McCune, *A Systematic Theology of Biblical Christianity,* Detroit Baptist Seminary).

The high priests of Israel were human and thus could identify with the people of Israel they served and for whom they interceded. But they were also flawed, sinful human beings like everyone else in the nation. Our Great High Priest is not only fully human and thus sympathetic to us, but He is also fully God and perfectly sinless (Heb. 4:15). He is far greater than Aaron or any of the high priests who were so important to Israel and the nation's relationship with God.

Because we have such a great High Priest, we can, as the author implores us, "hold fast our profession," or confession. This is an exhortation to cling to our confession of faith in Christ as our Saviour and Lord (cf. Heb. 3:1; 10:23).

When we are tempted to waver in our faith in the face of pressures, as many of the original Jewish readers of Hebrews were, we need to remember who Jesus is. He is God the Son, our sympathetic and perfect High Priest. He has offered the one final and sufficient sacrifice for our sins. He is infinitely greater than the greatest of human beings. To Him alone we can—and should—fully and unwaveringly entrust our lives for eternity.

—Jarl K. Waggoner.

Heart of the Lesson

A few weeks before I was to have surgery and my first-ever hospital stay, the niece of a woman at my church called to share her experiences with an identical surgery. She described the pain, the post-surgery nausea, and the recovery. She patiently answered my many questions. What a comfort to talk with someone who understood exactly what I was going through!

This week's lesson shows the wonder of having Jesus as our High Priest, a High Priest both perfectly human and perfectly God. He understands us perfectly.

1. Our High Priest is the Son of God (Heb. 4:14-16). Jesus provides access to God. After His resurrection, He ascended into heaven as the disciples watched and now is seated at God the Father's right hand. There He intercedes for us and assures us of God's forgiveness. Jesus represents us to God, and Jesus represents God to us.

Jesus, our High Priest, is not someone who lacks feelings and is unable to identify with us and our weaknesses. Rather, because of His time on earth as a man, He has experienced all the weaknesses and temptations that humans have. Yet He did not sin. Note that temptation—exposure to testing or seduction—is not sin in itself.

Having such a High Priest, we can approach God's throne boldly and confidently. There God offers us mercy, which means we do not get what we really deserve. And He offers us grace, His undeserved favor. Jesus will help us in our time of need, no matter how great or small that need may be.

2. Our High Priest is compassionate and gentle (Heb. 5:1-3). A desirable quality for a priest was a compassionate and gentle nature, especially toward those who had sinned ignorantly or had strayed from God but desired restoration. The priest's own experience of sinning would aid him in many cases to have compassion. Jesus, of course, had no personal experience with sinning, but He understands sin's allurement and is compassionate toward sinners.

The Old Testament high priest offered to God the people's gifts and sacrifices for sin. But first he had to offer sacrifices for his own sin. Jesus was without sin, so He had no need for personal sacrifices. Instead, He Himself was the sacrifice for sin.

3. Our High Priest was appointed by God (Heb. 5:4-6). Being a high priest was an honor and a calling from God, not a personal choice. Jesus did not assume the glory of being a high priest on His own. God the Father called Him to be a priest forever after the order of Melchizedek, the mysterious priest from Salem (Jerusalem) to whom Abraham offered sacrifices (cf. Gen. 14:18-20).

4. Our High Priest knows suffering (Heb. 5:7-8). In the Garden of Gethsemane, Jesus pled with the Father to allow the cup of suffering to pass from Him. God could have saved Jesus from death, but that was not the plan. Jesus ultimately said, "Not my will, but thine, be done" (Luke 22:42).

5. Our High Priest is the source of eternal salvation (Heb. 5:9-10). Jesus' obedience in going to the cross perfected Him, meaning that it made Him completely qualified to be our Saviour. Our salvation is eternal; nothing can pluck us from God's hand.

Knowing Jesus understands everything we face should give us confidence to present our needs to God. And Jesus' ability to withstand temptation should give us hope because His power lives in us.

—Ann Staatz.

World Missions

"Every day of those thirteen months was the same. Up at 5:00 A.M. Mop the floor. Clean up. Go to the restroom. Throw out the contents of the bucket. Then I had to sit cross-legged with my hands on my knees in the same position for the next seventeen hours."

For this young man in North Korea, a good day was the pain that came from sitting perfectly still until ten P.M. each night. A bad day, if he chanced to move or even flinch, meant torture.

His crime? When a friend struggling in his marriage asked him how he and his wife were so happy, he had answered, "We follow the Ten Commandments, and heaven is always watching. When you break them, you ask heaven for forgiveness. And when you receive food, you give thanks." That was all. He had not even said the word "God."

When we read about persecutions happening globally right now, the horror seems unimaginable.

The natural response to such stories is to feel sorry for those suffering, and such compassion is good, especially if it motivates us to pray or to act. (The Voice of the Martyrs at www.persecution.com offers ways churches and individuals can help fellow believers suffering persecution—including writing to encourage believers in prison, praying daily for the persecuted church around the world, and giving to outreach or widows or orphans of martyrs.) However, let us continue to read the account about the man in North Korea and see whether we can learn from it.

"During that time, I came to think a lot about my life. I thought about how I had forgotten God and failed to rely on Him. I thought about how I had relied only on my own brilliance. And so sitting there hour after hour, day after day, month after month, as one year yielded to its successor, I repented. And of all things, a spirit of thankfulness rose up in me. I became thankful to the Lord for this time in prison—His arresting me from my own pride. That is how I came to rely on only the Holy Spirit with faith."

This week's lesson tells us to "hold fast the profession of our faith" (Heb. 10:23; cf. 4:14). Millions have suffered in North Korea, yet when some North Korean Christians were asked how Americans could pray for them, they responded, "Pray for us? We pray for you!" Why would they be praying for us rather than for themselves—to be relieved of their suffering and be set free? When asked why, they answered, "Because Christians in the West still have some wealth and freedom and power. Most have not yet experienced what it is like when all you have in life is God."

It is worth pondering that it may be as difficult to hold fast our profession of faith when it is "safe" to be a Christian as when it is dangerous. How are we doing at obeying Hebrews 4:14 ourselves?

The Bible says, "He that is faithful in that which is least is faithful also in much" (Luke 16:10). If we will not speak of our faith now, when the punishment might mean ridicule or rejection, how can we expect to hold fast our profession if the penalty might one day be the loss of our lives?

Let us hold fast in the small tests so that we may develop faithfulness and strength to honor our Saviour no matter how big the tests may become.

—*Kimberly Rae.*

The Jewish Aspect

The writer of Hebrews used an intriguing and significant phrase when he wrote that Jesus "passed into the heavens" (4:14). More literally, the verse can be translated that Jesus "passed through the heavens." This brings two particular questions immediately to bear: First, what is the significance that Jesus passed through heavens? Second, how many heavens exist? The Jewish readers of the epistle would have particular thoughts as they read this verse.

The author of Hebrews had already established that Jesus is the superior High Priest (2:17; 3:1). In 4:14 he emphasized Jesus' high priestly ministry. In that ministry, He "passed through."

The Jewish Christian readers of Hebrews would immediately think about the ministry of the human high priest in Herod's temple. On the great Day of Atonement, the high priest followed a specific approach in his ritual. He "passed through" the Court of the Gentiles, the Court of Women, and the Court of the Israelites. Next, he "passed through" the court of the priests and came to the altar of burnt offering. Then he came to the laver.

The high priest next "passed through" the holy place. After that, he "passed through" a double veil and finally reached the empty Holy of Holies. The ark of the covenant, originally situated here, disappeared at the time of the Babylonian Captivity. Some believe it was hidden from the Babylonians (and is yet to be discovered). Others believe the Babylonians took it when they destroyed the temple.

The Lord Jesus also "passed through" in His ministry of achieving the perfect atonement for sins. He did not, however, pass through Herod's temple. He passed through the heavens until He reached the very throne room of God Himself.

Hebrews 4:14 specifically uses the plural word "heavens." How did ancient Jews view the "heavens"? The Hebrew word for heaven is *shamayim,* which appears 421 times in the Old Testament. The word is always used in the plural, and the context must determine what each use means. First, it can refer to the place where birds fly (Deut. 4:17) and from where rain falls (Gen. 8:2). Second, it may also refer to the place where the sun, moon, and stars are (1:14). Finally, it may refer to the place where God dwells (Ps. 2:4). In similar fashion the New Testament speaks of three "heavens"; Paul, notably, was caught up to the third one (II Cor. 12:2).

The ancient Jews, however, frequently expanded the number of the "heavens" beyond three. Jewish writings from the time of the New Testament refer to a belief in seven heavens. Seven heavens are specifically named in the book of Second Enoch (written before A.D. 70), which Enoch supposedly visited: *Vilon* ("curtain"), *Raqi'a* ("expanse"), *Shehakim* ("clouds"), *Zebul* ("habitation," where the New Jerusalem is), *Ma'on* ("refuge," where many angels are), *Makhon* ("city of angels"), and *Araboth* ("desert," home of God, who needs no moisture or air) ("Judaism's Seven Heavens," www.compellingtruth.org).

Other Jewish writings from New Testament times also make mention of seven heavens in God's creation ("The Testaments of the Twelve Patriarchs," www.earlychristianwritings.com). It may be that some of the original readers of Hebrews thought of seven heavens, or they may have thought of three heavens. In either case, Jesus "passed through" all of them to reach God's throne and complete our atonement.

—R. Larry Overstreet

Guiding the Superintendent

No human being is without sin. If you are familiar with what God's Word says about man's need for salvation and the extent of the price Jesus needed to pay for that salvation, that concept is nothing new. However, it can take time for that idea to fully sink in.

Consider what the qualifications would have to be for a mediator between you and God. As we will see from Scripture, such a divine job requires sinlessness. You could search across the globe, conducting interviews with every individual in every city of every country, and still you would not find a qualified individual. Nevertheless, that kind of person is necessary for anyone on this planet to have a relationship with God and see his sins forgiven—a sobering situation, to be sure. But we know from Scripture that the challenge is not impossible.

DEVOTIONAL OUTLINE

1. Our superior High Priest (Heb. 4:14-16). Only a divine, spotless high priest is capable of representing sinful man before God. As shown in this week's lesson text, we can have complete confidence in Christ to be the Intercessor we need.

Consider the dual elements of humanity and divinity expressed in this paragraph and how they speak of Jesus. He is both the Son of God and the Son of Man. He has passed through the heavens, showing that He is truly God. Moreover, He is able to fully sympathize with every spiritual weakness we suffer, except He is without sin. The fact that He experienced temptation shows that He can identify with our humanity.

2. Ancient high priests (Heb. 5:1-3). High priests in Old Testament times served a special purpose in God's plan for His people, but they were insufficient to accomplish God's redemptive plan for mankind. Even though they were able to sympathize with the people's weaknesses and point them to the Lord, they still needed to offer sacrifices to God for their own sins. A high priest who needed forgiveness himself could by no means accomplish forgiveness for others.

3. Our superior High Priest's credentials (Heb. 5:4-10). By contrast, however, Jesus offers infinitely greater credentials for being our Great High Priest. The writer of Hebrews again turned to Psalms to show that Jesus' messianic title also afforded Him high priestly duties.

This identity was fully expressed in Jesus' emotional turmoil at Gethsemane as He faced the cross. Enduring such physical pain on the cross and the infinitely painful separation from His Father shows beyond doubt that Jesus can intercede for His elect.

CHILDREN'S CORNER

Help children see that they can always turn to Jesus no matter what. Anytime, anywhere, and for any issue—Jesus will hear their cry.

Some of the children in your Sunday school may have trouble realizing that Jesus can completely identify with their struggles. Help them see that this is a powerful aspect of Jesus' role as our Great High Priest.

Since young children most likely will not understand the term "high priest," make sure it is explained to them that a priest is someone who talks to God for people. Jesus tells God the Father that we belong to Jesus because we trust in Him.

—Joshua A. Littler.

SCRIPTURE LESSON TEXT

GAL. 5:1 Stand fast therefore in the liberty wherewith Christ hath made us free, and be not entangled again with the yoke of bondage.

2 Behold, I Paul say unto you, that if ye be circumcised, Christ shall profit you nothing.

3 For I testify again to every man that is circumcised, that he is a debtor to do the whole law.

4 Christ is become of no effect unto you, whosoever of you are justified by the law; ye are fallen from grace.

5 For we through the Spirit wait for the hope of righteousness by faith.

6 For in Jesus Christ neither circumcision availeth any thing, nor uncircumcision; but faith which worketh by love.

7 Ye did run well; who did hinder you that ye should not obey the truth?

8 This persuasion *cometh* not of him that calleth you.

9 A little leaven leaveneth the whole lump.

10 I have confidence in you through the Lord, that ye will be none otherwise minded: but he that troubleth you shall bear his judgment, whosoever he be.

11 And I, brethren, if I yet preach circumcision, why do I yet suffer persecution? then is the offence of the cross ceased.

12 I would they were even cut off which trouble you.

13 For, brethren, ye have been called unto liberty; only *use* not liberty for an occasion to the flesh, but by love serve one another.

14 For all the law is fulfilled in one word, *even* in this; Thou shalt love thy neighbour as thyself.

15 But if ye bite and devour one another, take heed that ye be not consumed one of another.

16 *This* I say then, Walk in the Spirit, and ye shall not fulfil the lust of the flesh.

17 For the flesh lusteth against the Spirit, and the Spirit against the flesh: and these are contrary the one to the other: so that ye cannot do the things that ye would.

NOTES

Blessing of Liberty in Christ

Lesson Text: Galatians 5:1-17

Related Scriptures: John 8:31-36; Acts 15:1-21;
I Corinthians 7:17-24; II Corinthians 3:12-18

TIME: probably A.D. 48   PLACE: from Syrian Antioch

GOLDEN TEXT—"Stand fast therefore in the liberty wherewith Christ hath made us free, and be not entangled again with the yoke of bondage" (Galatians 5:1).

Introduction

For some people, freedom is a frightening concept.

The Israelites spent more than four hundred years in Egypt. Most of that time they suffered in slavery. But under the leadership of Moses, the Israelites were freed from Egyptian bondage by the mighty hand of God.

Probably over two million people left Egypt, bound for the Land of Promise. Yet only days after leaving the land of slavery, the multitude was complaining that they would have been better off remaining in Egypt. They were free, but when they encountered hardships under God's chosen leader, they longed to return to the bondage they had always known under the Egyptians.

Likewise, those who have known nothing but spiritual bondage often are tempted to return to what is familiar to them rather than fully embrace the responsibilities that accompany freedom in Christ.

LESSON OUTLINE

I. REMAINING IN LIBERTY—
Gal. 5:1-6

II. THE THREAT TO LIBERTY—
Gal. 5:7-12

III. THE PROPER USE OF LIBERTY—Gal. 5:13-17

Exposition: Verse by Verse

REMAINING IN LIBERTY

GAL. 5:1 Stand fast therefore in the liberty wherewith Christ hath made us free, and be not entangled again with the yoke of bondage.

2 Behold, I Paul say unto you, that if ye be circumcised, Christ shall profit you nothing.

3 For I testify again to every man that is circumcised, that he is a debtor to do the whole law.

4 Christ is become of no effect unto you, whosoever of you are justified by the law; ye are fallen from grace.

5 For we through the Spirit wait for the hope of righteousness by faith.

6 For in Jesus Christ neither circumcision availeth any thing, nor uncircumcision; but faith which worketh by love.

A command (Gal. 5:1). {Paul's command to the Galatians to "stand fast" in liberty was based on the truth that this was where Christ Himself had placed them. Through faith in Christ, they were freed from their terrible spiritual bondage. Now the apostle was telling them to keep on standing in that liberty they enjoyed—to stay free.}[Q1]

The other half of the command was not to let themselves be burdened down again under a yoke of slavery. Both Jewish and Gentile believers in Galatia had been enslaved by religion before their conversion to Christ. {But under the influence of the Judaizers, who were promoting adherence to the Mosaic Law as necessary for Christians, these believers were in danger of becoming entangled in the Jewish law.}[Q2] Although they were free in Christ, they were being told that more was needed for them to be rightly related to God.

A warning (Gal. 5:2-4). Paul issued a very strong warning to those who were thinking of adopting the Mosaic Law as a means of becoming or remaining righteous before God. Clearly, this was directed at Gentile converts who were being pressured by the false teachers to submit to circumcision and all the demands of the law. {To seek righteousness by submitting to circumcision was to declare that one was not fully trusting Christ alone.}[Q3]

When works of the law are added to grace, the very concept of grace, God's unmerited favor, is compromised. The Galatians were confused by the Judaizers. Some were thinking that adopting the law, and particularly the law of circumcision, was necessary or at least helpful in "establishing a right relationship with God" (Kent, *The Freedom of God's Sons,* BMH). But Paul warned that to truly seek righteousness through the law meant that Christ would be of no profit. His death and resurrection would have no value.

"Saving faith trusts Christ only and repudiates any attempt of man to produce a meritorious work. Paul warned that if anyone received circumcision as an additional means of salvation he would manifest that he was really an unsaved person" (Gromacki, *Stand Fast in Liberty,* Kress).

Furthermore, if one is required to observe the law of circumcision, he is obligated to keep the whole Law of Moses (cf. Jas. 2:10). The law is a unit. One cannot pick and choose what part of it to obey and what part to ignore. To place oneself under the law is to be required to keep it all and thus be condemned since no one can keep the law (Gal. 3:10).

Paul concluded his warning by repeating that Christ's work is of no value to those who are seeking to be justified by the law (5:4). "Are justified" does not suggest that a person could possibly be declared righteous by keeping the law; rather, it indicates an ongoing attempt at gaining righteousness through the law, which is fruitless. {One who insists on making such an attempt is "fallen from grace." To fall from grace is to fall into legalism.}[Q4] And "to choose legalism is to relinquish grace as the principle by which one desires to be related to God" (Barker and Kohlenberger, eds., *The Expositor's Bible Commentary, Abridged,* Zondervan).

An affirmation (Gal. 5:5-6). Much confusion was being sown among the Galatians by the false teachers, who were demanding adherence to the Mosaic law. Paul warned that such an approach to either salvation or the Christian life is contrary to the truth that salvation is "by grace . . . through faith" (Eph. 2:8). Thus the apostle affirmed, "We through the Spirit wait for the hope of righteousness by faith" (Gal. 5:5).

Rather than seek approval from God through observance of legalistic standards that offer no assurance, {those who have been born again by the Spirit through faith in Christ patiently wait in faith for the certain hope, or expectation, of righteousness. This refers to a future time when God will publicly declare the believer righteous.}⁰⁵ "Righteousness is already the believer's possession in justification, but its full realization will be experienced at Christ's coming to claim His own. For this the believer waits in faith. No performance of law could ever achieve it" (Kent).

Paul then affirmed that neither the practice nor nonpractice of the rite of circumcision was of any value. He was not opposed to the practice itself but rather to the idea that circumcision—or uncircumcision—had any spiritual value in making one righteous. The only thing that matters is faith that expresses itself in love.

We accept God's gift of salvation by faith (Eph. 2:8-9), and we live our lives by faith in Christ and His promises (II Cor. 5:7). That faith is not a stale, intellectual acknowledgment, however. True faith demonstrates itself in love. {Thus, while faith stands contrary to works with regard to one's relationship with God, genuine faith works; that is, it produces spiritual fruit in the believer's life.}⁰⁶ A person cannot claim to have faith and then live any way he wishes. His life will demonstrate "his loving gratitude for all that Christ has done for him" (Gromacki).

Paul's point was simple, and it is important to remember today when the temptation to replace God's grace and faith in Christ with works is just as great. Works do not produce salvation; rather, works are the evidence and product of true faith.

THE THREAT TO LIBERTY

7 Ye did run well; who did hinder you that ye should not obey the truth?

8 This persuasion cometh not of him that calleth you.

9 A little leaven leaveneth the whole lump.

10 I have confidence in you through the Lord, that ye will be none otherwise minded: but he that troubleth you shall bear his judgment, whosoever he be.

11 And I, brethren, if I yet preach circumcision, why do I yet suffer persecution? then is the offence of the cross ceased.

12 I would they were even cut off which trouble you.

Its source (Gal. 5:7-8). Using the metaphor of a race, Paul said that the Galatians had started out well in their Christian life. However, something was now hindering them, or literally cutting in on them, so that they were no longer obeying the truth. They were not eliminated from the race, but they were getting off course by mixing faith with various Jewish practices (cf. 3:10) and at least entertaining the thought that such practices were necessary for their acceptance before God. Having begun by faith, they were now turning to legalism to finish the race (cf. vs. 3).

Who had caused this hindrance? The answer should have been obvious to the Galatians. The enticement to turn to the law had come from the Judaizers. It certainly had not come from God, the One who had called them, for His gospel of grace was not the gospel the Judaizers taught (cf. 1:6-7).

Its danger (Gal. 5:9). {The danger presented by the false gospel of the Judaizers is expressed in the proverbial statement "A little leaven leaveneth the whole lump" (I Cor. 5:6; cf. Matt. 16:6). Like leaven in bread, the false teaching taking root in Galatia would spread and contaminate the whole church if measures were not taken to eliminate it.}[Q7] That is why the Galatians were to stand firm in their liberty and not become entangled in the bondage of legalism. Such a stand would put an end to the leavening process.

Its judgment (Gal. 5:10-12). For all the dangers presented by the legalism being taught in Galatia, {Paul was confident that his readers' faith was genuine and that they ultimately would agree with his teaching and not be carried away into error.}[Q8] He was also confident that the one who was teaching the error, whoever he was, would "bear his judgment." This could refer to the leader of the Judaizers, or it could be a general designation for all of them, since the plural is used in verse 12.

The judgment mentioned here is divine judgment. Error may have widespread and profound consequences, but it will not prevail in the end. God will see to that. We need to remember this truth and not be taken in by popular teachings that do not clearly align with the Bible. Error usually presents itself as popular and attractive, but it stands under the judgment of God.

Galatians 5:11 is difficult to interpret, but it is probably best understood as Paul's response to an accusation made against him; namely, that he had preached the necessity of circumcision but now was preaching a different message. Why such a charge would be leveled is unclear, but it was definitely untrue.

Paul pointed out that if he had taught that the rite was necessary for salvation, he would not have experienced such persecution from the Jews. The gospel of grace he preached was centered in the cross—the crucifixion—of Jesus as the payment for sin. This teaching was offensive to the Jews, who promoted works such as circumcision as the means of acceptance by God. Clearly, Paul was consistent and uncompromising in teaching salvation by grace through faith, apart from any works.

Paul was so adamant about the gospel of grace that he could tolerate nothing that would compromise it. He even wished that those who put such confidence in an act of the flesh would mutilate themselves as their pagan neighbors did in their twisted attempts to please their gods.

Paul's attitude might seem unduly harsh, but he recognized that anything that diminishes the gospel of Christ turns it into a gospel of man. And a manmade gospel is worse than worthless, for it leads people to eternal destruction.

THE PROPER USE OF LIBERTY

13 For, brethren, ye have been called unto liberty; only use not liberty for an occasion to the flesh, but by love serve one another.

14 For all the law is fulfilled in one word, even in this; Thou shalt love thy neighbour as thyself.

15 But if ye bite and devour one another, take heed that ye be not consumed one of another.

16 This I say then, Walk in the Spirit, and ye shall not fulfil the lust of the flesh.

17 For the flesh lusteth against the Spirit, and the Spirit against the flesh: and these are contrary the one to the other: so that ye cannot do the things that ye would.

Freedom to love (Gal. 5:13-15). It is imperative that believers remain grounded in their freedom in Christ, but that freedom is not a license to indulge any and all fleshly desires. The freedom Christ gives is freedom from sin and its power and consequences, as well as freedom from enslavement to a religious system that can offer no hope of victory over sin. Properly understood, liberty in Christ cannot promote sin. Instead, it should lead to loving service to others.

{Obedience to the biblical injunction to love one's neighbor as oneself (cf. Lev. 19:18) sums up the whole law. In fact, it fulfills, or completes, the law (Gal. 5:14). Love is the expression of faith (vs. 6), and when one by faith comes to Christ, that faith produces in the person the kind of love for others the law demanded but could not produce.}Q9

Galatians 5:15 assumes there was strife within the Galatian churches, whether it was over the teaching about the role of the law or something else. They needed to be reminded to love one another rather than to consume one another. This they had the power to do if they were truly men and women of faith.

The truth is worth fighting to preserve, but it does not give us the freedom to act in harmful and unloving ways.

Freedom to walk in the Spirit (Gal. 5:16-17). The key to avoiding the kind of conflict Paul described in verse 15 is applying our faith by walking, or living, in the Spirit. We who have placed our faith in Christ have the Holy Spirit dwelling within us. We must submit to His power and control, trusting Him to give us victory over temptation and to bring us into conformity with God's will.

{Walking by the Spirit is allowing Him to determine the course of our daily lives as He illuminates the teaching of Scripture to us.}Q10 This is not a passive stance on our part. "The principle of the Spirit does not make human effort unnecessary, but arouses it and equips it to put all its forces into the service of the Spirit" (Ridderbos, *The Epistle of Paul to the Churches of Galatia,* Eerdmans).

{When we walk in the Spirit, we will not fulfill the "lust of the flesh" (vs. 16). We will not give in to ungodly and selfish desires.}Q10 Verse 17 explains that there is a continuing internal conflict between the indwelling Spirit and the flesh. The flesh is the old disposition to sin that continues even in those who have been born again.

Freedom in Christ does not mean freedom to live apart from all restraint. True freedom comes from willingly submitting to the control of the Holy Spirit, and God the Spirit does not lead us into sin. To stand fast in the liberty Christ has given us is to be responsible for walking in the Spirit.

—Jarl K. Waggoner.

QUESTIONS

1. On what did Paul base his call to the Galatians to stand fast in liberty?

2. What threatened their freedom in Christ?

3. Why did Paul warn Gentile believers against submitting to circumcision?

4. What does it mean to be "fallen from grace" (Gal. 5:4)?

5. What righteousness do we hope for by faith?

6. How is faith related to works?

7. What danger did Paul express through the proverb about leaven?

8. Of what was Paul confident regarding the Galatian believers?

9. How does faith relate to the fact that love fulfills the law?

10. What is walking "in the Spirit" (vs. 16)? What results from it?

—Jarl K. Waggoner.

Preparing to Teach the Lesson

As you teach this lesson, be aware that you may have people in your class from very different persuasions. They may have been brought up in a tradition that tries to mix law and grace, or at least works and grace. Some may think we have to keep certain elements of the law or do certain good deeds to really be accepted in God's sight.

Sabbath observance was pretty carefully prescribed in my home church. We were allowed to talk and go for a leisurely walk on Sunday but not to play a softball game. It was to be a day of rest and a day of religious observance. We were always pressed to witness to unsaved people. There was a lot of talk about doing but not enough about resting in faith in the Lord.

TODAY'S AIM

Facts: to clearly see the contrasts drawn between a life under the law and a life under grace.

Principle: to understand that we are saved by God's grace, not by our works.

Application: to live a life of freedom in the Holy Spirit and love to others.

INTRODUCING THE LESSON

It is clear in Scripture that trusting in the Lord Jesus moves us from being under the law to being under grace. We have a freedom in Christ that we could never have under the law. There was a bondage under the law, a carefully outlined lifestyle that was actually designed to bring its followers to realize that they had to depend on God's gracious gift of salvation in order to be saved. The law was a schoolmaster to bring people to Christ and the salvation God provided instead of people trying to save themselves.

Freedom can be somewhat frightening. If we are freely accepted by God, what will we actually do with that freedom? This was enough of a problem that a large portion of the letter to the Galatians is devoted to it. How much of our salvation is provided by the Lord? Is there a portion we must do to make it effective?

DEVELOPING THE LESSON

1. Freed from the obligation to keep the law (Gal. 5:1-12). In such an important matter as eternal destiny, it is not surprising that some people want to "cover all the bases." If we keep all the law, the behavior God prescribed, will we not be more pleasing to Him?

Paul addressed the matter of circumcision. Abraham had been given this rite as the seal of the promise God had made to him as he walked by faith in God and His promise. All the faithful down through the ages since that time had received circumcision as physical and spiritual descendants of Abraham. It was perhaps very hard for people not to insist on the practice. However, Paul pointed out that if they did this, they were teaching that the whole law must be kept for salvation, which no one could ever do.

Trying to keep the law for our salvation makes us slaves to the law. It stands as a barrier to freedom in Christ. If we are slaves to the law, we have no standing in the grace of God. We cannot mix law and grace; it is either one or the other.

2. Freedom is not license to sin (Gal. 5:13-15). Our freedom is not freedom to sin but to do good apart from any thought of saving merits. We are free to love our brothers and sisters in Christ without relating it to having anything to do with saving us. If the law is fulfilled in loving our neighbors as ourselves, then as long as we have this attitude and follow through with deeds of kindness and love, we are effectually keeping the law.

Just as the Lord Jesus in His earthly ministry said that He was doing what He saw the Father do, so we can cooperate with the Holy Spirit and what He wants us to do for our neighbors. The alternative is to resist the Holy Spirit and fail to do that which is loving and kind. If we are critical and condemning in our relationships, we risk discouraging and crushing the spirits of our neighbors—that is, if we "bite and devour one another" (vs. 15).

3. Freedom in the Holy Spirit, not in the flesh (Gal. 5:16-17). Paul admonishes us to walk in the Spirit. This means that we should respond to the Holy Spirit's promptings as we live our daily lives. He will guide us to do what we can to show love and encouragement to our brothers and sisters in Christ. Our human nature—the flesh—is selfish, greedy, grasping, and usually negative in our relationships. As He dwells within us, the Holy Spirit is just the opposite. He loves and looks out for the well-being of other believers. The Holy Spirit will interest you in the salvation and spiritual growth of others.

It may be a struggle to listen for the Holy Spirit's promptings and put down our old fleshly desires. But the battle is the Lord's, and we can learn to obey the spiritually positive guidance of the Holy Spirit. Whatever your struggle may be, remember that others have gone this way before and that it is far better to persevere.

ILLUSTRATING THE LESSON

We should walk in the Spirit. In this way, we will allow no room in our lives for fleshly desires.

WALK IN THE SPIRIT

HE WILL GUIDE YOUR STEPS

CONCLUDING THE LESSON

It is easy to say that we must stand fast in the liberty we have in Christ and walk in the Spirit. It is much harder to do it. Remembering to listen for the promptings of the Holy Spirit and walking by them can be both difficult and easy things to do. We may understand the first time we hear His Word and do very well right from the start. Or we may have difficulty in understanding and take a lifetime to learn to do right.

It should be the natural state of mind for a Christian to obey the Holy Spirit, but sometimes it also feels natural for a Christian to follow the thought patterns and reactions of the unsaved people around us. We also have old thought patterns. We have choices to make every day as to which way we will go. The Lord Jesus loved you and died for you; it is now your turn to love others and build them up in faith and hope as much as you can. You are free to do this. You have the ability. It is the Holy Spirit within you who empowers you. If you do, you will not fulfill the desires of the flesh.

ANTICIPATING THE NEXT LESSON

In our next lesson, we will explore the blessings and significance of being members of Christ's body, the church.

—*Brian D. Doud.*

PRACTICAL POINTS

1. The freedom that Christ gives must be guarded so that the old ways do not enslave us again (Gal. 5:1).
2. Tradition, rituals, and customs cannot save us (Gal. 5:2-4; cf. Rom. 10:9).
3. Righteousness is an attribute of God. Our goal is to be like Him (Gal. 5:5; cf. II Tim. 4:8).
4. Love overcomes obstacles, breaks barriers, and creates opportunities. It unifies the body of Christ (Gal. 5:6; cf. I Pet. 4:8).
5. A bad influence can retard spiritual growth (Gal. 5:7-10).
6. Following Christ means a complete break with the past (vss. 11-17).
   —Lendell Sims.

RESEARCH AND DISCUSSION

1. Who did the Lord initially instruct regarding circumcision (cf. Gen. 17:9-14)? Why did the Lord command circumcision? Why was Paul now speaking against the custom in Galatians?
2. To the Jews of the day, what was the general feeling about those who were uncircumcised?
3. How can tradition and customs push us away from God? What are some of the things we celebrate that have become more of a tradition than a celebration of God?
4. It is important that we keep our focus on the things of God so that we understand His mind-set. How do we do this?
   —Lendell Sims.

ILLUSTRATED HIGH POINTS

Consumed one of another (Gal. 5:15)

The military strategy of "bait and bleed" is the practice of pitting enemies against one another. The strategist then simply waits on the sideline as his enemies engage in battle.

Russia's Catherine the Great said, "I am racking my brains in order to push the courts of Vienna and Berlin into French affairs . . . to be kept busy and out of my way." In 1941, United States Senator Harry Truman said, "If we see that Germany is winning we ought to help Russia, and if Russia is winning we ought to help Germany . . . let them kill as many as possible." Upon withdrawing from World War I, Russia's Vladimir Lenin said, "We can take advantage of their strife" (Bunyan and Fisher, *The Bolshevik Revolution, 1917-1918,* Stanford University).

The devil is a war strategist. Let us not play into his hands.

Contrary the one to the other (vs. 17)

Conflict, climax, and resolution—English teachers will tell you these are the three basic elements of plot development. Conflict is the struggle between opposing forces; climax is the most intense moment; and resolution is the conclusion of the matter.

Our spiritual journeys also contain these classic plot elements. Obviously, our major antagonist is the devil (cf. I Pet. 5:8), yet Paul identified another bitter enemy—our old man, or flesh (cf. Rom. 7:15, 18, 23). Believers fight a conflict not mentioned by English teachers—human flesh versus God's Spirit (cf. Gen. 6:3). The indwelling Holy Spirit brings this ancient conflict right into our hearts (cf. I Tim. 6:12).
—Therese Greenberg.

Golden Text Illuminated

"Stand fast therefore in the liberty wherewith Christ hath made us free, and be not entangled again with the yoke of bondage" (Galatians 5:1).

Liberty. Freedom. These are words we love to hear and talk about, especially those of us who live in the United States, "the land of the free." But what kind of liberty and freedom was Paul talking about, and what do we need to know about it?

Paul was writing to Gentile believers in Galatia who were being pressured by emissaries from Jerusalem to accept the rite of circumcision in order to become full-fledged members of God's covenant people under the law. These believers were being told that their faith in Jesus Christ alone was not enough to ensure their full acceptance by God; they had to become adherents to the law that God had given Israel in order to seal their salvation. And for men, this meant becoming circumcised.

We might think a small step such as circumcision would not pose significant difficulties. But the Galatian believers were put under great strain and perplexity by this requirement, for it was in direct variance with what Paul had preached to them in person. He had proclaimed freedom from the law's demands—and freedom from the penalty and bondage of sin—through faith in Jesus Christ and His sacrifice on their behalf.

Paul did not see circumcision as a small accommodation that the Gentile believers could make to keep the Jewish believers happy—or as a bit of added insurance to make their salvation more sure. He correctly saw that it went to the heart of the gospel: either you are saved by grace through faith in Christ, or you try to save yourself by keeping the law. If you choose the latter, you put yourself under an impossible bondage.

In Galatians 5:3, Paul declares that giving in to the demand for circumcision makes a person "a debtor to do the whole law." And if he puts himself in that position, "Christ is become of no effect" to him (vs. 4); he is "fallen from grace." It would be like telling Jesus, "Thanks, but I can take it from here." Such a person is taking back the whole crushing burden of sin and trying to pay for it himself, forgetting that the Lord has already freed him from all of it.

Paul warns unequivocally against getting "entangled again with the yoke of bondage." Why would anyone who has been graciously and supernaturally set free from the futility of trying to erase his debt of sin want to go back to that kind of enslavement? And yet, that is the pressure the Galatians found themselves under.

For them, it was circumcision. For us, it might be something entirely different that wants to drag us back into the cruel subjection of the law, of trying to merit God's grace by our own performance. Whatever it may be, Paul exhorts us, "Stand fast."

No one can force us back under the yoke of bondage that Jesus has freed us from. Satan cannot. Governments cannot. Friends, family, and coworkers cannot. No one has that power unless we cede it to them ourselves. We do not have to fight people to maintain our liberty; we only have to remain undeceived and look solely to Jesus to keep us walking in freedom with Him.

—Kenneth Sponsler.

Heart of the Lesson

Freedom. Emancipation. Shackles removed. Captives released. This is what the death and resurrection of Jesus Christ did for us. It set us free from the law of sin and death. When we stand before God on Judgment Day, Jesus will stand with us. He took upon Himself the punishment we rightly deserve. This is love.

1. Persevere in freedom (Gal. 5:1-6). We all have heard that bad habits are hard to break. Believe it or not, it is easier to acquire freedom than it is to maintain freedom. For instance, the first day of a diet is always the easiest. Why? Because it is only day one, and we are full of motivation. However, when day three or four arrives, and the boss brings in doughnuts, it is much more difficult to resist the temptation. If we choose to persevere and resist, on day sixty the doughnuts will be much less of an issue. We will have overcome our temptation.

In this passage, the Apostle Paul urged the Galatians to stand fast, or persevere, in the freedom that Christ gave them. Paul did not preach circumcision to the Galatians. Other Jewish Christians had convinced these Gentile converts that in order to truly become Christians, they had to follow the law and become circumcised. It was almost as if there were initiation rituals to becoming a Christian among these legalists.

Paul combated this philosophy, saying, "I testify again to every man that is circumcised, that he is a debtor to do the whole law" (vs. 3). In other words, we have a choice. We can try to follow the law and fail, or we can choose to be saved by grace.

2. No freedom in confusion (Gal. 5:7-12). If the truth were told, people are biased. We may not always want to admit it, but we are. When people ask our opinion or advice on an issue, we give it to them based on our knowledge, our experience, and our understanding. We can also base our answers on our emotions, our reactions, and our strengths or weaknesses.

This was why Paul asked the Galatians who it was that was hindering them in their race. Whoever they were, they were misinformed. The information they were providing did not line up with Paul's teaching. What once was clear had become clouded; the grace that had been freely given and freely received now had preconditions. One lie that sounds like the truth can pull us from the faith. This confusion does not originate with God.

3. Final warnings (Gal. 5:13-17). Contrary to some teaching, just because Jesus Christ came to give us freedom does not mean that we are free to do whatever we want. Be careful not to gratify the sin nature. The law is summed up with one simple yet profound command: "Thou shalt love thy neighbour as thyself" (cf. Lev. 19:18; Matt. 5:43). If we fight with one another, then we will ultimately be destroyed by one another. But if we keep in step with the Spirit, then we will be able to silence the cries of our flesh that so easily tempt us. Be aware that there is a constant war raging between our flesh and the Spirit. Thankfully, it is not an even contest. The Spirit is infinitely greater, but we must side with Him.

Jesus Christ came to set the captive free. Freedom always comes with a price. Jesus paid the debt; now we must sacrifice the will of our flesh to maintain our spiritual freedom.

—*Kristin Reeg.*

World Missions

There are numerous excellent articles and books about the incredible story of Eric Liddell, a devout Christian and Olympic champion. Eric was born in China in 1902 to Scottish missionary parents. Eric and his brother were sent to school in Scotland while Eric was a young child.

Eric showed an early interest in running. He received training up to the Olympic level and represented his country in the 1924 Olympics in Paris, France. Because a heat for the 100-meter race was scheduled for a Sunday, Eric refused to run. He did, however, run in the 400-meter race on another day and won the gold medal. He set several Olympic records that year. He also broke Scottish records in the 220-and 100-yard sprints. Eric went on to participate in a relay team that set a world record. Eric became known as the fastest man in Scotland. To this day his nickname remains "The Flying Scotsman."

After his success as an Olympian, Eric returned to China to be a missionary in 1925. Many people in sports and media disagreed with his decision to leave such a successful career in athletics to work on the mission field. In response to one inquirer, Eric said, "It's natural for a chap to think over all that sometimes, but I'm glad I'm at the work I'm engaging in now. A fellow's life counts for more at this than the other" (Keddie, *Running the Race*, Evangelical Press).

Eric's first assignment was teaching children and promoting Christian values. He integrated academic lessons with biblical teaching. He also worked after school with students who wanted to participate in athletics. The school where he started in Tianjin is still in operation. Eric stayed in China, expanding his missionary work and making a lasting impact on China.

In 1941, the Japanese invaded deeper into China. Eric and his brother were working in a rural medical mission. Despite warnings to accept furlough, Eric stayed to help distribute food, medicine, and supplies for the continuous stream of people needing care. In 1943, the Japanese took over the mission station and placed Eric and the other missionaries in an internment camp.

Eric Liddell died in 1945 at the camp. It is believed that a brain tumor, exhaustion, and malnutrition contributed to his death. According to a fellow missionary, Eric's last words were "It's complete surrender," referring to how he had lived his life for God.

Eric Liddell had been called into liberty. Because of his trust in Jesus as his Lord and Saviour, he stepped into the freedom that comes only with Christ. Though his freedom allowed him to pursue many avenues, Eric chose to spend his life serving others. A gifted athlete, Eric left us an example of one who made a higher choice—to answer the missionary call on his life. Such a life will always be remembered. Eric Liddell's daughter celebrated his life by visiting China in 1991 and presenting his school with one of his medals.

Though we may not be confronted with the choice to walk away from promising careers, we will be challenged to bring God into our chosen vocations. As Eric Liddell used his freedom in China, we are called to use ours to serve one another wherever God places us.

—Beverly Medley Jones.

The Jewish Aspect

Our theme for today, "Liberty in Christ," sounds the promise of joy for those in whom the Holy Spirit dwells.

Our Jewish friends pride themselves on following the teaching of the early fathers, particularly in respect to their care and concern for others. The Jewish community lives by the summary of the second tablet of the law, that portion dealing with responsibility to love others: commandments 6 through 10.

Jewish charity is seen in the word *tzedakah*. Its first meaning is righteousness, but Jewish scholars argue that it must also mean justice. The sages of Israel reasoned that since God owns the silver and the gold, to give it only to the rich is a violation of natural law. It has to belong to the poor as well. Therefore, to give to the poor is just and righteous (Ausubel, *The Book of Jewish Knowledge,* Crown Publishers).

The Jewish sages felt it was important to make benevolence giving a part of their religion. Rabbi Joshua Ben Korha said, "He that turns his eyes away from the needy worships idols!" (Ausubel).

At the same time, the Jews wisely thought it necessary to bestow some visible honor on the givers. They were careful to screen out those who gave for crass, personal reasons but lauded the righteous for their gifts.

In every synagogue in our city, prominent space is provided to list those who have made a substantial gift to the building of the sanctuary. One can be sure the benevolence giving there is also outstanding.

Rabbi Yechiel Eckstein, an eminent American Jewish religious leader, believed that American Christians might be open to provide humanitarian aid to Israel. Through the organization he founded, 20 to 50 million dollars are given annually for the poor and needy in the State of Israel. None of the funds go to the Israeli military.

Jesus exposed the scandalous giving of the Pharisees. He revealed how they would give a gift to the temple, declare it *corban,* and by that exempt themselves from supporting aged parents (Mark 7:10-13).

No race or group of people has ever outgiven the Jews. Their *tzedakah* is extended to maintenance of the State of Israel. No other nation in the world has ever existed largely on the freewill gifts of her people worldwide!

The Jews tell the delightful story of the *Lamed-vavniks. Lamed-vav* is the number thirty-six, and those who are among the righteous thirty-six in each generation are the *niks* in Yiddish. The fourth-century Talmud teachers held that there were thirty-six men in the world upon whom the Shekinah-glory rested. These men were unsung heroes, who by their righteousness kept the world turning. They did not know they were in such distinguished company, but in times of great need, they arose to deal with the matter. When their work was done, they fled the scene in order not to miss the blessing that God would extend to them (Ausubel).

It is doubtful the Jews would grant Lamed-vavnik status to a Christian Jew, but we have a nominee. Rachmiel Frydland, a Polish Jewish Christian, worked among the Jews of his home country. When Poland was occupied by the Nazis, Brother Rachmiel moved about quietly reaching out to his people, who were in great peril. Jews from all over Europe were enclosed in the Warsaw ghetto. Frydland crept in to minister to those marked for death. He went in again and again, until he was turned in to the Nazis.

—*Lyle P. Murphy.*

Guiding the Superintendent

There is a story of a bird that was held captive. It was chained by rope to a wooden stake. All the bird would do was circle the stake. A man observing the bird's dilemma sought its freedom. He paid a large amount for the bird's release. He quickly disconnected the bird from its rope. Sadly, the bird continued circling the stake. Although the bird was free, it failed to take advantage of its freedom.

This week's lesson teaches us that through Christ we are made free. We will discover that nothing can eradicate this reality. Through Him, we are recipients of grace that cancels our former bondage. But living in that freedom can be a challenge.

DEVOTIONAL OUTLINE

1. Freedom in Christ (Gal. 5:1-5). The Apostle Paul called the Galatian church to persevere in its freedom. He admonished the people to no longer be bound by the law.

Regrettably, the Jews tried to impose the old covenant law on the Galatians. They attempted to force circumcision on new believers. Paul admonished the Galatians that attempting to follow the law would never bring them a right relationship with God. A right relationship with God comes only by faith.

2. Misled Galatians (Gal. 5:6-12). Those who trust Christ as Saviour do not need circumcision. God desired the Galatians to have faith that expressed itself in love.

Paul commended the Galatians for their initial faith walk. However, false teachers had misled some of them. God's message of love and grace was being distorted. The false teachers attempted to circumvent the gospel message. Paul stated, "A little leaven leaveneth the whole lump" (Gal. 5:9). This meant a slight twist away from the truth could distort the gospel message.

Paul had a strong hope that the Galatians would not accept the false teaching. He declared that the false teachers would be penalized for their evil deeds. Some accused Paul of propagating erroneous doctrine. He asked if that was so, why was he being persecuted by false teachers? Apparently frustrated, he desired castration for the false messengers.

3. Wise use of freedom (Gal. 5:13-17). Although they were free, Paul cautioned the Galatians not to recklessly use their freedom. He directed them to love one another. Doing this was the true fulfillment of the law. They were instructed not to hurt one another. To avoid this, they had to allow the Holy Spirit to guide their lives.

CHILDREN'S CORNER

Although they are young, children need to know the benefits of being a believer. Help them understand the importance of allowing Jesus to guide their lives. As they yield to Him, they will exhibit godly behavior.

We might think that a passage such as this on spiritual liberty in Christ and the conflict between the flesh and the Spirit is above the comprehension level of children. It will be if it is presented in those terms. But if it is taught in simple language, the Spirit will enable children to grasp and follow God's Word. For instance, children can be told, "Because of Jesus, we are allowed to do many things, but not all things are good to do. Ask Him to show you what is good and what is not."

—*Tyrone Keith Carroll, Sr.*

SCRIPTURE LESSON TEXT

I COR. 12:14 For the body is not one member, but many.

15 If the foot shall say, Because I am not the hand, I am not of the body; is it therefore not of the body?

16 And if the ear shall say, Because I am not the eye, I am not of the body; is it therefore not of the body?

17 If the whole body *were* **an eye, where** *were* **the hearing? If the whole** *were* **hearing, where** *were* **the smelling?**

18 But now hath God set the members every one of them in the body, as it hath pleased him.

19 And if they were all one member, where *were* **the body?**

20 But now *are they* many members, yet but one body.

21 And the eye cannot say unto the hand, I have no need of thee: nor again the head to the feet, I have no need of you.

22 Nay, much more those members of the body, which seem to be more feeble, are necessary:

23 And those *members* **of the body, which we think to be less honourable, upon these we bestow more abundant honour; and** our uncomely *parts* **have more abundant comeliness.**

24 For our comely *parts* have no need: but God hath tempered the body together, having given more abundant honour to that *part* which lacked:

25 That there should be no schism in the body, but *that* **the members should have the same care one for another.**

26 And whether one member suffer, all the members suffer with it; or one member be honoured, all the members rejoice with it.

27 Now ye are the body of Christ, and members in particular.

28 And God hath set some in the church, first apostles, secondarily prophets, thirdly teachers, after that miracles, then gifts of healings, helps, governments, diversities of tongues.

29 *Are* **all apostles?** *are* **all prophets?** *are* **all teachers?** *are* **all workers of miracles?**

30 Have all the gifts of healing? do all speak with tongues? do all interpret?

31 But covet earnestly the best gifts: and yet shew I unto you a more excellent way.

NOTES

Blessing of Belonging in Christ

Lesson Text: I Corinthians 12:14-31

Related Scriptures: Romans 12:3-8; Ephesians 4:1-16

TIME: A.D. 55

PLACE: from Ephesus

GOLDEN TEXT—"Now ye are the body of Christ, and members in particular" (I Corinthians 12:27).

Introduction

One of the most important keys to the success of an organization is a proper division of responsibilities. All of us are familiar with the elaborate bureaucratic structures that characterize national, state, and local governments and big-business corporations. Educational institutions also require clearcut divisions among administrators, faculty, and supporting staff. Bureaucracy, of course, can become dysfunctional, but all recognize a need for organization appropriate to the purpose.

The church of Jesus Christ is more than an organization. It is a spiritual organism deriving its life from God and having Jesus as its Head. Nevertheless, its effectiveness depends on each member recognizing his or her spiritual gift and using it in harmony with others.

LESSON OUTLINE

I. THE WORTH OF THE MEMBERS—I Cor. 12:14-20

II. THE HARMONY OF THE MEMBERS—I Cor. 12:21-26

III. THE GIFTS OF THE MEMBERS—I Cor. 12:27-31

Exposition: Verse by Verse

THE WORTH OF THE MEMBERS

I COR. 12:14 For the body is not one member, but many.

15 If the foot shall say, Because I am not the hand, I am not of the body; is it therefore not of the body?

16 And if the ear shall say, Because I am not the eye, I am not of the body; is it therefore not of the body?

17 If the whole body were an eye, where were the hearing? If the whole were hearing, where were the smelling?

18 But now hath God set the

members every one of them in the body, as it hath pleased him.

19 And if they were all one member, where were the body?

20 But now are they many members, yet but one body.

Matthew Henry made the following comments on our lesson text for this week: "Christ and his church form one body, as Head and members. Christians become members of this body by baptism. The outward rite is of Divine institution; it is a sign of the new birth, and is called therefore the washing of regeneration [Titus 3:5].

"But it is by the Spirit, only by the renewing of the Holy Ghost, that we are made members of Christ's body. And by communion with Christ at the Lord's supper, we are strengthened, not by drinking the wine, but by drinking into one Spirit.

"Each member has its form, place, and use. The meanest makes a part of the body. There must be a distinction of members in the body. So Christ's members have different powers and different places. We should do the duties of our own place, and not murmur, or quarrel with others.

"All Christians are dependent one upon another; each is to expect and receive help from the rest. Let us then have more of the spirit of union in our religion" (*Matthew Henry's Concise Commentary,* biblehub.com).

The principle stated (I Cor. 12:14). After explaining the concept of gifts bestowed by the Holy Spirit to glorify Christ (vss. 1-11), Paul likened the church to a body of many members unified in Christ (vs. 12). It has been brought together in one Spirit from many backgrounds (vs. 13). This spiritual unity is a remarkable phenomenon, unmatched by any human unifying force. But then he began to stress the need for diversity in the unified body in order to achieve its spiritual goals: "For the body is not one member, but many" (vs. 14). The point he was about to develop is that to function as a body, the body needs the contribution of each separate part.

Illustrations from the human body (I Cor. 12:15-17). To illustrate problems that can hinder the church, Paul offered a whimsical but pertinent speculation on what would happen if bodily organs refused to accept their proper functions. The foot, for example, might say, "Because I am not the hand, I am not of the body." The foot would therefore stop functioning as it should and deprive the body of an essential ability.

Something like this was happening in Corinth. {Those who had spectacular gifts (tongues) were exalting themselves. Those who lacked such gifts became discouraged and assumed they had nothing to contribute, depriving the church of gifts they *did* have.}[Q1]

Extending his illustration, Paul imagined the ear saying, "Because I am not the eye, I am not of the body" (vs. 16). As the foot denigrated itself because it considered the hand superior, so the ear sees itself as inferior to the eye. All would agree that hands and eyes are essential. But no one would argue from this that feet and ears are unnecessary. Yet equivalent arguments in the church left some members discouraged or disgruntled and the church impoverished.

Paul showed how nonsensical such thinking is. If the entire body were an eye, where would the hearing be? If the entire body were an ear, what would happen to the sense of smell? Each organ is important, but there would be no point to its ability without the rest.

So it is with members of a church who think their gifts are the only important ones. {By despising others' gifts or trying to force them all into one mold, they are actually destroying the spiritual body of which they are a part.}[Q2] Church leaders ought to encourage all their people to discover, develop, and use their gifts.

God's sovereign distribution (I Cor. 12:18). "But now" turns attention from hypothetical illustrations to the actual facts. Instead of fashioning the body of just one or two organs, God has "set the members every one of them in the body, as it hath pleased him." We marvel at the body's efficiency in spite of its complexity. All parts cooperate to achieve what it was intended to do.

If God has the wisdom and power to design our bodies to operate efficiently, can He not fashion Christ's spiritual body, the church, in the same way? {It is not our prerogative to question His design or impose our own interpretation of how it should work. We should welcome the diversity of spiritual gifts and seek wisdom in how they can be used.}Q3

The summary of the argument (I Cor. 12:19-20). Paul now recapitulated his major point—that the body cannot exist apart from its many members. "And if they were all one member," he asked, "where were the body?" The unstated answer is that there would be no body. But he immediately asserted, "But now are they many members, yet but one body." This is a self-evident truth about the physical body, and it is true of Christ's church as well.

THE HARMONY OF THE MEMBERS

21 And the eye cannot say unto the hand, I have no need of thee: nor again the head to the feet, I have no need of you.

22 Nay, much more those members of the body, which seem to be more feeble, are necessary:

23 And those members of the body, which we think to be less honourable, upon these we bestow more abundant honour; and our uncomely parts have more abundant comeliness.

24 For our comely parts have no need: but God hath tempered the body together, having given more abundant honour to that part which lacked:

25 That there should be no schism in the body, but that the members should have the same care one for another.

26 And whether one member suffer, all the members suffer with it; or one member be honoured, all the members rejoice with it.

The necessity of harmony (I Cor. 12:21-23). Paul now resumed his illustration but shifted the emphasis from body parts that feel useless or deprived to those that feel independently sufficient. If the eye says to the hand or the head says to the feet, "I have no need of thee," they are deceiving themselves. The eye looks at the desirable object, but without the hand to pick it up, the desire is left unfulfilled. The head, with all its reasoning powers, cannot move at all without the cooperation of the feet.

So it is with members of the body of Christ. {The Corinthians needed this admonition because some of them were glorying in their gifts and despising all who lacked them. Factions had developed (I Cor. 1:10-11) and were evident even at their observances of the Lord's Supper (11:18-22). Their inordinate emphasis on tongues had led to disorderly services (chap. 14). Their abuse of Christian liberty caused them to wound weak consciences (8:9-12).}Q4

Thus, Paul reminded them that, rather than to be despised, those members of the body that seem weak or feeble are all the more necessary. {Many bodily organs are not visible and, in fact, need to be protected inside the skin and bone structure—the heart, lungs, digestive organs, and kidneys. Yet they are essential to human life.

Likewise, in the body of Christ, many members who never minister publicly are nevertheless the "lifeline" of the church. They may actually be more important to the church than those who have a public ministry.}[Q5]

Paul went even further: "And those members of the body, which we think to be less honourable, upon these we bestow more abundant honour; and our uncomely parts have more abundant comeliness" (I Cor. 12:23). This describes parts of the body that modesty tells us should not be exposed; so we bestow on them more abundant honor through clothing. Thus, the more presentable members bestow comeliness on those that are unpresentable.

God's provision of harmony (I Cor. 12:24). God recognizes that "our comely parts have no need." To conceal them would be to hinder their effectiveness. But He has put the body together in such a way as to give extra honor to the parts that lacked it. God has interspersed the weaker members with the stronger, the less presentable with the more attractive, so that all members partake of a common honor. {As a result, the entire body presents an attractive, unified appearance. All are blended into a harmonious whole, and all members can rejoice that the body not only works smoothly but also presents a pleasing appearance to others.}[Q6]

The outworking of harmony (I Cor. 12:25-26). God has blended the members together so "that there should be no schism in the body, but that the members should have the same care one for another." In the church, as in our bodies, God has arranged the members in a way that will promote unity, not division. He has given all members the opportunity and responsibility to lavish on one another the same kind of care they bestow on themselves.

Sadly, the Corinthian church was not experiencing this harmony (I Cor. 1:11; 11:18). The members had all the gifts necessary to do so, but their spiritual maturity did not match their giftedness.

The Corinthian church had difficulty experiencing what comes naturally to the physical body. If one part suffers, the rest of the body suffers with it; or if one part is honored, the rest of the body rejoices with it.

The same principle should be true of the church. Paul urged the Romans, "Rejoice with them that do rejoice, and weep with them that weep" (Rom. 12:15). To feel no reaction to either one is evidence of a serious spiritual problem. {Ironically, it is often easier for believers to sympathize with those who weep than to rejoice with those who rejoice. Some of us are too self-centered to rejoice when another is honored.}[Q7]

THE GIFTS OF THE MEMBERS

27 Now ye are the body of Christ, and members in particular.

28 And God hath set some in the church, first apostles, secondarily prophets, thirdly teachers, after that miracles, then gifts of healings, helps, governments, diversities of tongues.

29 Are all apostles? are all prophets? are all teachers? are all workers of miracles?

30 Have all the gifts of healing? do all speak with tongues? do all interpret?

31 But covet earnestly the best gifts: and yet shew I unto you a more excellent way.

A listing of gifts (I Cor. 12:27-28). From his use of the human body as an illustration, Paul moved to his intended lesson: "Now ye are the body of Christ, and members in particular." The church is an organism that is to live out and manifest the life of Christ.

Within this organism, individual believers make up its various members. Each believer has a vital role to fulfill. But each must know that he or she is but one member, not the whole body, and therefore needs the contributions of all the others to make the congregation's ministry glorifying to Christ.

Paul then listed spiritual gifts that contribute to the church's health. The list is not exhaustive, but it gives a good representation of gifts known to the Corinthians. Paul made it clear that God does the giving. He also indicated that there is a definite ranking to the gifts. Paul saw that the Corinthians were exalting lesser gifts precisely because they were showier. He therefore had to set things straight.

{The first rank belonged to the apostles. These were the men who had seen the risen Christ and were commissioned by Him to plant churches and give them His authoritative teaching.

Second, God gave the church prophets. These were people who received new revelation from God and passed it on to the churches as occasion required before the New Testament canon was completed. The third group is teachers, who have the ability to expound and apply truth that has already been revealed. These first three gifts are ranked ahead of the others because they are involved in communicating the content of the Christian message.}Q8

In the latter part of I Corinthians 12:28, Paul listed gifts such as miracles, healing, helps, governments, and diverse tongues. "Helps" refers to all kinds of ministrations to other members of the body. "Governments" refers to administration, and it is instructive that what is regarded as a high office in human organizations is given a lower ranking in the church. {Finally, "tongues" (languages) is pointedly ranked last.}Q9

The importance of diversity (I Cor. 12:29-30). Paul now posed a series of rhetorical questions, all of which anticipate a negative answer. Choosing a sampling of the gifts just enumerated, he showed the folly of thinking everyone in the church should have them all. God has bestowed gifts on all His children, but He has left in each of us a vacuum that can be filled only by the gifts of others.

Advice to the church (I Cor. 12:31). {Paul ended this discussion with a command: "But covet earnestly the best gifts." He was saying, "You are right in wanting God's gifts, but ask Him for those that are most useful in edifying the church as a whole." These would be especially prophecy and teaching.}Q10

But Paul was about to show them something even better: the way of love, which he would expound in the next chapter. So, in effect he was saying, "Desire the most useful gifts. But, more important, show love to one another in using the gifts you have."

—Robert E. Wenger.

QUESTIONS

1. What potential problem in the church did Paul illustrate through the foot and the ear?
2. How were self-important church members harming the church?
3. Why should we welcome the diversity God has given the church?
4. How were the Corinthians destroying the harmony of the church?
5. How does the vital importance of physical organs that are hidden relate to spiritual gifts?
6. How can a church of diverse elements present a unified witness?
7. Is it easy for Christians to rejoice and sympathize with each other? Explain.
8. In Paul's list of spiritual gifts, which ones did he rank higher? Why?
9. How was Paul's ranking of gifts a rebuke to the Corinthians?
10. What was Paul's advice to believers at the end of this passage?

—Robert E. Wenger.

Preparing to Teach the Lesson

According to some estimates, there are approximately 33,000 Protestant denominations in the world today. How does this variety of denominations correlate to Paul's teaching that all believers are in one body in Christ? What do Paul's words "Now ye are the body of Christ, and members in particular" (I Cor. 12:27) mean?

John Gill has commented, "The church of Christ is not one person only, or does not consist of one sort of persons; as only of Jews, or only of Gentiles, or only of rich and freemen, or only of men of extraordinary gifts and abilities, or greatly eminent for grace and spiritual knowledge: but many; . . . so in the mystical body of Christ, the church, there are many members, . . . yet all one in Christ the head, and all related to each other" (*Gill's Exposition of the Entire Bible,* biblehub.com).

TODAY'S AIM

Facts: to understand the biblical emphasis on believers being one body in Christ.

Principle: to accept that unity in the church is achieved through the work of God, not people.

Application: to minister effectively in our local churches with oneness of heart.

INTRODUCING THE LESSON

Have you ever watched an orchestra tuning up before a concert? How do all the diverse instruments tune up in order to play in unity? The first-chair oboe player keeps his instrument tuned to A 440, the standard. All the other orchestra members tune their instruments to that oboe.

The body of Christ is similar to an orchestra. The standard for us is the Lord Himself. The Holy Spirit places us, as His instruments, into Christ's body by His baptism. Whether Jew or Gentile, we are united in one body (I Cor. 12:12-13). Each local church should reflect the characteristics of that one body.

DEVELOPING THE LESSON

1. We are the body (I Cor. 12:14-20). Paul used the example of a human body as an analogy for the body of Christ as seen in the local congregation. A human body is not limited to one member but is composed of many that all function together. In a similar way, a church is not one member, but many. Individuals in a church have many different gifts, but together they are one body.

Paul elaborated on his analogy by showing how inconceivable it should be that a person with a particular gift would be envious of another with a different gift. You cannot imagine your foot refusing to cooperate in your body because it is not a hand; nor can you imagine your ear refusing to be recognized as part of your body because it is not an eye. It is just as foolish to think that because you do not have one certain gift, you are not valuable in the local church.

Without question, differences in the members of our body exist, but each has its own purpose. How functional would a body be if it were only an eye, or an ear, or a nose? The differences in the various members are what give advantage to the physical body. The same is true of church members, who have various gifts in the spiritual body.

The whole arrangement of having different members in a human body was God's doing. Differing gifts for those in a local church is likewise God's divine purpose. The gifts are not placed in the body randomly; they are arranged by God for His purposes. Some Christians feel that they are not appreciated because they do not have the gifts that would put them in the limelight. God, however, makes no mistakes. He placed diversity within the church for His purposes, using each part for His glory. There is no inferior gift in God's plan.

2. We share in the body (I Cor. 12:21-26). Paul continued his analogy of the human body. He showed how unthinkable it is that any one part would think it can function alone. Try to imagine an eye getting any work done without the hands or the head moving anywhere without the feet. In the church, likewise, no one person can fulfill God's purposes without the others functioning alongside in the ministry.

All parts of a human body are essential to its functioning capabilities. This includes parts that seemingly are "feeble" (vs. 22), "less honourable," "uncomely" (vs. 23), or "comely" (vs. 24). God is the one who put the body together, and He did it for a threefold purpose. His purpose was for harmony, for mutual care, and for mutual sympathy.

3. We function in the body (I Cor. 12:27-31). All parts of the spiritual body are to function like a physical body. The church at Corinth was of the same quality as the whole body of Christ. Just as the human body should work together, so should the church.

As parts of God's church, we must recognize that He gives gifts according to His sovereignty. Paul began by listing the most important gifts by naming those who possessed them. Gifts differ in their apparent value, and God chooses which Christians receive which gifts. All Christians, however, must be faithful in exercising their gifts (cf. I Pet. 4:10). The apostles came first, followed by the prophets, and then by the teachers. All these were involved with directly communicating God's truth and establishing His church. After these came the gifts of lesser impor-

tance—miracles, healings, helps, governments, and tongues (I Cor. 12:28).

In addition to giving gifts according to His sovereignty, God also gives them in diversity. He gives the gifts to whom He pleases. No Christian receives them all. Since none of us has all the gifts, what should we do? We should "covet earnestly the best gifts" (vs. 31). The verb "covet" means "to earnestly desire." Corinth exalted tongues, a lesser gift. Paul exhorted them to instead desire to use the greater gifts.

ILLUSTRATING THE LESSON

Each person in the local church cooperates to further Christ's work.

CONCLUDING THE LESSON

God gave spiritual gifts as it pleased Him. No matter what your gift may be, you have a vital part to play in your local church. Any attitude of grumbling or of superiority is out of place. The goal is for each of us to exercise our gifts and cause the body to function properly.

ANTICIPATING THE NEXT LESSON

Next week our attention focuses specifically on blessings amid trials from James, chapter 1.

—*R. Larry Overstreet.*

PRACTICAL POINTS

1. The Holy Spirit unites many members into one body to do God's work (I Cor. 12:14).
2. Believers should neither boast of nor belittle their status in the body of Christ (vss. 15-19).
3. Every gift is critical to the healthy functioning of the church (vss. 20-21).
4. Behind-the-scenes work is often most critical to the success of a ministry (vss. 22-24).
5. The members of Christ's body are inseparably bound to one another (vss. 25-26).
6. Believers must accept God's gifts for them and not envy those of others (vss. 27-31).

—Cheryl Y. Powell.

RESEARCH AND DISCUSSION

1. How does the Christian church respond to the member who really does not feel that he is a part of the church's ministry? Why is it important to address this issue?
2. What, if any, is the difference between a natural ability or talent that God blesses someone with and a spiritual gift?
3. What types of church work are seen as more honorable than others? What types may be considered less honorable? How do the different categories of service work together for the good of the whole?
4. What does it mean that all members suffer with the member who suffers? How does this attitude prevent division in the church?

—Cheryl Y. Powell.

ILLUSTRATED HIGH POINTS

Not one member (I Cor. 12:14)

The family unit is a wonderful entity that God has created. Although each member has a different personality, each one adds to the whole, which has a personality of its own. When family members know Jesus Christ as Saviour and submit to Him, each individual learns to love, respect, and support the others. Forgiveness is practiced when relationships become strained. Through submission to Christ, the family lives in harmony, and God is glorified.

It should be the same way in the larger family—the family of God, the local church. Having experienced Christ's new life through having faith in Him and submitting to Him, each person learns to love, respect, and support the others. When sin arises, forgiveness is the norm. I trust that in your local church family, you experience being God's family as you serve Him together.

No schism in the body (vs. 25)

Sometimes young people can become very exclusive and form their own little groups. They look down on others their age, thinking that they are better because of how they dress or what they accomplish in school. In addition, such a group can become mean as the members make fun of others.

Sometimes, sad to say, such an exclusive group can be found in a local church. Certainly, a local church can have different groups whose members share specific interests or life experiences. But when a group starts thinking that it is better than another group, the local church family will be injured spiritually, for each person and each spiritual gift is needed in the local church. No cliques allowed!

—Paul R. Bawden.

Golden Text Illuminated

"Now ye are the body of Christ, and members in particular" (I Corinthians 12:27).

"Not his natural body, which his Father prepared for him, in which he bore our sins on the tree, and which was offered up once for all; . . . but his body mystical, the church; not that the Corinthians were the whole of the body, only a part of it, as every single congregational church is of the church universal. . . . the sense is, that they were not only members of Christ, and of his body, but were particularly members one of another, in strict union and close communion, and of mutual use and service to each other" (*Gill's Exposition of the Entire Bible,* biblehub.com).

The truth expressed in our golden text was one the Corinthian believers desperately needed to understand. It is equally important for the church today to grasp this truth.

The Corinthian church was a church in conflict. There was division around various personalities—specifically, Paul, Peter, and Apollos. Various groups in the church elevated one of these godly men over the others (I Cor. 1:12-13). Likewise, certain spiritual gifts, particularly the more spectacular ones, were elevated over other gifts.

Paul condemned such attitudes, for they engendered pride and a false concept of the value of God's people. Pride is as much a temptation today as it was in Paul's day, and it is very subtle.

With his illustration of the church as a human body (I Cor. 12:12-27), Paul put everything in perspective. Every part of the body is essential to the proper functioning of the whole body. Thus, every part is to be properly honored and appreciated.

The same is true of the church. If all Christians possessed the same gift, the church could not function as it should. This is why the Spirit has given many different gifts to the church body. All are to be honored as essential.

Paul summed it up by saying, "Ye are the body of Christ." "Ye" is plural and refers to the entire Corinthian church. They were the one spiritual "body of Christ." The apostle then stated that they were "members in particular." Just as together they were the body of Christ, so individually they were members of the body.

Thus, no one is to be despised because of his or her gift, and no one is to be elevated above others as more important because of his or her gift. The church as a whole functions effectively when each member humbly employs the gift or gifts the Spirit has given and everyone recognizes that only Christ is the true Head of the body, the church (Col. 1:18).

As the Apostle Paul pointed out in his epistle to the Ephesians, "The whole body [the church] fitly joined together and compacted by that which every joint supplieth, according to the effectual working in the measure of every part, maketh increase of the body unto the edifying of itself in love" (4:16). Such spiritual growth and edification of the church cannot take place as they should if some members of the body are considered of no importance.

The church Christ established is designed to function effectively only when every member understands his or her role and is ministering to others within the church.

—Jarl K. Waggoner.

Heart of the Lesson

Our lesson this week speaks of the unity and diversity in the body of Christ, to which all those who put their faith in Him belong. We are all different, yet we are all one because the love of Jesus binds us together. There are no lesser servants in the church, for we are equal partners in ministry, using the gifts we have to serve the body of Christ in the very best way we can under His leadership.

1. Many members (I Cor. 12:14-17). Paul compared the local body of believers to the human body and showed how all the parts are very different. But each of the parts has a specific place in the local body of the church. One cannot claim superiority over the others. Every part has a specific task to do, having been given a special gift (or gifts) in order to bless and edify the local church. The local church could not fulfill its mission if everyone had the same gift.

Differing gifts in different people are crucial in order to do what Christ wants us to do. So every part is equally important in the service of the local church. If one person in the church does not use his or her gifts, then the local body suffers. All the areas of ministry are covered when every church member uses the gifts that God has given him or her. Their gifts are valuable in ministry, even though they may not consider them as important as the gifts another has. All are important in His work.

2. One purpose (I Cor. 12:18-26). It only takes us one close look to see how intricately our body has been woven together in its many parts. Every part has its special place and its special function. One part cannot do the work of another. Yet it is all these very different parts that make up one totally functioning unit. It is simply amazing to see how all this works, and God is the Divine Mastermind that put it all together. It is the same in the local church.

No part, no matter how seemingly insignificant, is without value. God can use us in ways we cannot imagine and bless the others we worship with. No gift is wasted in the economy of God when it is given to us. God has a definite purpose behind the gifts He has chosen for each of us in the body of Christ. What we think is not so important is really very important in the eyes of God. Some parts are more visible than others, and all are equally of use to Him.

Some members are more vulnerable than others and may need extra care. Some parts are honored, and others have less dignity; but God has put us all together in the same place so that we may serve and build up one another. Mutual care is the mark of the body of Christ. Because of the integral unity between the members, it is important to see that when one suffers, the whole body suffers. When one rejoices, the other parts also rejoice because we are one body, woven together in love.

3. Many gifts (I Cor. 12:27-31). The abilities of apostles, prophets, teachers, miracle workers, helpers, healers, and those who speak in tongues—these are only some of the special gifts that are given to the church (cf. Rom. 12:6-8; I Cor. 12:8-11). We all do not have the same gifts, and this is done deliberately by God. We should, however, earnestly desire the gifts that will be most helpful in the body of Christ.

—A. Koshy Muthalaly.

World Missions

The attack on Pearl Harbor in 1941 shocked the nation. Afterward, many were seething for revenge. One of those was a young bombardier named Jake DeShazer, who participated in the Doolittle raid on Japan.

After their successful bombing mission, Jake and his fellow crewmates were forced to bail out of their aircraft. They landed in Japanese-occupied territory in China. He was given a life sentence as a prisoner of war.

Already filled with hatred toward the Japanese, Jake's situation only deepened those feelings. He was tortured and mistreated seemingly every minute of the day. The only thing that kept him alive was his desire for revenge.

However, things began to change when he received an opportunity to read the Bible. In the three weeks he was given to read it, he stayed awake day and night and could not put it down.

The Living Word captured his heart like nothing else. Before, he had had no comprehension why someone like Jesus would command someone to forgive his enemies, even as he was being tortured to death.

The day came when Jake prayed, "Lord, though I am far from home and though I am in prison, I ask for Your forgiveness." He knew he was a new man as his heart filled with the joy and presence of Jesus.

As his mistreatment continued, Jake understood that God was asking him to reach out to his tormentors with forgiveness and love.

Unknown to Jake, God was also working in the hearts of others. One was the leader of the first wave of attackers on Pearl Harbor, Mitsuo Fuchida.

The war finally ended, and those who fought and suffered in it made their way home to a new life in peacetime. For Jake, it truly was a time of peace as he continued to grow in Christ and serve Him in new ways. For Mitsuo, the external war ended, but an internal one still held him in its grip.

Even though Mitsuo's life had been miraculously spared many times during the war, he had no peace in his heart. He listened to the testimony of a young woman whose parents had been killed by the Japanese in the Philippines, yet who showed great love to the Japanese.

He also read Jake's account of life as a POW and how he had found love and forgiveness through Jesus. Jake was now married, and he and his wife were missionaries in Japan. Thousands came to Christ through his witness, including two of Jake's former guards.

Mitsuo decided to study the Bible, and soon the gospel was planted deep in his heart. He spoke to his countrymen, sharing Jesus with them.

Jake and Mitsuo met and began ministering together. They shared their testimonies of God's grace all over Japan.

Only Jesus can heal the hurts and disappointments of our past and bring them all together for the good of others and for His glory.

"Therefore if any man be in Christ, he is a new creature: old things are passed away; behold, all things are become new. . . . Now then we are ambassadors for Christ, . . . we pray you in Christ's stead, be ye reconciled to God" (II Cor. 5:17, 20).

—Christina Futrell.

The Jewish Aspect

"Now ye are the body of Christ, and members in particular" (I Cor. 12:27). The concept in this golden text has no counterpart in Jewish religious experience. At the same time, "peoplehood," or community, is what makes Jewish society tick.

When the synagogue is experienced up close and personal, we find it to be a gathering place where Jews express their heritage to other Jews. There is the lady who loves the hora and other Jewish dances, some that may date from the days of David. There is the man who is really nonreligious. He is, however, politically motivated. Arguing fine points by the hour, he joins a pro-Jewish faction.

Religious Jews do not agree on the kashruth (the system of kosher foods and dietary rules). Nevertheless, there are plenty of pareve foods (that is, those that are not restricted by even the most observant Jews).

Rabbi Kertzer wrote, "Jewish community is positive, not negative; it is open, not closed; anyone who wishes to link his or her own personal destiny to that of the community . . . may join it." And yet the single, unifying factor for Jews the world over seems to be that they must stand together in resistance to anti-Semitism—hatred of the Jews.

It was once said that the degree of anti-Semitism depended on the number of Jews in a given district. At the time of the rise of the Nazis in the 1930s, anti-Semitism had already been deeply ingrained in the European psyche. And yet, not long before, German Jews were quite loyal to the Fatherland, calling themselves "Germans of the Mosaic persuasion."

One very damaging aspect of Jewish behavior were instances of hatred of other Jews. German Jews dressed like other Germans, spoke German, and were content to be Jews one day a week. But many of them detested the Jews of Poland, who dressed in wide hats, side curls, and beards and spoke Yiddish. In 1944, when young Jews in the Warsaw ghetto sought to arm their people to resist the Germans, these long-standing divisions within Jewish life were exposed.

Anti-Semitism is satanically inspired. The wicked one has provoked many to strike out against the descendants of Abraham (cf. Ezra 4:4-7; Neh. 4:7, 11; Esther 3:8-15).

Sadly, many who are called Christians have been hostile toward the Jews. Jules Isaac, a secular Jew who lived through World War II, asked, "Did the Nazis spring from nothing or from the bosom of a Christian people?" (*The Teaching of Contempt,* Holt, Rinehart and Winston).

Jews remember that in the past, certain Christian institutions charged their whole race with deicide—killing God. The Bible, however, teaches that our sin was the reason Christ died. Scripture specifically indicts only Herod, Pilate, and the Gentiles and Jews in Jerusalem who worked with them (Acts 4:27). Their guilt remains, but ultimately, the wicked unwittingly did what God had "determined before to be done" (Acts 4:28; cf. 2:22-23).

Remember Paul's passion toward his fellow Jews: "I could wish that myself were accursed from Christ for my brethren, my kinsmen according to the flesh: who are Israelites; to whom pertaineth the adoption, and the glory, and the covenants, . . . and of whom as concerning the flesh Christ came, who is over all, God blessed for ever. Amen" (Rom. 9:1-5).

—*Lyle P. Murphy.*

Guiding the Superintendent

The human body, having many parts that make up the one body, is often used as an analogy of the body of Christ.

DEVOTIONAL OUTLINE

1. God values every member (I Cor. 12:14-19). There is much that one can accomplish in the church, and the church's effectiveness is multiplied tremendously when all of its members harmoniously combine their gifts and talents, in the one Spirit, toward the fulfillment of God's desire "that all should come to repentance" (II Pet. 3:9). Whoever seeks to become a Christian must confess faith in the one true and living God. When the new convert trusts in Christ as Saviour and Lord, he receives the baptism of the Holy Spirit and is indwelled by that same Spirit. Every convert experiences these same blessings, but all are not given the same assignment in the body. God in His sovereignty endued each member as it pleased Him.

2. God knows every member (I Cor. 12:20-27). One of the greatest challenges in church leadership is attending equally to each member of the one body. Some members are more confident than others and require less guidance. Their gifts are frequently used in carrying out the ministry of the church. It is not unrealistic to have members who feel inferior or inadequate; they need encouragement.

The truth is that every member wants to feel useful and appreciated. The highly gifted must not shun the less confident ones but embrace them and assure them that there is no division in the body of Christ. Each member, though different, is mutually dependent on the others and shares in the others' joy and sorrow.

3. God loves His members (I Cor. 12:28-31). In God's church, there are no "Big I's" and "Little You's." He knows precisely what the church's needs are and has fitly joined together every area of church ministry (cf. Eph. 4:16). Looking around your church, you will notice that all members are not pastors and all are not teachers; rather, they are diverse, multigifted servants operating in their God-given grace. With God, no gift or office is more honorable than any other.

Calvin observes, "The symmetry of the Church consists, so to speak, of a manifold unity, that is, when the variety of gifts is directed to the same object, as in music there are different sounds, but suited to each other with such an adaptation, as to produce concord. Hence it is befitting that there should be a distinction of gifts as well as of offices, and yet all harmonize in one. Paul, . . . commends this variety, that no one may, by rashly intruding himself into another's place, confound the distinction which the Lord has established. Hence he orders every one to be contented with his own gifts, and cultivate the particular department that has been assigned to him" (*Calvin's Commentaries,* biblehub.com).

CHILDREN'S CORNER

Assure the children that God has placed them in the church where they can best honor Him with their gifts.

Children should easily see the humor in Paul's words about the eye saying to the hand, "I don't need you!" or the head saying the same thing to the feet. Play up the absurdity of such talk, and let the youngsters realize it is just as absurd for one Christian to tell another, "I can get along fine without you!"

—Jane E. Campbell.

Scripture Lesson Text

JAS. 1:1 James, a servant of God and of the Lord Jesus Christ, to the twelve tribes which are scattered abroad, greeting.

2 My brethren, count it all joy when ye fall into divers temptations;

3 Knowing *this,* that the trying of your faith worketh patience.

4 But let patience have *her* perfect work, that ye may be perfect and entire, wanting nothing.

5 If any of you lack wisdom, let him ask of God, that giveth to all *men* liberally, and upbraideth not; and it shall be given him.

6 But let him ask in faith, nothing wavering. For he that wavereth is like a wave of the sea driven with the wind and tossed.

7 For let not that man think that he shall receive any thing of the Lord.

8 A double minded man *is* unstable in all his ways.

12 Blessed *is* the man that endureth temptation: for when he is tried, he shall receive the crown of life, which the Lord hath promised to them that love him.

13 Let no man say when he is tempted, I am tempted of God: for God cannot be tempted with evil, neither tempteth he any man:

14 But every man is tempted, when he is drawn away of his own lust, and enticed.

15 Then when lust hath conceived, it bringeth forth sin: and sin, when it is finished, bringeth forth death.

16 Do not err, my beloved brethren.

17 Every good gift and every perfect gift is from above, and cometh down from the Father of lights, with whom is no variableness, neither shadow of turning.

18 Of his own will begat he us with the word of truth, that we should be a kind of firstfruits of his creatures.

NOTES

Blessings amid Trials

Lesson Text: James 1:1-8, 12-18

Related Scriptures: Matthew 4:1-11; 5:10-12;
I Peter 1:3-9; 3:13-18; Revelation 2:8-11

TIME: about A.D. 45   PLACE: from Jerusalem

GOLDEN TEXT—"Blessed is the man that endureth temptation: for when he is tried, he shall receive the crown of life, which the Lord hath promised to them that love him" (James 1:12).

Introduction

Since there are several men with the name "James" mentioned in the New Testament, Bible scholars are not in complete agreement concerning which James wrote the book that bears his name. While two of the twelve apostles had this name (Luke 6:14-15), the epistle of James has been traditionally identified with "James the Lord's brother" (Gal. 1:19). Even though the half brothers of Christ did not believe in Him during His earthly ministry (John 7:3-5), James later became a prominent leader in the Jerusalem church (Acts 12:17; 15:13; 21:18).

All the books we will study this quarter concern God's blessings. This week, we look at God's blessings amid the trials we all face in life.

The book of James was probably one of the earliest epistles of the New Testament to be written. It is usually dated somewhere between A.D. 45 and 62, the year that James was martyred according to the Jewish historian Josephus.

LESSON OUTLINE

I. PRAYING FOR WISDOM—
   Jas. 1:1-8

II. PERSEVERING IN TRIAL—
   JAS. 1:12-15

III. PERFECT GIFTS FROM ABOVE—
   Jas. 1:16-18

Exposition: Verse by Verse

PRAYING FOR WISDOM

JAS. 1:1 James, a servant of God and of the Lord Jesus Christ, to the twelve tribes which are scattered abroad, greeting.

2 My brethren, count it all joy when ye fall into divers temptations;

3 Knowing this, that the trying of your faith worketh patience.

4 But let patience have her per-

fect work, that ye may be perfect and entire, wanting nothing.

5 If any of you lack wisdom, let him ask of God, that giveth to all men liberally, and upbraideth not; and it shall be given him.

6 But let him ask in faith, nothing wavering. For he that wavereth is like a wave of the sea driven with the wind and tossed.

7 For let not that man think that he shall receive any thing of the Lord.

8 A double minded man is unstable in all his ways.

Servant of God (Jas. 1:1). One of the reasons scholars debate the identity of James is that there are few clues in the book itself to aid us in discovering who he was. {He simply called himself a "servant of God."}Q1 While there are several Greek words translated "servant," this one referred to a slave and was often used by Paul to describe his own relationship to Christ (Rom. 1:1).

{Since we know that the twelve tribes of Israel did not exist in the same manner in the days of the early church as they did in the time of Moses, there are two major views concerning what James meant by this particular designation of his readership.}Q2

{Some think James was addressing Jewish Christians throughout the Gentile world.}Q2 During the centuries after the Babylonian Captivity and preceding the coming of Christ, Jews had been scattered over a wide area. This is often referred to as the Dispersion or Diaspora. In favor of this view is the fact that there is a definite Jewish flavor to the book of James.

{A second view is that James was simply writing to all believers throughout the Roman Empire, both Jew and Gentile.}Q2 In favor of this view is the fact that Old Testament terminology is frequently applied to Christians in the New Testament (cf. Rom. 2:28; Gal. 3:29; I Pet. 2:9).

Various trials (Jas. 1:2-4). Trials and temptations are a part of life, though we usually do not count them "all joy" when we encounter them. Why some people have more trials than others is a mystery. If we get sidetracked into trying to discover why we face the trials we do, we will never gain the greater blessing of growing stronger because of them.

The word rendered "temptations" in verse 2 is used and translated variously in the New Testament. Sometimes it is used in the sense of solicitation to commit sin, as when Christ was "tempted (the verb form of the same word) of the devil" (Matt. 4:1). In other passages, though, it is used of trials we undergo because of our faith. Such troubles often arise because of our stand for Christ. James's readers were probably being persecuted for their faith. Whether facing physical persecution or not, all believers will have their faith tested in various ways.

{This being the case, "the trying of your faith" (Jas. 1:3) has the capability of producing spiritual growth. The word translated "patience" carries the idea of steadfastness or patient endurance.}Q3 Once we have encountered and overcome a trial, we are stronger because of the experience. Such spiritual development prepares us for future encounters with both Satan and the inevitable uncertainties of life.

Trials should not destroy us but develop us. Hence, our Christian faith will be mature and fully developed, free from many deficiencies. Overcoming trials enables us to be victorious in Christian living.

Promise of wisdom (Jas. 1:5). While we all need wisdom in general, the context suggests that wisdom was especially needed to understand the divine purpose behind the trials being faced by these early saints. As we will see later, God is not the source of our temptations (vss. 13-15). He can, however, use them to stimulate spiritual growth in us (Rom. 5:3).

While the words "wisdom" and "knowledge" are sometimes used interchangeably in the Bible, it has been suggested that wisdom is the correct use of knowledge. For example, a person may study the Bible and know many facts. This is knowledge. Knowing how to apply that knowledge is wisdom. {Since most of us know more of the Bible than we are using, we need to pray for such wisdom from on high.}Q4

"Wisdom is more than wide knowledge . . . As a Jew, James viewed wisdom as related to the practice of righteousness in daily life. It is the moral discernment that enables the believer to meet life and its trials with decisions and actions consistent with God's will" (Hiebert, *James,* Moody).

With regard to this divine insight that God desires to impart to His children, James assures us that God gives wisdom generously, without a hint of resentment or criticism, to those who ask Him.

Ask in faith (Jas. 1:6-8). {Faith is at the foundation of all effective praying. Asking for wisdom without faith is futile. If our faith wavers, we are "like a wave of the sea driven with the wind and tossed."}Q5

Prayer, however, is not a means to manipulate God. Nor does it involve some magical formula that assures one of instant access to God's throne. Prayer is an act of faith. To attempt to communicate with God on any foundation other than faith is to ensure that our prayers will remain unanswered.

Those who approach God with doubts concerning His ability to respond are depicted as "double minded" (vs. 8). Representing one Greek word, "double minded" literally means "two-souled." It is as if a person had two minds living in one body. "The one is turned Godward, while the other is turned toward the world; the one believes God, but the other disbelieves. . . . His double-mindedness reveals itself in his conduct as a whole; he is 'unstable in all he does'" (Hiebert).

PERSEVERING IN TRIAL

12 Blessed is the man that endureth temptation: for when he is tried, he shall receive the crown of life, which the Lord hath promised to them that love him.

13 Let no man say when he is tempted, I am tempted of God: for God cannot be tempted with evil, neither tempteth he any man:

14 But every man is tempted, when he is drawn away of his own lust, and enticed.

15 Then when lust hath conceived, it bringeth forth sin: and sin, when it is finished, bringeth forth death.

Crown of life (Jas. 1:12). While many blessings are pronounced upon believers (cf. Matt. 5:3-12), certainly a great blessing comes to those who endure trials. {The primary blessing is not to be received in this life, though; rather, those who pass the test will receive the crown of life.}Q6

The word translated "crown" in James 1:12 was commonly used in the athletic games of that day and referred to a wreath of victory granted to the winner of a contest. It would be equivalent to a blue ribbon or gold medal today. While some see this crown as representing a reward consisting of life in its fullness, others understand it as a symbol for eternal life itself.

The crown of life is promised only to those who love the Lord. While there may be several ways to measure our love for Christ, the Lord Jesus singled out obedience to His teachings as one way to declare our devotion to Him. In John 14:15 He said, "If ye love me, keep my commandments."

No temptation from God (Jas. 1:13). The word translated "tempted" can mean either a test or a trial, but here it seems to be used in the traditional sense of a temptation to commit sin.

{While it is true that temptations come upon us all, it is equally true that God does not send them. It is true that in His sovereignty and omniscience He allows them to occur, but He is not the source of them.}[Q7]

Trials come from a variety of sources, including our own bad decisions. In the case of James's readers, however, they were likely facing trials because of their faith in Christ (Heb. 10:32-34).

In stark contrast, temptations to commit sin come from Satan, whom the Bible describes as "the tempter" (Matt. 4:3). They also come from our own inner sinful desires (Jas. 1:14). James was adamant that we should not blame God for temptations we experience.

Lust, sin, and death (Jas. 1:14-15). The word translated "lust" refers to a strong desire of any kind, whether good or bad. In modern English we usually think of lust in reference to a desire to commit some immoral act. Yet any kind of desire, whether wrong in itself or satisfied in wrong ways, can lead us into sin. {It is through our desires that we are frequently "enticed," a word that was originally used of catching fish using bait.}[Q8] Of course, what entices one person may not even be considered a temptation to another.

James emphasized that the desire to commit sin comes from within. Christ stressed this same truth when He said that evil actions originate in an evil heart (Mark 7:20-23). Later in his letter, James urged his readers, "Resist the devil, and he will flee from you" (4:7). The devil may play a part in temptation, but at this point James wanted to stress man's culpability in choosing to sin. In short, we sin because we want

to! Admitting our sins is not easy, but it opens the door to full pardon.

"Christian living is a matter of the will, not the feelings. . . . This explains why immature Christians easily fall into temptation: they let their feelings make the decisions. The more you exercise your will in saying a decisive no to temptation, the more God will take control of your life" (Wiersbe, *The Bible Exposition Commentary,* Victor).

We should not, however, make the mistake of confusing temptation with sin. Sin occurs only when we yield to temptation. Using the language of conception and childbirth, James declared that once lust has been conceived, it ultimately gives birth to sin.

Left unchecked and unforgiven, sin will eventually bring death to the sinner. Since we are all sinners (Rom. 3:23), we must all face physical death in this world (5:12). However, the "wages of sin" (6:23) involves more than dying. Eventually, all those who have rejected Christ will suffer the "second death" (Rev. 20:14), which is eternal separation from God in hell (Matt. 25:41).

PERFECT GIFTS FROM ABOVE

16 Do not err, my beloved brethren.

17 Every good gift and every perfect gift is from above, and cometh down from the Father of lights, with whom is no variableness, neither shadow of turning.

18 Of his own will begat he us with the word of truth, that we should be a kind of firstfruits of his creatures.

Caution against deception (Jas. 1:16). A warning was given by James to those he endearingly called his "beloved brethren." It is not clear whether this verse should be considered the conclusion to what James had just said about temptation and sin or whether it is an introduction to what he was about to say concerning God's good gifts.

Either way, it is a warning not to go astray in our thinking. The word translated "err" can mean to "wander away" or "be deceived." There are, of course, many ways of being deceived. Some are deceived by being lured away into thinking that God is the source of their temptations. Others, however, are deceived into thinking that the good gifts they receive have some source other than God above. The Lord does not send temptation; He sends good gifts upon His children.

Gifts from above (Jas. 1:17). {While some distinctions can be made between the words "good" and "perfect," the idea is that all blessings come from our heavenly Father.}Q9 All good things can be traced back to God. On the other hand, evil is from the evil one (John 8:44).

{God is here described as the "Father of lights" (Jas. 1:17). Concerning the material universe, God is the Creator of the heavenly lights: the sun, moon, and stars. Spiritually speaking, God is the source of knowledge, wisdom, and purity, which are depicted as light in Scripture. "God is light, and in him is no darkness at all" (I John 1:5).}Q9

The God we serve is One "with whom is no variableness, neither shadow of turning" (Jas. 1:17). Unlike the changing shadows cast by the sun, God is unchanging. Even though God has acted variously at different times in history, His essential character remains unchanged (Mal. 3:6; Heb. 13:8).

Begotten by the Word (Jas. 1:18). In contrast to being born into death by sin (vs. 15), {James here stressed the fact that we have been born anew from above through the "word of truth." As Peter declared, "This is the word which by the gospel is preached unto you" (I Pet. 1:25).}Q10

While it is true that we must respond to the call of God, He chose us before we chose Him (cf. Acts 16:14; Eph. 1:4; II Thess. 2:13).

"The plan is His, and came from His heart's desire. Our salvation is the result of the deliberate choice of God. This plan He foreordained before the foundation of the world; and there is none other that can take a single ounce of credit for God's wonderful plan" (Fream, *A Chain of Jewels from James and Jude,* College Press).

The firstfruits were the first crops harvested. Those early Christians who had been born again were a "kind of firstfruits of his creatures" (Jas. 1:18), an indication that many more would follow.

—John A. Owston.

QUESTIONS

1. How did James describe himself?
2. To whom was James writing? What might he have meant with his particular designation?
3. What does the testing of one's faith produce?
4. What specific thing did James tell his readers to pray for?
5. In what way should we approach God? What are we like without this quality?
6. What is promised to those who endure trials?
7. Does God tempt us? Why or why not?
8. What was one original use of the word for "enticed" (Jas. 1:14)?
9. Where do all good gifts come from? What is meant by "Father of lights" (vs. 17)?
10. Through what has God begotten us to new life?

—John A. Owston.

Preparing to Teach the Lesson

It is not easy for anyone to go through long periods of trials and temptation. In this week's text, however, James has taught us that good can come even out of such difficult times for the faithful Christian believer.

TODAY'S AIM

Facts: to understand that the purpose of trials and temptations is to develop patience.

Principle: to teach that trials and temptations in the lives of believers help make them strong in their faith.

Application: to help students learn to endure trials and temptations, knowing that the Lord is perfecting their faith.

INTRODUCING THE LESSON

This week's lesson introduces us to the truth that there is a purpose in the trials we face. That purpose is to make us strong in our faith. Almost everyone knows someone who is a faithful and strong believer in Jesus but whose problems in life never seem to go away. We all wonder why such a good person has to go through those difficult circumstances. It is truly a mystery until we begin to realize the ways God uses to perfect us.

DEVELOPING THE LESSON

1. An informative greeting (Jas. 1:1). Here we see James identifying himself to his readers as the author of this letter. It is interesting that even though he was our Lord's earthly half brother, he did not take on that designation here but instead identified himself with his fellow believers as a servant of the Father and the Son. He put himself on equal terms with his brothers and sisters who were being persecuted for their faith.

James wrote in particular to those who were scattered beyond Palestine when the persecution of the Christians arose in Jerusalem (Acts 8:1).

2. Trials—an opportunity for character development (Jas. 1:2-4). James gave the suffering Christians a very strange message. He asked that they count it a reason for joy when they experienced difficult situations, or trials, which seems to be the meaning of "temptations" here.

Notice the unique perspective of the strong Christian. James told believers that suffering brings forth the fruit of patience in our lives. Underlying this truth is the fact that nothing happens to the Christian believer without a divine purpose.

For the one who trusts in God, suffering comes only with God's permission and has a definite purpose—to make us strong in the faith. Patience comes only when faith is really tested and tried. In other words, faith has to be put under extreme pressure. The Christian who knows life's trials is the one who is being perfected and purified.

3. Seek wisdom from God (Jas. 1:5-8). It was within the context of suffering and persecution that James encouraged the Christian to seek God's help. When the Christian's faith is being tested, he needs the wisdom to know how to respond. This wisdom comes from God alone.

James talked about the character of God here. He said that it is the nature of God to give very liberally to people. He does not hold back. We see the utmost example of God's giving in the incarnation and in His giving His only Son to die on the cross for our salvation.

James also pointed out the part that

man must play. He is to ask for wisdom in simple faith, without wavering. This means that he must take God at His word and trust Him completely. God always keeps His promises to His children. Man must learn to trust Him as a child trusts his father.

James pointed out that one who does not trust God fully is like a wave of the sea that is unstable. It is there one moment and gone the next without any apparent goal in mind. Faith is the prerequisite to receiving wisdom from a generous God.

4. The reward for those who endure (Jas. 1:12-16). Endurance through trials is not without reward for the faithful Christian. The reward that James talked about is the crown of life for all those who love the Lord and endure suffering. The imagery comes from the Greek Olympic races, in which the runner who won received a wreath of olive leaves. It was a great public honor to win.

In this section James also discussed the nature of temptation (vs. 13), here meaning temptation to sin. This is not something that God brings about, for God is beyond all temptation. God does not tempt anyone; nor can He be tempted Himself. James stated that temptation stems from our evil desires and what remains of our sinful nature.

James ended this section with a warning. He told Christians to be on their guard and not to go astray, for lust leads to sin. When sin has completed its course, the end is always death. (See also Romans 6:23, which says that "the wages of sin is death.")

5. Everything perfect comes from God (Jas. 1:17-18). Here James showed us something about the nature of God. After pointing out that God is perfect and cannot be tempted, James declared quite naturally that everything that is truly perfect comes from God. He is the Father of lights. Light in Scripture is indicative of purity.

Unlike man, God does not change. He can be trusted. He made us His children by choosing us and giving us His Word. It was an act of His will. We became His choice possession.

ILLUSTRATING THE LESSON

The Christian goes through trials, but the end result is eternal glory. The glory does not come without the trials. Christ's glorious resurrection, which came only after the cross, illustrates this.

TRIALS BEFORE GLORY

THE CROSS THE GLORY

CONCLUDING THE LESSON

The lesson this week has brought home some very important truths. The Christian goes through trials for a divine purpose. The crown of life awaits him when he has finished the race. It is through those times of trials and temptations that God develops Christian character in each of us. With wisdom from God, we can endure even the most difficult of times. He has promised to stay with us to the very end.

ANTICIPATING THE NEXT LESSON

Next week's lesson deals with II Corinthians 1:3-11 and the blessings of God's comfort to us so that we are equipped to comfort others.

—A. Koshy Muthalaly.

PRACTICAL POINTS

1. It is our Christian duty to find joy in difficult and trying circumstances (Jas. 1:1-2).
2. The key to accepting afflictions in a positive manner is knowing they can produce something good in us (Jas. 1:3-4; cf. Rom. 5:3-5).
3. Another key to coping with times of testing is seeking God's wisdom on how to handle the situation (Jas. 1:5-8).
4. It is love for God that enables us to endure whatever He allows in our lives (vs. 12).
5. We must be careful not to confuse our lusts with God's will (vss. 13-15).
6. A godly life begins with a proper understanding of the nature of God (Jas. 1:16-18; cf. Hos. 4:6).

—Darrell W. McKay.

RESEARCH AND DISCUSSION

1. Why did James not use the word "if" instead of "when" when talking about trials (Jas. 1:2; cf. I Pet. 4:12)?
2. What enables a person to pray without wavering (Jas. 1:6)?
3. What is it about double-mindedness that makes one unstable in everything (vs. 8)?
4. What other crowns does God have to give to faithful Christians (Jas. 1:12; cf. I Cor. 9:25; II Tim. 4:8; I Pet. 5:4; Rev. 2:10)?
5. What might be the basis for referring to God as the "Father of lights" (Jas. 1:17), and what effect should this have on our lives?

—Darrell W. McKay.

ILLUSTRATED HIGH POINTS

A double minded man (Jas. 1:8).

Everyone liked Don. He was always calm and never contentious. Don's popularity in the church quickly catapulted him to a seat on the governing board. Things went well for a time, but then the members began to notice that he always sided with the majority. On close votes, Don would abstain. He was more concerned about being liked than in taking a stand. He was not reelected when his term expired.

When lust hath conceived (vs. 15)

A young family moved into our neighborhood when I was in primary school. The Smiths had one child, Bobby. We often played together. Mrs. Smith was always cheerful and always made me feel welcome when I visited. As far as I could tell, everyone admired the Smiths.

The Smiths were close friends of the Joneses, with whom they often socialized. Sometimes when the two couples went out for an evening, Bobby would stay at my house. He did not seem fond of the Joneses.

Once Bobby told me about the times Mr. Jones would come to his house during the day while Bobby's father was at work. His mother would tell Bobby to go out and play for a while. Bobby did not know what was going on, but he did not like it.

One day when Bobby came home from school, an ambulance was parked in front of his house. Neighbors tried to keep Bobby out of the house, but he went in anyway. His mother was lying on the floor, a suicide victim. Bobby was devastated.

Years later, Bobby confided to me that his mother had become pregnant. This had posed a scandal, since his father was sterile.

—Albert J. Schneider.

Golden Text Illuminated

"Blessed is the man that endureth temptation: for when he is tried, he shall receive the crown of life, which the Lord hath promised to them that love him" (James 1:12).

In the Beatitudes, Jesus set the ultimate standard in pronouncing blessings that sound odd or even downright bewildering: "Blessed are the poor in spirit" (Matt. 5:3); "Blessed are they that mourn" (vs. 4); "Blessed are they which are persecuted" (vs. 10). In our golden text, Jesus' half brother James follows His lead in declaring, "Blessed is the man that endureth temptation." What are we to make of this?

If we have read from the beginning of James 1, we should not be too surprised, for in verse 2 he starts things off with the equally puzzling "Count it all joy when ye fall into divers temptations." There seems to be a theme developing here.

Indeed, there is. But what exactly is it? Both in verse 2 and in verse 12, James speaks of "temptation." The Greek word in both cases essentially means "trial" or "test," and it covers external trials brought upon us in the form of difficult circumstances or persecution as well as the internal ones that we normally associate with the word temptation.

Either way, we do not normally think of enduring trials or temptation as a blessing. But James looks ahead to a blessed outcome. Once a person is "tried," an unimaginably good thing follows. The word for "tried" means "approved through testing" and here indicates a believer who has passed the test and comes out of it stronger in faith and godliness than before.

James then declares that such a person will "receive the crown of life." The Greek term for "crown" referred to the wreath awarded to winners of athletic contests and thus signifies recognition and reward. The New Testament speaks of wreaths or crowns made of gold (Rev. 4:4; 14:14) or even thorns, such as was placed on Jesus before His crucifixion. We might say that Jesus wore a crown of disgrace in order that we might wear one of honor.

"The crown of life" thus points to the ultimate recognition and glory that God is pleased to bestow on His children. Of course, it comes solely by His grace, for even our successful endurance of life's trials and temptations is achieved only by His work within us. God deserves all the glory for what He does in our lives, but He graciously lifts us up beyond what we deserve.

James says that this crown of life has been promised by the Lord "to them that love him." Where did he find this promise? The one place we see it explicitly mentioned in the New Testament is Revelation 2:10: "I will give thee the crown of life." That book, however, was penned long after James wrote his epistle. It is likely that he simply knew of Jesus' teaching on the subject, teaching not recorded in the Gospels. Or he may be summarizing extended promises found in such passages as Mark 10:29-30.

At any rate, to receive the crown of life is to receive a gift so inconceivably glorious that any trials gone through beforehand pale in comparison. Paul says the same thing as James in slightly different terms: "Our light affliction, which is but for a moment, worketh for us a far more exceeding and eternal weight of glory" (II Cor. 4:17).

—*Kenneth Sponsler.*

Heart of the Lesson

As Christians we are saved by faith, but we also live by faith. Faith is an integral part—an essential part—of our spiritual lives. In this lesson we will see the important part faith plays in understanding and profiting from the trials and temptations that are common to everyone.

1. The value of temptation (Jas. 1:1-4). No one likes trials and temptations. We would much prefer to live happy and serene lives, with never a care in the world. Yet if we did that, we would miss one of the greatest opportunities for spiritual growth and blessing.

After all, what is the goal of the Christian life? Is it not to stand before God "perfect and entire, wanting nothing" (vs. 4)? How do we get to that point? James tells us we get there by weathering the trials and temptations of our Christian life.

2. Understanding temptation (Jas. 1:5-8). If we would like to completely avoid trials and temptations, we are failing to understand their nature. We are prone to ask, "Why me, Lord? Why this, and why now?" God is more than willing to give us understanding, or wisdom. All we have to do is ask. When we ask, however, we must ask in faith. That is the crux of the matter.

Too often our requests to God are driven by doubt, not faith. We know we are supposed to go to Him with our requests, so we do. But in the back of our minds, we are thinking, He's not going to listen to me on this. I'll believe it when I see it! And then when the answer we desire does not materialize, we tell ourselves, I knew it wouldn't happen!

If we really want to gain the wisdom and understanding God offers, we must ask in unfailing confidence that He can and will give it to us for the asking.

3. A promise in temptation (Jas. 1:12). Earlier, James had said that the result of trials and temptations is to make the Christian complete. Now he adds the promise that the one who endures temptation will receive "the crown of life." It is axiomatic that the one who stands before God complete will receive the crown of life. We understand that the crown of life is the eternal life that every believer will enjoy with God in heaven. That is a prize worth having, and it comes to the one who endures temptation.

If we say that the crown of life comes to the one who endures temptation, dare we say that it comes only to the one who endures temptation? That may be saying too much, and yet experience teaches us that everyone is subject to temptation. The only alternative to enduring temptation is to yield to it, and that is sin. A life dominated by sin leads to spiritual death.

4. The source of temptation (Jas. 1:13-18). A major factor in enduring temptation is understanding its source. James tells us emphatically that it does not come from God. God is holy. He calls us to holiness. He has no interest in leading people to sin.

Temptation, James says, arises out of our own desires. When we understand that, we can better withstand the temptation.

Here, then, is the paradox of temptation in the Christian life: While God is not the author of temptation, He uses it to accomplish spiritual completeness in the heart of the sincere believer (cf. Rom. 8:28).

—*Ralph Woodworth.*

World Missions

Our lesson this week focuses on the trials and afflictions of believers. Often these times turn out to be blessings in disguise. In the very beginning of his epistle, James described his relationship to the Lord. He spoke of himself as "a servant of God and of the Lord Jesus Christ" (1:1). Countless thousands of God's people have suffered and died because of their association with the Lord and His Word.

I had the privilege of serving the Lord as a missionary in Africa for many years. Some of my African coworkers eventually became martyrs because of their stand for the Lord and Bible principles. They would not bow to their government's demands to return to the old tribal ways and send their young people with the witch doctors for their tribal initiation ceremonies. Because of their refusal to go along with the government's "cultural revolution," they were executed.

It is interesting to note that James did not focus on the fact that he was a kin in the flesh to Jesus. He chose to identify himself as a servant to Christ. There is an important lesson for us in this spiritual association between James and Jesus. We should focus on being His servants even though He is our Saviour. Being saved obligates one to serve. The epistle of James points this out perhaps more than any other book in the Bible.

Our lesson speaks not only of trials, temptations, and afflictions but also of patience. James wrote, "My brethren, count it all joy when ye fall into divers temptations; knowing this, that the trying of your faith worketh patience" (1:2-3). We are told to exercise the Christian grace of joy even amid afflictions. The world's philosophy tells us to be calm in our troubles, but Christianity tells us to be joyful. Trials can bring unusual joy at times when the ordinary calls for sorrow and sadness.

Another virtue that is mentioned in our Scripture text is wisdom. Practically everything that touches our lives requires some degree of wisdom. Regarding this subject, we read, "If any of you lack wisdom, let him ask of God, that giveth to all men liberally, and upbraideth not; and it shall be given him" (vs. 5). Our God is the source of all wisdom, and only He can bestow upon us that which we need. We must not fear to ask Him for wisdom. To waver in asking Him shows doubt and an insecurity about His promise. The writer of Hebrews wrote, "Let us therefore come boldly unto the throne of grace, that we may obtain mercy, and find grace to help in time of need" (4:16).

Afflictions and trials must not cause Christians to become unsteady and shaken. One who is driven and tossed about by the wind, not exercising unwavering faith, will not receive anything of the Lord. That lack of solid grounding indicates a double-minded man who is unstable in all his ways. Missionaries report that some of the most stable Christians they know are among primitive tribal people. They exercise childlike faith and trust in the Lord.

Trials, temptations, afflictions, and more are part of life here on earth. Amid all these shine the promises of God. Nehemiah wrote, "For the joy of the Lord is your strength" (Neh. 8:10). The psalmist said, "Weeping may endure for a night, but joy cometh in the morning" (Ps. 30:5). Our faith must be put into practice.

—V. Ben Kendrick.

The Jewish Aspect

James wrote his epistle "to the twelve tribes which are scattered abroad" (1:1). The historical background of this statement is slightly more complicated than might be expected at first glance.

Everyone knows Israel had twelve tribes. In some ways, though, there actually were thirteen tribes. The twelve tribes of Israel were descendants of the twelve sons of Jacob (Gen. 49). One of Jacob's sons was Joseph, but it is not customary to refer to the tribe of Joseph. Instead, Joseph's two sons, Ephraim and Manasseh, became separate tribes (48:5), making the total thirteen.

In the listing of the tribes in Revelation 7:5-8, the tribe of Dan was left out, bringing the total back to twelve. The book of Joshua records that Dan never occupied their allotted territory (Josh. 19:47; Judg. 18:1). Part of the tribe migrated north and made their own territory. The group that remained in the south seems to have been absorbed into Judah while the northern group was taken away by the Assyrians (II Kgs. 15:29). Perhaps John left them out of Revelation 7:5-8 because their descendants will be too small to seal twelve thousand men.

During the conquest of the land, only twelve received an inheritance. Levi received the priesthood and the service of the sanctuary. God alone was their portion (Josh. 13:33). During the sealing of the 144,000, Dan is left out so that there are again twelve tribes; but during the messianic age, Dan will have a portion. There will again be thirteen tribes and thirteen territories (Ezek. 48:1-27). In spite of this complex issue of the number of the tribes of Israel, they always are referred to in the Bible as the twelve tribes. Ephraim and Manasseh are thought of as half tribes.

When James wrote to the twelve tribes, he used a traditional phrase to refer to the Jewish people. They were the "twelve tribes which are scattered abroad." "Scattered abroad" roughly approximates the Jewish term *galut* ("exile"), which has also been called the Diaspora, or the Dispersion.

The Jewish people are acutely aware of being scattered from their land. God, through Moses, foretold that the Jewish people would be scattered "among the nations" (Deut. 4:27). James wrote from Jerusalem, where he was the leader of the church. He was in the land. He wrote to the Jewish communities scattered throughout the Roman empire.

From James 1:1, then, we learn that the book was probably a letter to Jewish Christians. While applying to all Christians, the specific concerns and issues of the book were directed to a Jewish audience who believed in Jesus.

James, whose Hebrew name was Jacob, wrote a Jewish letter to a Jewish audience. Throughout the letter, that Jewishness can be seen. The book of James deals with wisdom (vs. 5), a Jewish concept rather than a Roman one. The apostle referred to the "fatherless and widows" (vs. 27), a common Old Testament concern. Many of his sayings sound like proverbs (4:10). Blessed are the doers of he Word, James said. His words, written first to Jewish believers, are God's Word to all believers.

Let us pray for the grace of God, that we may be the doers of His Word, as James described, and be blessed.

—*Derek Leman.*

Guiding the Superintendent

During the month of February 2018, the Winter Olympics were held in Pyeongchang, South Korea. For a period of approximately two weeks, the nations of the world watched as their best amateur and professional athletes competed against one another.

It is never an easy process for athletic contestants to endure to eventually qualify to participate in the Olympic Games. Before being selected for their respective teams, athletes have to survive the competition of Olympic trials. This process involves a time of testing that determines whether the athletes are qualified to compete against the best athletes in the world.

Not many people welcome trials or view them as a necessary part of their personal development. For the believer in Jesus Christ, though, God has determined that godly spiritual character development will include struggling through trials.

DEVOTIONAL OUTLINE

1. A challenge to persevere (Jas. 1:1-4). As a called servant of "God and of the Lord Jesus Christ," James challenged his readers to remain joyfully resolute in the midst of many kinds of trials.

The reason for James's daring challenge was the revealed truths that the trial of personal faith results in godly patience and that the development of patience results in personal spiritual fulfillment.

2. A challenge of single-minded faith (Jas. 1:5-8). James challenged his readers to ask God for His gift of wisdom. The spiritual foundation of their communication was to be an established faith that would please God and cause Him to liberally respond to their petitions.

3. A challenge to personal accountability (Jas. 1:12-18). When God's people struggled with temptations, James reminded them that God was not the source. The source was their own lust, and James challenged his readers to assume personal responsibility for dealing with their sin. He then reminded his readers that God's personal interaction with them as His begotten people was good and would result in a blessed life.

CHILDREN'S CORNER

The spiritual development of children often begins with simple but profound foundational scriptural truths. Use James 1:16-18 to encourage your Sunday school teachers to emphasize God's goodness to their children. His inviting and attractive attitude of goodness will deeply impact their young minds and hearts.

Remind your teachers that children are masters of the art of rerouting blame. When confronted with personal acts of selfishness, they quickly divert attention to someone else.

Use James 1:13-15 to challenge your teachers to undertake the difficult but necessary task of training their youngsters in the spiritual discipline of accepting personal responsibility for their actions, including dealing with the consequences.

Another thing that many children —and adults too—have difficulty with is meeting trials and difficulties with patience. James says to "count it all joy" when we fall into various trials. No one finds that a natural thing to do. It has to be taught—and better, modeled. If children see you consistently showing joy amid trials, they may eventually catch on and, by grace, learn to do so as well.

—*Thomas R. Chmura.*

SCRIPTURE LESSON TEXT

II COR. 1:3 Blessed *be* God, even the Father of our Lord Jesus Christ, the Father of mercies, and the God of all comfort;

4 Who comforteth us in all our tribulation, that we may be able to comfort them which are in any trouble, by the comfort wherewith we ourselves are comforted of God.

5 For as the sufferings of Christ abound in us, so our consolation also aboundeth by Christ.

6 And whether we be afflicted, *it is* **for your consolation and salvation, which is effectual in the enduring of the same sufferings which we also suffer: or whether we be comforted,** *it is* **for your consolation and salvation.**

7 And our hope of you *is* stedfast, knowing, that as ye are partakers of the sufferings, so *shall ye be* also of the consolation.

8 For we would not, brethren, have you ignorant of our trouble which came to us in Asia, that we were pressed out of measure, above strength, insomuch that we despaired even of life:

9 But we had the sentence of death in ourselves, that we should not trust in ourselves, but in God which raiseth the dead:

10 Who delivered us from so great a death, and doth deliver: in whom we trust that he will yet deliver *us;*

11 Ye also helping together by prayer for us, that for the gift *bestowed* upon us by the means of many persons thanks may be given by many on our behalf.

NOTES

144

Blessing of God's Comfort

Lesson Text: II Corinthians 1:3-11

Related Scriptures: Psalm 71:1-24;
John 14:15-27; 15:18-27; I Peter 4:12-19

TIME: probably A.D. 55

PLACE: from Macedonia

GOLDEN TEXT—"Our hope of you is stedfast, knowing, that as ye are partakers of the sufferings, so shall ye be also of the consolation" (II Corinthians 1:7).

Introduction

Since the Apostle Paul was widely traveled and very well known around his world, he was highly respected and thus enjoyed life to the fullest every day—right? He had it made and smiled every day—right? Wrong!

In II Corinthians we find the most extensive autobiographical writing of all Paul's letters. It might also have been the most difficult letter he had to write, for the Corinthian culture was very corrupt and the church had been far too influenced by it. He had already faced some major tension with this group.

Although he had evidently been attacked by some opponents in the church in Corinth and would spend a great deal of time in this letter defending his apostleship, Paul began with an encouraging note about how God comforts His people.

LESSON OUTLINE

I. THE VALUE OF COMFORT— II Cor. 1:3-7

II. THE VALUE OF PRAYER— II Cor. 1:8-11

Exposition: Verse by Verse

THE VALUE OF COMFORT

II COR. 1:3 Blessed be God, even the Father of our Lord Jesus Christ, the Father of mercies, and the God of all comfort;

4 Who comforteth us in all our tribulation, that we may be able to comfort them which are in any trouble, by the comfort wherewith we ourselves are comforted of God.

5 For as the sufferings of Christ abound in us, so our consolation also aboundeth by Christ.

6 And whether we be afflicted, it is for your consolation and salvation, which is effectual in the enduring of the same sufferings which we also suffer: or whether we be comforted, it is for your consolation and salvation.

7 And our hope of you is stedfast, knowing, that as ye are partakers of the sufferings, so shall ye be also of the consolation.

God comforts us (II Cor. 1:3-4). After his greeting, which in this case was brief and somewhat abrupt, {Paul immediately expressed adoration and praise to God.}[Q1] There are several truths about God in this statement. {First, He is the Father of the Lord Jesus, mentioned here with His most complete title.}[Q2] The word "Lord" indicates that the Son of God is the Master and Ruler of His kingdom. "Jesus" is His human name, meaning "Yahweh saves." The last word in His name, "Christ," is the translation of the Greek word for Messiah.

{Second, God is called the Father of mercies.}[Q2] He is the source of all mercies. Warren Wiersbe explained it this way: "To the Jewish people, the phrase *father of* means 'originator of.' Satan is the father of lies (John 8:44) because lies originated with him. According to Genesis 4:21, Jubal was the father of musical instruments because he originated the pipe and the harp. God is the Father of mercies because all mercy originates with Him and can be secured only from Him" (*The Bible Exposition Commentary,* Cook).

{Third, God is called the God of all comfort. This means He is also the ultimate source of encouragement.}[Q3] The Greek word *parakalēsis* means "comfort" and "solace" and is derived from the word *parakaleō,* which means "to draw near" in order to provide consolation or encouragement. We are familiar with the word *paraclete,* referring to one who comes alongside to help. It is used of the Holy Spirit (cf. John 14:26).

{The fourth truth about God is the fact that He comforts us personally when we go through difficult times.}[Q3] The theological truth that He is the God of all comfort suddenly becomes very real and close to our hearts. {But the comfort He gives us has an even greater purpose than just our own encouragement. Paul added that we are comforted "that we may be able to comfort them which are in any trouble, by the comfort wherewith we ourselves are comforted of God" (II Cor. 1:4).}[Q4]

Matthew Henry comments on our text for this week: "We are encouraged to come boldly to the throne of grace, that we may obtain mercy, and find grace to help in time of need. The Lord is able to give peace to the troubled conscience, and to calm the raging passions of the soul. These blessings are given by him, as the Father of his redeemed family.

"It is our Saviour who says, Let not your heart be troubled. All comforts come from God, and our sweetest comforts are in him. He speaks peace to souls by granting the free remission of sins; and he comforts them by the enlivening influences of the Holy Spirit, and by the rich mercies of his grace. He is able to bind up the broken-hearted, to heal the most painful wounds, and also to give hope and joy under the heaviest sorrows" (Matthew *Henry's Concise Commentary,* biblehub.com).

When we have been comforted in hard times, we are to share that comfort with others who are going through similar times. Some years ago, a young wife lost her third child at five months of development. She and her husband were heartbroken but sensed God's presence with them. It was just a few months later, after they had begun a ministry at a new church, that a young mother lost her firstborn shortly before he was to be born. Guess which woman ministered most effectively to that young wife, just as God's comfort was shared with her!

We are comforted (II Cor. 1:5). "Paul explained how he knew this principle to be true. Christians are so intimately joined with Christ that experiences flow from Christ, to believers, through believers, and to others" (Anders, ed., *Holman New Testament Commentary,* Broadman & Holman). Any believer who lives in a close relationship with the Lord is going to have the opportunity to share His comfort with others when they experience hard times. This is especially true when we ourselves have gone through such hard times.

The difficulties Paul experienced were largely due to his public stand for Jesus. Jesus had suffered mockery, rejection, and ultimately death because of the unbelief of His people. Paul was experiencing mockery and rejection, and he would also suffer death in the end. We should not be surprised when we and the message we share with the world are rejected by the people we talk with. In view of the fact that the world is becoming more anti-Christian, we should be prepared for greater persecution and perhaps even martyrdom.

Paul said that the sufferings of Christ abound in us. He used a Greek word that means "to superabound" or "be in excess." The phrase in which this word is found means "overflow unto us so that we suffer like sufferings and become fellow sufferers with Christ" (Robertson, *Word Pictures in the New Testament,* B&H). Paul used the same word to describe our consolation. It also abounds because of our relationship with Him. Are you suffering today? Are you experiencing His consolation?

"The favours God bestows on us, are not only to make us cheerful, but also that we may be useful to others. He sends comforts enough to support such as simply trust in and serve him.

"If we should be brought so low as to despair even of life, yet we may then trust God, who can bring back even from death" (Matthew Henry).

We comfort you (II Cor. 1:6). In this statement we see Paul's explanation of what he said in verse 3. Paul used

himself as the example in his use of "we," giving the Corinthians and us the understanding that this is the kind of love and concern each believer should have for others. His point is that when we are afflicted, it is for the purpose of giving us the opportunity to experience something that we can pass on to others, particularly the "consolation and salvation" we receive.

The word "consolation" refers to the solace or comfort we receive as we go through trials. The word "salvation" refers to the rescue or deliverance that we eventually experience. The wife who lost a baby prior to his birth experienced the comfort of God's presence and eventually the reduction of pain and disappointment. When she sat down with the newlywed mother who had experienced loss, she could reassure her of the Lord's presence and care and that the pain would gradually diminish and even strengthen her future ministry.

God is always in control. "We must never think that trouble is an accident. For the believer, everything is a divine appointment. There are only three possible outlooks a person can take when it comes to the trials of life. If our trials are the products of 'fate' or 'chance,' then our only recourse is to give up. . . . If *we* have to control everything ourselves, then the situation is equally as hopeless. But if *God* is in control, and we trust Him, then we can overcome circumstances with His help" (Wiersbe).

We hope for you (II Cor. 1:7). Paul was very confident in this truth. He had said in the previous verse that the comfort and deliverance the church was experiencing was "effectual in the enduring of the same sufferings which we also suffer." To endure meant to remain constant in their trust and therefore hopeful for what was yet to come. Paul was filled with a strong hope for them. God had worked for him in providing consolation and salvation, and He would also work for them in doing the same thing.

It is somewhat surprising that Paul had such a confident hope for the people in the Corinthian church. We discover in his letters to this church that he had to deal with sectarianism, a lack of unity among the members, serious immorality, their allowance of worldly attitudes among themselves, and the distrust they developed toward him, along with other issues and needs for instruction. {In describing his hope, he used a word that means "to wait with expectation and patience." His hope for them was thus a steadfast one.}[Q5]

Paul's assurance to the church was that just as they were sharing in the same kind of suffering he had experienced (they were partakers), so they would share (be partakers) in the comfort he had experienced. This was also an expression of his confidence that they were not going to allow their trials to turn them away from God. That can be a temptation, for we sometimes come to doubt God's goodness when our trials are extremely difficult and unending.

THE VALUE OF PRAYER

8 For we would not, brethren, have you ignorant of our trouble which came to us in Asia, that we were pressed out of measure, above strength, insomuch that we despaired even of life:

9 But we had the sentence of death in ourselves, that we should not trust in ourselves, but in God which raiseth the dead:

10 Who delivered us from so great a death, and doth deliver: in whom we trust that he will yet deliver us;

11 Ye also helping together by prayer for us, that for the gift bestowed upon us by the means of many persons thanks may be given by many on our behalf.

Burdened beyond measure (II Cor. 1:8). In the previous verses Paul wrote extensively about how God comforts and encourages people when they are experiencing trials. Now he changed subjects, moving from the principle of comfort in general to an explanation of his personal experience. He referred to what he considered to be a life-threatening situation in Asia, but he gave no explanation of what it was. It is often the mark of a mature believer not to speak constantly of his own experiences but to focus on the needs of others.

{His reason for writing about this was probably to let the Corinthians know that he had indeed experienced deep trial. He had said that the comfort he had received he could pass on to them, just as they could do the same for others. Referring to his own severe trial assured them that he was speaking from real experience and not just philosophizing or spouting truth from an academic viewpoint. They could put confidence in his instruction because it had grown out of deep experiences in which he had needed God's presence and help.}[Q6]

{Paul's reference to this trial is described with three phrases in II Corinthians 1:8. First, he had been "pressed out of measure," meaning he had been under great pressure and burdens. Second, he had found it to be "above strength," meaning it was beyond the endurance of normal human stamina. It was the kind of situation in which many would emotionally collapse. Third, it was so threatening he feared for his life.}[Q7]

"We do not know what the specific 'trouble' was, but it was great enough to make Paul think he was going to die. Whether it was peril from his many enemies . . . serious illness, or special satanic attack, we do not know; but we do know that God controlled the circumstances and protected His servant. When God puts His children into the furnace, He keeps His hand on the thermostat and His eye on the thermometer (I Cor. 10:13; I Pet. 1:6-7). Paul may have despaired of life, but God did not despair of Paul" (Wiersbe).

Delivered from death (II Cor. 1:9-10). Whatever the threat was that Paul had faced, it was real. He had truly thought he was not going to survive. One of the benefits of not knowing the exact situation is that it allows us to identify with Paul no matter what we are facing. Maybe it was some kind of serious illness, perhaps some threats by enemies, or even one of his beatings (11:24). It could have been any one of a number of possibilities. Whatever you might be facing today, you can hope in God for a similar kind of deliverance.

{What Paul learned was that we cannot trust in ourselves when certain things are out of our control. Instead, we must trust in the God who is capable of raising the dead!}Q8 In this case, Paul was spared death, and he realized that was a deliverance from God. There is no impossible situation with God; whatever predicament we find ourselves in, we can always have the hope of His working on our behalf. What is humanly impossible is not even a challenge to God. He knows how to deliver us.

Paul's exclamations give the impression that whatever he faced, it was something outside the realm of human help. He had no choice but to cast himself completely upon God; otherwise, his life would have been over. {During such impossible times, our natural propensity is to become afraid, because that is how our human nature tends. In the midst of such fear, however, we can always have hope as long as we are alive. Paul said about God, "We trust that he will yet deliver us"}Q9 (1:10).

Thanks through prayer (II Cor. 1:11). Paul recognized that what God had done for him was an answer to the prayers of the Corinthian—and perhaps other—believers. There is a challenge for continued prayer in the future in this statement. It is connected to the thought at the end of verse 10: "He will yet deliver us; ye also helping together by prayer for us." And in the future, {whenever God answers prayer, there will be rejoicing and thanksgiving from His people. When many pray, many will give thanks for answers.}Q10

Paul had learned firsthand that God is a good and faithful God who never leaves or forsakes us. We find consolation through prayer, both in the middle of a trial and in daily communicated dependence on Him.

—Keith E. Eggert.

QUESTIONS

1. What did Paul express at the beginning of this letter in spite of having problems to deal with?

2. What two things did Paul say God was the Father of?

3. What else did Paul attribute to God, and how did he apply that to us?

4. What is one of the greatest benefits of receiving comfort from God in hard times?

5. What was steadfast in Paul relative to the Corinthian believers?

6. How did Paul let them know he understood their need for consolation and salvation?

7. How did he describe his trial?

8. What did Paul say he learned in his extremely difficult trial?

9. How can we keep from being afraid in times of extreme trial?

10. What did Paul say about prayer and its importance for believers?

—Keith E. Eggert.

Preparing to Teach the Lesson

Not one of us likes to suffer. But if there is some meaning behind the struggle—some greater good that will come out of it—that would help a lot in enduring the suffering. We look now at what God teaches us, through the inspiration of the Holy Spirit, concerning the suffering and consolation of Paul. Paul and some of his traveling and ministering companions suffered in many ways: shipwreck, imprisonment, beatings, verbal abuse, sleepless nights, hungry days, and much more. What did it all mean? Was their suffering the result of Paul's taking a religious stance that was politically incorrect, or his bad choices, or just the variations of circumstance that life seems to provide? In all the suffering, Paul saw a divine purpose that made it all worthwhile.

TODAY'S AIM

Facts: to see God as the source of all comfort.

Principle: to understand that God comforts and consoles us to equip us to comfort others.

Application: to use the comfort we have experienced to actively seek to comfort others.

INTRODUCING THE LESSON

"Suffering for the cause" is common among people. Whether it is a protest march or a sit-in or an outright war with people dying, we have all seen the suffering hero. We may wonder of what use it will be in the long run. Even if we sympathize with the person and the cause, we may think it was the wrong way to go about promoting the cause. We may wonder if it was worth it. Especially when we see suffering missionaries, we may struggle to understand the value of it all.

Our Scripture leaves no such doubt or need for explanation. Emphatically, yes, there is great value in suffering for Christ!

DEVELOPING THE LESSON

1. The God of all comfort (II Cor. 1:3-4). Paul started by blessing the Lord for His mercy and comfort. Mercy usually is brought out as a withholding of penalty due someone, but in this case it may have been the mercy of God in keeping Paul and the others from even worse calamity than that which they did experience. Likewise, we thank God for His mercy in a narrowly missed accident or an illness we do not contract when an epidemic is raging all around us.

Paul had been traveling and preaching the gospel of Christ. It had not proved to be popular. He had suffered much, but he said he had also been comforted much. God is not the God of some comfort once in a while. He is the God of all comfort. This comfort is so great that it can be shared by others to their own great comfort. Paul saw his suffering and comfort as something he could use to comfort others.

"The Apostle . . . reckoned, that whatever favors God conferred upon him, were not given for his own sake merely, but in order that he might have more in his power for helping others. And, unquestionably, when the Lord confers upon us any favor, he in a manner invites us by his example to be generous to our neighbours" (*Calvin's Commentaries,* biblehub.com).

2. Our suffering and consolation (II Cor. 1:5-7). Our suffering and subsequent consolation is, in part, given to us by God to share with others for their consolation. Paul even included the idea that it is also for their salvation. This is not the eternal salvation of their souls but rather their preservation from discouragement and turning from following the Lord. When someone sees you suffer and hears of your comfort, victory, and thankfulness to the Lord, it will greatly lift his spirits and console him. That means suffering is not entirely negative but has the highest use—helping others. There are very few things you and I can do to help others. Suffering is one of them.

Paul mentioned that "our hope of you is stedfast" (vs. 7). He was confident that they would be consoled in their suffering. He was sure they would continue to trust the Lord when the going got tough because he knew the Lord would console them just as He had consoled Paul and his companions. He said this was all for them! When suffering, an immature Christian says, "Why me?" A mature Christian says, "Praise the Lord! This will bring comfort and consolation to others."

3. A great opportunity (II Cor. 1:8-11). Paul did not want to hide the facts of the trouble, even despair, and that it was severe. He may have entertained thoughts that death would be a better alternative to what was going on. Then he remembered that we are all going to die sometime but that meanwhile we can trust in the Lord because He will raise us from the dead. He delivered us from death and hell when He saved us, He continually delivers us from the deathly things of this life, and He will deliver us after death in this physical life to enduring spiritual life with Him in heaven. God has the past, present, and future covered when it comes to death. So we are comforted, consoled, and joyous about living and even suffering for Him.

The huge bonus here is in II Corinthians 1:11: "Ye also helping together by prayer for us." We need not wring our hands in despair at the suffering of others. We can help by prayer. Our problem is that we do not believe praying accomplishes anything. Did not Jesus pray for you when He prayed for those who would later believe (John 17:20)? You and I can pray for the comfort, consolation, and salvation of those who are suffering. We may then be able to help them physically. Nevertheless, physical assistance means less if we are not also lifting them up in prayer.

ILLUSTRATING THE LESSON

When we suffer and God comforts us, it is like a sandwich and a bowl of soup on a cold day.

COMFORT

IN THE MIDST OF DISTRESS

CONCLUDING THE LESSON

I hope that you are not suffering now or that if you are, you are suffering for the right reason. If you are suffering, thank God for the great opportunity to trust Him and receive His comforting hand and presence. You can then share your experience with others who are having a hard time.

ANTICIPATING THE NEXT LESSON

In the next lesson, we will look at II Peter 1:3-14 and the blessing of godliness. Christians need to cultivate godly behavior.

—Brian D. Doud.

PRACTICAL POINTS

1. Ultimately, all true comfort comes from God, no matter what the intermediate means (II Cor. 1:3).
2. God's comfort is not to be hoarded but shared (vs. 4).
3. Those who suffer for Christ shall ultimately be comforted by Christ (vss. 5-7).
4. Be careful of minimizing others' suffering; theirs is as real as yours (vs. 8).
5. God often uses suffering to cause us to lean upon Him even more (vss. 9-10).
6. Never underestimate God's use of your prayers in the deliverance of others (vs. 11).
   —Don Kakavecos.

RESEARCH AND DISCUSSION

1. What do the verses in this week's lesson teach us about the reality of suffering in the life of the Christian (II Cor. 1:4, 8-9)? How does this compare with the teachings of present-day "health, wealth, and prosperity" preachers?
2. How can the comfort God gives us in our suffering be helpful in comforting others? Can you give some examples?
3. How does Paul's sharing his experience with suffering encourage us to be open and honest in our troubles (vss. 8-10)?
4. Why does God allow the believer to suffer (II Cor. 1:9; cf. Rom. 5:3; II Cor. 12:9-10; Jas. 1:3)? What should the Christian remember about the sufferings of this world (Rom. 8:18)?
   —Don Kakavecos.

ILLUSTRATED HIGH POINTS

Partakers of the sufferings (II Cor. 1:7)

Annie Johnson Flint (1866–1932) was a partaker of suffering. As a young woman, she developed a severe case of arthritis that left her crippled and unable to care for herself. In much pain, she suffered greatly for forty years before being received into heavenly comfort (Flint, *Annie Johnson Flint Poems: Volume I,* Eerdmans).

My favorite Annie Flint poem is "What God Hath Promised." It has been set to music and speaks to the heart.

> God hath not promised skies always blue,
> Flower-strewn pathways all our lives through;
> God hath not promised sun without rain,
> Joy without sorrow, peace without pain.
> But God hath promised strength for the day,
> Rest for the labor, light for the way,
> Grace for the trials, help from above,
> Unfailing sympathy, undying love.

In whom we trust (vs. 10)

When I was a teenager, I challenged my parents to trust God for their financial needs, since my father had recently been laid off at work.

At the time, my parents were unbelievers; however, when I asked to conduct a daily devotional time, they agreed. We would read a chapter of the Bible and pray. We would ask the Lord to help others we knew and then to remember the needs of our home.

God was faithful to supply our requests during that trying time. After school one day, my parents became excited when the mail came. There was a letter with a check enclosed, telling them they had overpaid a bill. Their records did not indicate the mistake, but this event was a testimony to my parents of what God could do.
   —James O. Baker.

Golden Text Illuminated

"Our hope of you is stedfast, knowing, that as ye are partakers of the sufferings, so shall ye be also of the consolation" (II Corinthians 1:7).

The whole letter of Second Corinthians is about suffering and consolation. Paul outlines God's promise that the consolation we receive in the Christian life will be much greater than the suffering we are asked to bear. In this most personal of all of Paul's letters, he explained that he found this to be true in his own life.

Paul suffered much in his life (cf. II Cor. 4:8-10; 11:24-28). He at times even despaired of life and felt he had a sentence of death on him (1:8-9). Yes, even the great apostle was brought low by his troubles! I guess we should not feel so bad if things get us down from time to time. Still, it is important that we learn to come through such seasons, experiencing the grace and consolation of the Lord.

One of the ways we receive consolation in our suffering is through others in the body of Christ. We are to bear one another's burdens, and one of the ways we do that is to pray for each other as we experience difficulty, hardship, and suffering (II Cor. 1:11).

"It is evident from this, that the Corinthians had been subjected to trials similar to those which the apostle had endured. . . . Such trials were common in all the early churches; and they served to unite all the friends of the Redeemer in common bonds, and to make them feel that they were one. They had united sorrows; and they had united joys; and they felt they were tending to the same heaven of glory. United sorrows and united consolations tend more than anything else to bind people together. We always have a 'brotherly' feeling for one who suffers as we do; or who has the same kind of joy which we have" (*Barnes' Notes on the Bible,* biblehub.com).

Paul expressed clear confidence that consolation greater than our suffering is available in the Christian life. We experience suffering. We shall experience consolation. What can we do to ensure this?

First, we can make sure we are deeply involved in the body of Christ. Paul certainly was. He prayed for Christians and was prayed for by Christians all over the known world! We want to be locked in and known by our brothers and sisters in the body of Christ so that we can bear the burdens of others and they can bear ours. It is tempting to remain on the fringes these days and not commit ourselves to accountable relationships in the body of Christ, but that will not do in times of suffering. So let us be deeply connected in the body of Christ.

Second, we have to be open about our troubles and difficulties. Each of us should have brothers and sisters we can share our hearts and burdens with. We have to be willing to love others. And there are times when we have to be willing to let others show love to us.

Finally, we have to pray for one another. Paul expressed confidence that consolation would come. He believed in a prayer-hearing and prayer-answering God. Much of our consolation comes mysteriously from God as He upholds us through things we never thought we could bear. Prayer, then, becomes a mighty source of consolation.

—*Jeff VanGoethem.*

Heart of the Lesson

The title of this lesson states correctly that consolation is God's blessing. Our need for comfort, for consolation, is experienced often, and there are different ways to satisfy that need. "Swedish hymnist Lina Sandell Berg served with her father in an evangelistic ministry. As they were traveling by ship, he accidentally fell overboard and drowned. In need of comfort that only God can supply, she wrote the following words that are still sung by Christians around the world: Day by day and with each passing moment, Strength I find to meet my trials here; Trusting in my Father's wise bestowment, I've no cause for worry or for fear" (Zuck, *The Speaker's Quote Book,* Kregel).

1. The comfort of God (II Cor. 1:3-7). This is the heart of this lesson. How encouraging it is to realize that even the Apostle Paul, used so mightily by God, needed His comfort at times! Perhaps this will give you help when you find yourself in need of consolation to help you to go on loving and serving God even when trouble and trials seem to surround you.

We Christians use the word "bless" a lot as we pray. We want God to bless us and others we pray for. We usually want God to give good things to us and to those we pray for.

As used in the Bible, however, and especially in II Corinthians 1:3, "blessed" means God is to be praised. Paul was not asking God for anything; rather, he was telling the Corinthians and us by application that our Heavenly Father is to be praised for who He is and what He has done and is doing for us.

2. The prayer of Paul and God's people (II Cor. 1:8-11). Paul's friends needed to know they were not the only ones who faced difficulties. He too,

while hazarding his life for the cause of Christ, faced problems. Some of those were even life-threatening. Warrior though he was, he was not exempt from discouragement. He referred to a specific instance to encourage the Corinthians in their walk with the Lord.

The apostle's reflection on that past experience reminded him that since God had delivered him and his helpers from death, He would do so again in the future if that was His will. It is a good thing for us to never forget all that God has done for us in the past as we battle the storms of life in the present and in the future. God never forsakes His own. We do not always get what we think we need or want, but God knows what is best for us. We need to trust Him through thick and thin.

"[Paul] declares . . . that he entertains the assured hope that it will not be vain, that he has been afflicted, and has received consolation for their advantage. . . . He endured with fortitude so many hardships for the sake of the gospel" (*Calvin's Commentaries,* biblehub.com).

The Corinthian Christians needed to know that their earlier prayers for Paul when he faced great conflict had been of help to him. God answered their prayers, and Paul's life was saved. Apparently, Titus had brought a good report to him about the folks back at Corinth. They had interceded on behalf of the apostle and his work, and God had brought deliverance to him and those with him.

Think of it! We can and should intercede on behalf of those we support with our money to carry the message of the gospel to faraway lands. God expects us to do this. He is praised, and we are blessed as we hold each other up in prayer.

—*Robert P. Lightner.*

World Missions

Hopefully, we all know how it feels when we learn that a desperately needed prayer has been answered. It is a mixture of excitement, joy, and awe. We know that God can do all things; yet when we hear of His work, it seems unbelievable!

We also know how it feels when someone we love is facing insurmountable troubles. When he is suffering, we suffer with him. Our heart breaks with his. How true II Corinthians 1:7 is when it says, "Ye are partakers of the sufferings"!

Two stories that exemplify this come from India. There is a terrorist organization called the Rashtriya Swayamsevak Sangh. It is also known as the RSS. It is a Hindu-based terror network, whose mission is to subvert and drive out all religions that are not Hindu.

"Hindu-nationalist informants live in nearly every village and report on the activities of Christians, resulting in attacks and arrests. When Christians are attacked, they often drop charges against their attackers to show forgiveness as a witness for Christ. Churches have been demolished and burned, worship gatherings have been disrupted, crosses in graveyards have been vandalized, and Bibles and other Christian literature have been confiscated and burned. Many pastors have been beaten and jailed, and several are martyred each year. Christians are often arrested and held for up to three weeks after being falsely accused of forcing Hindus to convert to Christianity" (persecution.com/india).

The RSS actively burns down churches and pastors' homes. They attack, beat, and even kill followers of Jesus. For over thirty years, the RSS has attacked a particular Indian pastor's family and his ministry. For the purposes of this article, we will call them the Titus family. The RSS burned down the ministry's facility twice and has tried to harm the Titus family many times, using many different schemes. They even promised a year's wages to any Hindu who killed the pastor.

Recently, two main leaders of the RSS went to the pastor's home, wishing to speak to him. You can imagine Pastor Titus's surprise when the men started confessing to the many years of plots and schemes in their effort to stop the work God was doing in their area. They told him of a recent plot that was hatched to harm their childrens ministry; in the end, the leaders had refused to carry it out.

Do you think the Titus family ever thought this peace would be achieved? For so many years, they had offered their prayers to God over this persecution. They and their friends all over the world had prayed and knew the second part of II Corinthians 1:7: "So shall ye be also of the consolation." When God works, He does things that are so amazing that no man can take credit for them.

In another part of India, the village elders agreed to let a foreign ministry dig a much-needed well. The few Christians in the village believed that this would be a great outreach to the area. But after digging six hundred feet, there was nothing but dusty rocks. The little group of Christians gathered weekly to pray at the dry well, asking God for a miracle.

A year passed. One morning, the village woke to streams of water coming out of the well's pipe! When the foreign ministry returns to enhance the well system, the Christians are going to baptize fifteen new believers at the well site. When we pray for others, we partake in their suffering. But when God moves, we also share in their joy.

—*Christina Futrell.*

The Jewish Aspect

When Paul experienced extreme sufferings, he praised the church at Corinth for standing by him through prayer (II Cor. 1:11). As a well-trained Jew, Paul appreciated intercessory prayer. Jews today also emphasize intercession in their prayer lives. Like Christians, Jews recognize various elements in prayer, including petition, confession, praise, meditation, thanksgiving, and adoration, as well as intercession.

The Hebrew words for intercession are the verb *palal (pll)* and its corresponding noun *tefillah*. Jewish scholars recognize that in "Scripture the stem *pll* signifies 'to interpose, judge, hope.' These meanings are eminently suited to the biblical conception of prayer as intercession and self-scrutiny leading to hope" (Abrahams and Jacobs, "Prayer," www.jewishvirtuallibrary. org). Examples of intercession in the Scriptures include Abraham, the first instance of one who interceded. He interceded for Ishmael (Gen. 17:18) and for Sodom (18:23-33), and he "is called a prophet . . . at the precise moment when his intercessory powers are invoked (Gen. 20:7)" (Unterman, "Forgiveness," www.jewishvirtuallibrary. org). Other examples are Job (Job 1:5; 42:8), David (II Sam. 24:17), Solomon (I Kgs. 8:12-53), Elijah (17:20-23), Daniel (Dan. 9:3-19), and Nehemiah (Neh. 1:4-11).

The classic example for Jews, however, is Moses. He was a man characterized by passionate intercession on behalf of others. He did so on behalf of Pharaoh and Egypt (Ex. 9:27-33), even though he knew Pharaoh would continue with a hard heart. He interceded on behalf of Miriam after she challenged his authority (Num. 12:10-15). "And the Lord said unto Moses, . . . Now therefore let me alone, that my wrath may wax hot against them, and that I may consume them: . . . And Moses besought the Lord, . . . Remember Abraham, Isaac, and Israel, thy servants, . . . And the Lord repented of the evil which he thought to do unto his people" (Ex. 32:9-14).

Moses' climactic example was his intercession for Israel at the time of their rebellion with the golden calf (Ex. 32). This event was emphasized by the psalmist (Ps. 106:23). "According to the Talmud, Moses felt that Israel's sin was so serious that there was no possibility of intercession on their behalf (Rosh Hashanah 17b). At this point, God appeared to Moses and taught him the Thirteen Attributes, saying: 'Whenever Israel sins, let them recite this [the Thirteen Attributes] in its proper order and I will forgive them.' Thus this appeal to God's mercy reassures us that repentance is always possible and that God always awaits our return" (Eisenberg, "The 13 Attributes of Mercy," www.myjewishlearning.com).

During the Israelites' failures, Moses continued to intercede with God because he believed God's mercy and forgiveness are part of His unchangeable nature (cf. Ex. 34:6-9; Num. 14:13-21; Deut. 9:16-29). Jews believe that God is near "to all that call upon him in truth" (Ps. 145:18). Since this is the case, why is an intercessor needed?

Jews recognize that merely having an intercessor is no guarantee that God will respond favorably. They observe that both Jeremiah (15:1) and Ezekiel (14:13-20) testify that "God will reject even the mediation of the most righteous when Israel's sins have exceeded the limit of His forbearance" (Unterman). All of God's people should live so as to glorify His precious name.

—R. Larry Overstreet.

Guiding the Superintendent

Of top priority for believers is offering comfort to others. A quick read of II Corinthians 1:3-11 will reveal a repeated use of the idea. Paul used one word that gets translated by two words—"comfort" and "consolation." The root word, *paraclete,* usually refers to the Holy Spirit coming alongside a person for comfort and encouragement.

The believer is encouraged to come alongside another person to offer comfort as that person is going through struggles. This week's text is the opening section of II Corinthians. In this section the Bible explains how God allows the believer to go through struggles so that he can, in turn, help others.

DEVOTIONAL OUTLINE

1. Suffering enables us to comfort others (II Cor. 1:3-7). As our suffering level goes up, so does our ability to comfort. If we are to help others bear their burdens, we need to experience suffering ourselves.

To experience suffering leaves a believer with an indebtedness to help others. Paul did not seek prayer to remove his sufferings. He prayed that others would be helped through his sufferings.

2. Suffering enables us to be patient (II Cor. 1:8-9). Patient endurance is a mark of spiritual maturity (Heb. 12:1-7). If we become bitter or critical of God, our trials work against us instead of for us. The comfort of God can be felt only as it comes through patient endurance. Suffering is a vital and necessary part of the Christian process.

Because we know that God has purposes for our suffering, when suffering does come, we can trust God to do what He knows is best for us.

3. Suffering enables us to pray (II Cor. 1:10-11). It is only as we suffer that we will experience true community with other believers. Paul felt that he would never have made it through his sufferings without the prayers of believers; the people in the Corinthian church were one with Paul because of their prayers.

"[Paul] declares his confidence in the Corinthians to be such, that he entertains the assured hope that it will not be vain, that he has been afflicted, and has received consolation for their advantage. The false apostles made every effort to turn to Paul's reproach everything that befell him. Had they obtained their wish, the afflictions which he endured for their salvation, had been vain and fruitless; they would have derived no advantage from the consolations with which the Lord refreshed him. . .

"His afflictions tended to promote the comfort of believers, as furnishing them with occasion of confirmation, on their perceiving that he suffered willingly, and endured with fortitude so many hardships for the sake of the gospel. (*Calvin's Commentaries,* biblehub.com).

When we understand the true nature and purpose of prayer, we are well prepared to go to God in prayer for our struggling brothers and sisters.

CHILDREN'S CORNER

Most children want to steer as far away from suffering as possible. This lesson will help them understand why God allows suffering.

Suffering often leads to disunity. Yet children can also learn that suffering could actually help them and their friends and family stand closer together, like soldiers who keep watch on their buddies in battle.

—*Martin R. Dahlquist.*

SCRIPTURE LESSON TEXT

II PET. 1:3 According as his divine power hath given unto us all things that *pertain* unto life and godliness, through the knowledge of him that hath called us to glory and virtue:

4 Whereby are given unto us exceeding great and precious promises: that by these ye might be partakers of the divine nature, having escaped the corruption that is in the world through lust.

5 And beside this, giving all diligence, add to your faith virtue; and to virtue knowledge;

6 And to knowledge temperance; and to temperance patience; and to patience godliness;

7 And to godliness brotherly kindness; and to brotherly kindness charity.

8 For if these things be in you, and abound, they make *you that ye shall* neither *be* barren nor unfruitful in the knowledge of our Lord Jesus Christ.

9 But he that lacketh these things is blind, and cannot see afar off, and hath forgotten that he was purged from his old sins.

10 Wherefore the rather, brethren, give diligence to make your calling and election sure: for if ye do these things, ye shall never fall:

11 For so an entrance shall be ministered unto you abundantly into the everlasting kingdom of our Lord and Saviour Jesus Christ.

12 Wherefore I will not be negligent to put you always in remembrance of these things, though ye know *them,* and be established in the present truth.

13 Yea, I think it meet, as long as I am in this tabernacle, to stir you up by putting *you* in remembrance;

14 Knowing that shortly I must put off *this* my tabernacle, even as our Lord Jesus Christ hath shewed me.

NOTES

Blessing of Godliness

Lesson Text: II Peter 1:3-14

Related Scriptures: Ephesians 4:17-32; I John 2:28—3:10

TIME: about A.D. 64

PLACE: unknown

GOLDEN TEXT—"For if these things be in you, and abound, they make you that ye shall neither be barren nor unfruitful in the knowledge of our Lord Jesus Christ" (II Peter 1:8).

Introduction

The list of God-breathed books listed in our Bibles form the authoritative canon of Scripture. These books are considered equally inspired, but since they were produced over a long period of time, they were recognized as authoritative at different points of history.

While the Old Testament took over a thousand years to be completed, the entire New Testament was written in only about a fifty-year time span.

Since there were other books circulating in the early church (Luke 1:1-4), certain tests were applied to decide whether a book was canonical. Among these were apostolicity, orthodoxy, and universality. This meant that a book came from an apostle or one closely associated with an apostle, contained sound doctrine, and was universally accepted by the church.

For whatever reason, II Peter was not as well-known or as quickly accepted as Peter's first letter. But none of the reasons offered to argue that Peter is not the author are ultimately convincing. In time, II Peter was recognized as canonical.

LESSON OUTLINE

I. DIVINE POWER—II Pet. 1:3-4

II. DISCIPLESHIP PRIORITIES—II Pet. 1:5-9

III. DILIGENT PERSEVERANCE—II Pet. 1:10-11

IV. DEPARTURE PREDICTED—II Pet. 1:12-14

Exposition: Verse by Verse

DIVINE POWER

II PET. 1:3 According as his divine power hath given unto us all things that pertain unto life and godliness, through the knowledge of him that hath called us to glory and virtue:

4 Whereby are given unto us exceeding great and precious promises: that by these ye might be partakers of the divine nature, having

escaped the corruption that is in the world through lust.

Particular privileges (II Pet. 1:3). Peter opened this letter in a fashion characteristic of the letter writing of the day. He did not identify his recipients as in his first letter, but they were most likely the believers addressed there (I Pet. 1:1; II Pet. 3:1).

As will be mentioned in next week's lesson, many New Testament epistles begin with a doctrinal section followed by more practical matters. In this letter, though, Peter began with some very practical matters related to Christian living. Before encouraging his readers to be diligent in Christian living, he reminded them that the mighty power of God had been given to believers, enabling them to live according to God's will.

Some claim that God always wants us to be healthy and wealthy. In contrast, II Peter 1:3 says that God's power enables us to have everything that we need for "life and godliness." All that is needed for spiritual health—and especially what is necessary to please God—has been given to us through knowing Christ (II Tim. 3:16-17).

As God's children, we have been called "to glory and virtue" (II Pet. 1:3). This can mean that God called us to live good lives here in order to share in His glory later. Some manuscripts read "to glory," while others read "by his own glory," indicating that it is God's glory and virtue (or goodness) calling us to Himself. As Paul said, "The goodness of God leadeth thee to repentance" (Rom. 2:4). Either way, "the apostle is making their divine call the ground for his appeal for holy living" (Green, *2 Peter and Jude,* InterVarsity).

Precious promises (II Pet. 1:4). As God's people, we have "great and precious promises." {Among these are the promise of eternal life (I John 2:25), answered prayer (5:14), the forgiveness of sins (Acts 10:43), the presence of the Holy Spirit (2:38; 5:32), and God's providential care (Rom. 8:28), to name a few.}Q1

{Not only are we recipients of "divine power" (II Pet. 1:3), but we are also "partakers of the divine nature" (vs. 4). This does not mean that we can evolve into gods, as one cult teaches; nor does it mean that we will ultimately be absorbed into the divine, as some Eastern religions claim.

Peter was merely saying that when we come to Christ, commit our lives to Him, and diligently pursue holy living, we become more like the Lord Himself.}Q2 Consequently, people should be able to see something of the Lord Jesus in us as they observe our lives. This is possible only because we have escaped the corruption that permeates the world because of lust. "By *the world* Peter means society alienated from God by rebellion" (Green).

The Greek word for "lust" in the New Testament refers to a strong desire, usually an evil one. But context will determine whether it is a good or bad desire. For example, this same word is used twice in Luke 22:15 when Jesus told the Twelve, "With desire I have desired to eat this passover with you before I suffer." Peter obviously used it in a negative sense when describing the evil desires of this world. "Peter did not see the material world itself as evil; what corrupts is the selfish desire that dominates human beings" (Schreiner, *1, 2 Peter, Jude,* Holman).

DISCIPLESHIP PRIORITIES

5 And beside this, giving all diligence, add to your faith virtue; and to virtue knowledge;

6 And to knowledge temperance; and to temperance patience; and to patience godliness;

7 And to godliness brotherly kindness; and to brotherly kindness charity.

8 For if these things be in you, and abound, they make you that ye shall neither be barren nor unfruitful in the knowledge of our Lord Jesus Christ.

9 But he that lacketh these things is blind, and cannot see afar off, and hath forgotten that he was purged from his old sins.

Add to your faith (II Pet. 1:5-7). Although the "divine power" (vs. 3) and the "divine nature" (vs. 4) are essential in the entire scheme of redemption, {Peter encouraged his readers to put forth diligent effort to add to their initial faith— that is, to grow as disciples of Christ.}Q3

To be sure, faith is at the root of salvation, but faith does not stop at the point of one's coming to Christ. Our faith must grow and develop. This includes adding various Christian graces to our faith in Christ. The list given by Peter is similar to what Paul called the fruit of the Spirit (Gal. 5:22-23).

The first quality to be added to our faith is virtue. Virtue can be understood as goodness or moral excellence. Greeks often used this word to describe those who were morally virtuous.

While unsaved people may not be morally virtuous—although some may appear to be so—they can usually recognize this quality in others. When professed Christians are not morally virtuous, their failures are quickly highlighted by unbelievers as a sure sign of hypocrisy. It therefore behooves us to live as blamelessly as possible. This will not only benefit us in our own spiritual growth but also serve as a vibrant testimony for Christ.

{To virtue, knowledge needs to be added. While we may think of the knowledge of the Scriptures, which is invaluable, that may not be what Peter had in mind. As used in the ancient world, "knowledge" often meant practical wisdom—namely, the ability to distinguish good from evil.}Q4

As used by the Gnostic-anticipating false teachers in Peter's day, "knowledge" meant a secret knowledge given only to a privileged few. But as Peter makes clear, knowledge is available to all and should be pursued in our faith development.

Of course, certain types of knowledge have no value for the believer and should not be embraced (Rom. 16:19). At the other extreme, however, Christians may develop an anti-intellectual attitude and even glory in ignorance. Since all truth is God's truth, we have nothing to fear from true knowledge, whether it is about God, His Word, or His creation (cf. I Tim. 6:20-21).

{Temperance has often been understood in reference to alcohol. Although this is included, temperance is not limited to self-control in just this one area. "It meant controlling the passions instead of being controlled by them" (Green).}Q5 Elsewhere (ch. 2), the apostle described the false teachers as anything but temperate. They are depicted as presumptuous, sensual, animal-like, filled with adulterous thoughts, and servants of corruption.

True believers are to be examples of self-control. To be sure, most of us have to admit that there are numerous areas in our lives that need restraint. That being so, the exhortation to add temperance to our faith is even more relevant.

Patience is better understood as endurance or perseverance. While we can all think of people or situations that try our patience, Peter was primarily dealing with steadfastness. This is another virtue that most of us feel we need to develop more fully.

Michael Green described this virtue as "the temper of mind which is unmoved by difficulty and distress, and which can withstand the two Satanic agencies of opposition from the world without and enticement from the flesh within." This same word is used in Hebrews 12:2 to describe the fact that Jesus "endured the cross" for us. Godliness must also be added to our faith if we are to grow in Christ. This particular word in Greek is not often found in the New Testament, as it was used of religion even among pagans. It was, however, used of people who were conscientious in performing their religious duties. The word describes Cornelius and is translated "devout" (Acts 10:2).

"Christ has given believers everything to be godly, and yet believers must pursue godliness. The term godliness refers to piety or, more simply, to living a life that is like God" (Schreiner).

"Brotherly kindness" (II Pet. 1:7) translates the Greek word *philadelphia*. It literally means "brotherly love."

Since Christians are all part of the family of God, we need to love our brothers and sisters in the Lord in a manner befitting a loving family. Obviously, not all family members get along with each other, but in the family of God, brotherly love must be the norm. Even when we disagree, we must not be disagreeable!

{"Charity" in II Peter 1:7 is the Greek *agapē* and is frequently translated "love" (cf. Matt. 5:44; Rom. 13:8-9; Eph. 2:4; 4:16; 5:25). Being God's motivation for sending His Son into the world (John 3:16) and the identifying mark of true believers (13:35), love is the crowning virtue to be added to our faith (Col. 3:14).}[Q6] As Paul pointed out, we can be extremely gifted, possess great faith, and even make great sacrifices (I Cor. 13:1-3), but without love we are nothing.

Abound in your faith (II Pet. 1:8-9). When a person comes to Christ, he does not need a lot of faith—just a simple faith willing to trust in the crucified Christ to forgive his sins. Such a person is a true Christian, but he is only a babe in Christ. {To remain in that state is to be "barren" and "unfruitful," certainly not a description of a growing disciple (I Cor. 3:1-3).}[Q7]

To abound in the qualities listed above

means we are increasing in measure, like a tree growing taller each year and producing an increasing amount of fruit. Of course, we should not view the aforementioned graces in a checklist fashion, trying to complete one, then moving on to another. All these virtues need to be developed and increased as we make progress in the Christian life (I Pet. 2:1-2).

Since Peter emphasized knowledge in this letter, it is likely that this was in contrast to the false teachers, who were stressing an esoteric knowledge of which they boasted. These false teachers likely claimed their knowledge was already complete, so there would be no need for them to add to their faith. Significantly, Peter's last exhortation in the letter is to grow in knowledge (II Pet. 3:18).

On the other hand, if a believer lacks the things Peter said need to be added to faith, it reveals grave inadequacies. Hence, this person is "blind, and cannot see afar off" (1:9). How can a person be both blind and nearsighted? "Such a man is blind to heavenly things, and engrossed in the earthly; he cannot see what is afar off, but only what is near. This makes excellent sense in view of the immorality and earthiness of the false teachers" (Green).

How can a person forget that he has been forgiven? Peter here was specifically referring to sins committed prior to conversion. For whatever reason, this person deliberately puts out of his mind the fact that he has been pardoned. That being so, there is a diminished desire to add the graces previously enumerated.

DILIGENT PERSEVERANCE

10 Wherefore the rather, brethren, give diligence to make your calling and election sure: for if ye do these things, ye shall never fall:

11 For so an entrance shall be ministered unto you abundantly into the everlasting kingdom of our Lord and Saviour Jesus Christ.

Someone has said that the proof of the profession is in the perseverance of the professor. This is the emphasis of Peter when exhorting his readers to certify their position in Christ.

"*Make your calling and election* sure is an appeal that goes to the heart of the paradox of election and free will. The New Testament characteristically makes room for both without attempting to resolve the apparent antinomy. So here; election comes from God alone—but man's behaviour is the proof or disproof of it" (Green).

Though Christ was "foreordained before the foundation of the world" (I Pet. 1:20) to be our Saviour, He also had to come to earth, obey the Father's will, and secure our redemption on the cross. So it is with the Christian. We were "elect according to the foreknowledge of God" (vs. 2). Or as Paul put it, "He hath chosen us in him before the foundation of the world" (Eph. 1:4). We must nevertheless repent, believe the gospel (Mark 1:15), and then live according to the gospel (Acts 2:41-42; 13:43; Phil. 1:27).

{Living as we should, abounding in Christian virtues, gives us assurance that our profession of faith is genuine.}Q8 "Those who live ungodly lives show no evidence that they truly belong to God, that they have genuinely received forgiveness" (Schreiner).

{For those who persevere in the faith, "the everlasting kingdom of our Lord and Saviour Jesus Christ" (II Pet. 1:11) awaits.}Q9 We are already a part of Christ's kingdom, but one day we will be welcomed into the eternal kingdom (II Tim. 4:18).

DEPARTURE PREDICTED

12 Wherefore I will not be negligent to put you always in remembrance of these things, though ye know them, and be established in the present truth.

13 Yea, I think it meet, as long as I am in this tabernacle, to stir you up by putting you in remembrance;

14 Knowing that shortly I must put off this my tabernacle, even as our Lord Jesus Christ hath shewed me.

When Peter wrote these words, he knew that his days were numbered and that before long he would be executed—something Christ had predicted many years earlier (John 21:18).

{Knowing that he was going to lay aside his "tabernacle" (II Pet. 1:14)—his earthly body—Peter wanted his fellow saints to have a written record of his instructions.}Q10 Like Peter's readers, we may "be established in the present truth" (vs. 12), but we need ongoing reminders.

—*John Alva Owston.*

QUESTIONS

1. What are some of the great promises given to us as believers?

2. What does it mean that we are "partakers of the divine nature" (II Pet. 1:4)? What does this *not* mean?

3. What does it mean to "add to your faith" (vs. 5)?

4. What kind of knowledge was Peter likely talking about?

5. What is temperance? Why is this important?

6. Why is love so vital for the Christian?

7. Why is a barren and unfruitful believer a contradiction?

8. What is involved in making our calling and election sure?

9. What are the results of being diligent in Christian living?

10. Why did Peter write this letter? What did he know about his own future?

—*John Alva Owston.*

Preparing to Teach the Lesson

Our lesson this week reminds us that the Christian life is truly difficult to live out every day. But as Christians we are also provided with all the tools and resources we need so that we can be successful in any situation. Our lesson reminds us of the power of God's Word to build us up and provide us the victory we need daily.

TODAY'S AIM

Facts: to show the resources we have as Christians to live godly lives.

Principle: to understand that God has already provided us with all that we need to live godly lives.

Application: to learn to use the resources God gives us to live the way God wants us to.

INTRODUCING THE LESSON

Over and over again we hear the claim that Christianity takes the fun out of life. But in reality, that is not true. It is exciting to discover what God can do for us daily when we fully trust Him. When we lean on our Lord Jesus for all that we need, we can live a godly life of exciting faith. Our lesson this week shows us that God has not left us alone to somehow find a way to live a godly life. He has already put all the resources in place for us to succeed.

DEVELOPING THE LESSON

1. Jesus has already given us His resources for godly living (II Pet. 1:3-4). No believer has any excuse for living an ungodly life. Peter declared that Jesus has given us the divine power we need to live a godly life. When He called us, He gave us all we needed to reflect His glory. With His power also came all His wonderful promises. These tell us that when we follow Him we will share in His holy nature and have His power to resist wrong desires.

Help your students to see that on our own we cannot be victorious over sin. We need to trust Jesus to take charge and sustain us. Without Him, we will be defeated. Have class members share experiences of defeat that were turned to victory through trusting Jesus.

2. Growing in Christ leads to productive godliness (II Pet. 1:5-9). Here Peter was talking about the application of God's promises to our lives. "Virtue," or moral excellence, comes from knowing our Lord Jesus. As we grow in our knowledge of Him, we grow in "temperance," or self-control. Remind the students that we now have His power for this. This self-control leads to patient endurance, which is where we fall short quite often. But it is this endurance that is making us more godly, more like Jesus. Remind the class how patient our Lord is with us.

We have not yet reached our goal. Our godliness shows us how to love others, and the more we love, the closer we grow in likeness to Jesus. When we learn to genuinely love others, we are more useful to our Lord and bear more fruit for Him. This will slowly increase as we learn more and more about Jesus. If we are not growing, we are stagnant. We have forgotten how God has cleansed us from our old, sinful ways. We are therefore lacking in our vision, being unable to see fully how good God has been to us.

Remind the class that it is dangerous to forget how far our God has brought us from our old lives. We dare not forget His grace to us, for doing so will become a roadblock in our growth toward Christlikeness.

3. Show yourselves as Christians as you enter the eternal kingdom (II Pet. 1:10-11). Too many people in the world are kept from following our Lord because they have not seen Him in us. This is sad. Peter knew how we can fall so easily, so he challenged his readers to work hard to live as Jesus did. Jesus called us to be His children. As we prove our holy calling, we will not stumble along the way or drop out of the journey. We can then expect a glorious welcome "into the everlasting kingdom of our Lord." Such a reward is worth waiting for.

4. Remember the Word of God (II Pet. 1:12-14). In the Christian life, the Word is exceedingly important. Too many Christians think they can be solid Christians without studying the Word. Peter reminds his readers to pay attention to Scripture. That is where the truth of God is. Peter wanted to keep reminding his readers of that. We can stand firm in the truth only when we read Scripture and know it deep down in our hearts. As a leader of the early church, Peter knew it was his responsibility to constantly point people to the Word as long as he was alive. He was very aware that his days on earth were short. Therefore, he was all the more fervent in passing on the truth to believers.

Note the fervor of Peter in his passing on the truth of God's Word so that his hearers might grow in Christ. Should we not have the same kind of passion both for God's Word and for growing more like Jesus? Peter told his readers that he was going to work hard at this in the little time he had left. It was his desire that long after he was gone, they would remember what he had taught them about standing firm in the truth and living a godly life.

Emphasize to the class that as Christians we are called to equip one another with the truths of God's Word. That is

what builds pure and godly lives. When we study the Bible seriously, truths become cemented in our hearts and have room to grow in our lives day by day.

ILLUSTRATING THE LESSON

God has already given us all that we need to live godly lives. It is simply a matter of our using these resources—applying His Word and its promises and acting in His power.

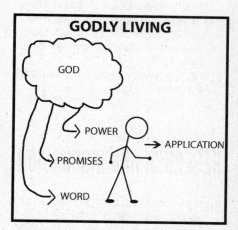

CONCLUDING THE LESSON

Strength in the Christian life comes only by drawing close to God. We draw close to God as we allow Him to speak to us as we study His Word. When we neglect the truths of Scripture, we become weak Christians. We soon become ineffective in our Christian lives and in our daily task of witnessing to others. The body of Christ is only as strong as its individual members. When we seriously study the Word, it makes the entire body stronger.

ANTICIPATING THE NEXT LESSON

In our lesson next week, we will examine Galatians 5:18—6:10 and the blessings of bearing abundant spiritual fruit to the glory of God.

—A. Koshy Muthalaly.

PRACTICAL POINTS

1. We should never complain that the Christian life is too hard; we have been given all we need to live it gloriously (II Pet. 1:3).
2. God has given us His nature; we must live it out in practice (vss. 4-7).
3. To neglect the qualities of the Spirit that we have been given is to inexcusably rob ourselves (vss. 8-9).
4. Living daily in God's power brings assurance that we are really His (vss. 10-11).
5. We will never outgrow the need for reminders of the truth (vss. 12-14).
—Kenneth A. Sponsler.

RESEARCH AND DISCUSSION

1. How do God's promises make us partakers of His nature (II Pet. 1:4)? What is our part in this relationship?
2. How do we add to our lives virtues that can be received only from God (vss. 5-6)?
3. Why does love stand last in Peter's list while it is first in Paul's (II Pet. 1:7; cf. I Cor. 13:13)? Why is there no discrepancy in this?
4. What is the spiritual condition of a person who has forgotten that he has been cleansed from past sins (II Pet. 1:9)?
5. How is it possible to make our "calling and election sure" (vs. 10)? Is that within human capacity? Explain.
6. What can we do to refresh each other's memory of the truths we have received (vs. 13)?
—Kenneth A. Sponsler.

ILLUSTRATED HIGH POINTS

Given unto us all things (II Pet. 1:3)

Today's supermarkets can average 46,000 square feet in size and offer an average of 38,718 different items. We can usually find everything we want at the local store.

I grew up in a small town. Sixty-five years ago, our local, 900-square-foot store provided all that we needed. Back then, our mothers cooked more from scratch than from boxes.

Peter declared that God has given every believer all that is needed for life and godliness. He then mentioned a list of specifics that will enable us to be effective servants of the Lord.

Blind, and cannot see afar off (vs.9)

Christ has opened the eyes (mind) of those who have believed. It is possible, however, for one to shut his eyes to what he does not wish to see.

There is an old story about a desert nomad who woke up hungry. He lit a lamp and began eating some dates. He noticed one had a worm in it, so he threw it out. He tried another, but it also had a worm, so he threw that one out. Then, reasoning that if this continued, he would not have any dates left to eat, he put out his lamp and continued eating.

And so it is—many prefer denial and ignorance instead of the truth, continuing in the direction that only causes grief.

In remembrance of these (vs. 12)

It seems that Christians regularly need reminders of previously learned biblical truths. Indeed, much of what we read and hear on Sundays is something we have heard before. There is little that is absolutely new. Even so, sometimes we feel our minds are like a sieve. The information goes in, but it is soon forgotten.
—David A. Hamburg.

Golden Text Illuminated

"For if these things be in you, and abound, they make you that ye shall neither be barren nor unfruitful in the knowledge of our Lord Jesus Christ" (II Peter 1:8).

Our golden text for this week concisely illustrates the truth that, to understand any statement of Scripture, it is necessary to look at its context. Peter speaks of "these things"; to what things is he referring? The answer in this case is easy, although it may take a lifetime to fully grasp. In verses 5-7 we find a list of eight character qualities that the apostle urges us to diligently cultivate. They are quite similar to the ninefold fruit of the Spirit listed by Paul in Galatians 5:22-23.

Other features covering this lesson will delve into the gist of these qualities; here we will focus on what Peter promises if they "be in you, and abound." What happens if the preceding eight qualities are present in our lives in increasing measure?

The phrase "they make you that ye shall neither be" is a somewhat fancy way of saying, "they will keep you from being." What is important are the two words that Peter next uses in telling us what the diligent cultivation of the qualities mentioned above will prevent. Let us focus on these key terms.

"Barren" and "unfruitful" are close synonyms that reinforce each other with subtle distinctions in nuance. "Barren" here does not refer to women who are unable to have children (a different Greek word is used in those cases); it rather speaks of being useless and unproductive in one's work or lifestyle. The word has been applied to trees that bear no fruit and to fields in which nothing grows.

"Unfruitful" conveys the same essential meaning, with the added nuance of being idle and lazy, of not being employed in any useful service. James uses the term to speak of a faith that is useless (2:20), and an extrabiblical source warns against speaking a "careless" word, that is, one better left unsaid.

Needless to say, if we bear the name of Christ, none of us should ever want to be characterized by these traits or known for them in any way! And the promise of our text is that if we by God's grace cultivate the qualities listed earlier, we will be spared from unfruitfulness and useless futility.

But Peter's concern is not merely focused on our lives in general. Most unbelievers would rather not be characterized by uselessness and insignificance. Peter specifically promises that walking in the aforementioned qualities of grace will keep us from being unfruitful "in the knowledge of our Lord Jesus Christ." Does this imply that there is a knowledge of Christ that can be useless, availing nothing? That seems to be precisely Peter's point.

Wherever the gospel of Jesus Christ is proclaimed, knowledge of Him is imparted in varying degrees to all who hear. For many, that knowledge affects little more than theoretical thinking processes; it consists of facts to be stored away. For others, that knowledge is accepted personally, but not always with full faith and commitment. The soil of such people's hearts is rocky or filled with thorns.

Then there is knowledge of Christ that transforms the lives of all who receive it. That is the knowledge that Peter exhorts us to make sure we have and live by. May we heed his words!

—*Kenneth Sponsler.*

Heart of the Lesson

There is nothing God would like to see more in His children than a display of His divine nature. Since they have been reborn by Him and indwelt by His Spirit, it seems quite natural that there should be evidence of godliness in them. If there is not, it certainly is not the fault of God.

1. Godliness is possible (II Pet. 1:3-4). The Apostle Peter was explicitly clear in stating that Christians have been given the things that enable them to be godly. Through knowing the Lord and believing His precious promises, they can exhibit moral traits that reflect the divine nature. Believers in Christ no longer have to show the deficiencies of the old nature that characterized their past. They are new people with the ability to live new lives.

As a result, there is no need for people who truly know Christ to live as though they did not know Him. Christians are people God has created, called, and converted. The path they now tread should be 180 degrees different from their former way of life.

2. Diligence is necessary (II Pet. 1:5-11). The recipients of Peter's epistle were people of faith in that they knew the Lord. That was fundamental to their being able to develop godly behavior. God had given them what was necessary to do so, but at this point they needed to make the decision to pursue a deep relationship with the Lord.

To their faith they needed to add additional virtues, each one being built upon the previous one. After listing them, Peter said that only a spiritually blind person does not see their value, and for a second time he said his readers must be diligent to obtain them. The decision must be made to begin the quest.

One often hears the phrase "a mile wide and an inch deep" when speaking of the shape of the Christian church in various places. In other words, many in those places have come to faith in Christ, but they remain largely untaught and are thus shallow in their understanding of the faith.

How would others define you or your church in this regard? How would you define yourself? When looking at Peter's list of virtues to add to one's faith, where would you place yourself? This can be a sobering exercise.

3. Reminders are helpful (II Pet. 1:12-14). Peter knew that Christians need reminders, for life has a way of diverting the attention in a multitude of directions so that one's focus can be lost. He made it his ministry in the closing period of his life to do what he could to keep his fellow believers on the track to godliness. This brings to mind the Lord's charge to him beside the Sea of Galilee, when He told him three times to "feed" His "sheep" (John 21:15-17).

The command to feed and tend the lambs of God (believers) was taken seriously by the apostle, and we can draw a lesson from this charge as well. Some are better soul-winners than others, while some are better able to nurture those new or young in the faith. Both kinds of people are needed in God's work, so let each of us who know the Lord seek to do as Peter did and fulfill the calling Jesus has given us with the gift He has given for that purpose.

—Darrell W. McKay.

World Missions

God promises to give His divine power to every believer so that all may live godly lives (II Pet. 1:3). To this end, He assures His servants with "exceeding great and precious promises" (vs. 4). Everything that is needed to live a victorious life is freely given by God.

These promises, like a coin, have two sides to them. There is God's side, by which He imparts His divine nature to the believer. Then there is man's side: "And beside this, giving all diligence, add to your faith" (vs. 5). Taken together, the seven additional qualities mentioned in verses 5-7 result in an abounding and fruitful life (vs. 8).

Missionaries and Christian workers around the world have grappled with this call to holy living. Realizing that godliness is the standard that the Lord requires, those who have fully surrendered to God have served Him wherever He has led. This consecration requires a faith in God to supply needs and give divine direction.

No missionary desires to be either "barren" or "unfruitful" in his or her work (vs. 8). The work of winning souls requires each of the characteristics listed in verses 5-7: virtue, knowledge, temperance, patience, godliness, brotherly kindness, and charity. These all culminate in producing spiritual offspring. However, spiritual barrenness calls for self-examination (vss. 9-10).

Basil Miller, in his book *How They Were Won* (Beacon Hill Press), related how well-known Christians were won to Christ. Sometimes it is believed that one must be a great Christian in order to evangelize others. Often, Satan uses this excuse to keep believers from trying to win others for Christ.

Hudson Taylor, the great missionary to China, was won by a tract written by an anonymous writer. An unknown believer wrote a gospel message to unknown individuals, and God used it to save a young man who ultimately reached thousands of Chinese for the Saviour.

A young boy was won by the kind words of two preachers who came into the forest in England to tell the gypsies of Jesus. After speaking to a certain family, one of the ministers placed his hand on the boy's head and prayed for God to make a great preacher out of him. These words burned into the boy's soul.

After the family contracted smallpox and the boy's mother died, he finally yielded to God. He entered the ministry when only seventeen. For more than fifty years he preached and sang around the world, always taking time to do personal work. Who was this boy whom God equipped? It was none other than famed evangelist Gypsy Smith.

John G. Paton was won by family prayers. Each morning and evening, his father would gather his eleven children together, read the Bible, and pray. This left such an impact on young John that he came to know his father's God. When he volunteered for mission work among the cannibals of the New Hebrides Islands, many told him not to go. But his father stood behind young Paton and prayed for him. His work on the islands reads like a novel. For fifteen years he labored, with two of the islands becoming Christianized.

Even though the servants of the Lord have faced many obstacles throughout history, God has equipped yielded lives for godly service. When God calls these faithful servants home, they will experience a wonderful entrance "into the everlasting kingdom of our Lord and Saviour Jesus Christ" (II Pet. 1:11). It will be a future day of great rejoicing for God's servants.

—*James O. Baker.*

The Jewish Aspect

In our text this week, Peter offered his prescription for Christian living. We should remember that the majority of those he was addressing were Jewish believers. The elements called for in Peter's prescription (II Pet. 1:5-7)—faith, virtue, knowledge, temperance, patience, godliness, kindness, and charity, or love—were long-standing admonitions for Jews. We may assume Peter was taught these virtues by his parents and in a synagogue in Galilee.

Many Jews of the Dispersion lived under relentless oppression and poverty. But conscientious Jews bound themselves to teach and model the qualities Peter set forth here. To this day, thoughtful Jewish parents devote themselves to living out these principles.

Two prominent characteristics of observant Jews have been a remarkable sense of responsibility for caring for others and prodigious acts of personal kindness. These characteristics are described by writer Danny Siegel, whose admonitions match those in Peter's prescription (Nemitoff, ed., *A Basic Judaism Reader,* Congregation Beth Israel). Their application aided in Jewish survival in hostile lands through the centuries.

As Siegel explained, these character qualities make up the Jewish conception of *tzedakah* (zed-ah-kah), meaning justice or that which is right. This righteousness is expressed through the giving of one's resources, possessions, time, and energy to help others.

Many Jews are warmly openhanded in helping others. They take very seriously their responsibility to provide for those in need. They usually take very good care of their own Jewish poor, sick, and disadvantaged. And the highlight of their philanthropy is that they also readily give aid to non-Jews.

It is better to give than to receive, but sometimes it is also *easier* to give than to receive. I encountered a Jewish man in our evangelistic calling who badly needed a new pair of shoes. I ended up calling the local Jewish Family Services office and reported the case. They were plainly distressed to learn of a Jew's need from a Christian.

The Jews look upon acts of kindness toward others as a means of bringing about *tikkun Olam,* literally, "the repair of the world." They look upon violence, bloodshed, pain, and tears as evidence of a broken world that only good works can change. Siegel said this requires "taking the initiative to find the people and times and situations where we can best apply our powers."

Few Gentile cultural traditions in ancient times helped people apply Peter's points. In those days, because of the terrible immorality practiced almost universally by Gentiles (*goyim*), Jews generally viewed non-Jews as filthy vermin. But "with the rise of Christianity and Islam, a number of rabbis sought to distinguish between the dissolute heathens of the past and those Gentiles who were subject to religious values and morality" (Unterman, *Dictionary of Jewish Lore and Legend,* Thames and Hudson). Peter's message had much in common with Jewish moral teachings, but he addressed both Jews and Gentiles. All those indwelt by the Holy Spirit have the spiritual capacity to think the thoughts of God after Him and to approve the things Peter outlined, things that are excellent.

The theme of our lesson emphasizes that we are equipped for godliness. Do the Christians you know exemplify Peter's points?

—Lyle P. Murphy.

Guiding the Superintendent

When God gives something, He never skimps on the amount. Over the centuries many believers have experienced the full amount of grace and love that only God can give. God does not just squeak by when it comes to our salvation. The lesson this week will focus on godliness and the means God gives us to be godly. Peter put it this way: "According as his divine power hath given unto us all things that pertain unto life and godliness" (II Pet. 1:3).

There are always two sides to godliness.

DEVOTIONAL OUTLINE

1. God's side of godliness (II Pet. 1:3-4). When an individual becomes a believer, he receives all that he might need to develop a life of godliness. He is especially given the needed divine power. Nothing that a person has is his own. It is all the result of God's gracious gift.

As part of the process, every believer has been given a special destiny. We have been called to "glory and virtue" (vs. 3). We are recipients of all the "precious promises" (vs. 4) in the Bible, so we can live lives of godliness free from the corruption of the world.

2. Man's side of godliness (II Pet. 1:5-7). It is always important to remember that there must be a balance between the divine and the human side of spiritual growth (godliness). Spiritual growth is never automatic. Spiritual diligence and discipline are required.

Visible growth should be obvious in the life of a true believer. Peter exhorted believers to give "all diligence" (vs. 5) to add to their lives several key qualities that build on each other: faith, virtue, knowledge, temperance, patience, godliness, brotherly kindness, and charity (love).

This is quite a list, but it indicates that as God is working in us, we must respond by working out these qualities in our lives.

3. Results of godliness (II Pet. 1:8-14). As God is at work in us and as we are working on these qualities ourselves, certain results will follow. These results become further affirmations that God is truly in our lives.

The text suggests three key signs that spiritual growth is taking place. First, there will be fruit, or progress (vs. 8). Second, there will be vision (vs. 9). We will start to see the world as God sees it. Third, there will be a sense of assurance about our salvation (vss. 10-11) and also about our eternal rewards. If we are growing in the Lord, we will have a sense of the divine presence in our lives and look forward to a fuller relationship with God hereafter: an abundant entrance into heaven.

The text goes on to show how God's Word is an integral part of our spiritual growth. Then Peter told his readers that he had written this material down to remind them of the truth.

CHILDREN'S CORNER

The lesson this week covers a list of Christian virtues. Perhaps it would be wise to concentrate on just one of them. You could leave it up to your teachers to discern which of these needs the most attention by the children in their classes. Or it may be appropriate to focus on the first of the virtues, "virtue" itself (vs. 5). This quality essentially refers to moral excellence, or goodness. Children should learn that they can trust God to enable them to be good. He will always help them do the right thing.

—Martin R. Dahlquist.

SCRIPTURE LESSON TEXT

GAL. 5:18 But if ye be led of the Spirit, ye are not under the law.

19 Now the works of the flesh are manifest, which are *these;* **Adultery, fornication, uncleanness, lasciviousness,**

20 Idolatry, witchcraft, hatred, variance, emulations, wrath, strife, seditions, heresies,

21 Envyings, murders, drunkenness, revellings, and such like: of the which I tell you before, as I have also told *you* **in time past, that they which do such things shall not inherit the kingdom of God.**

22 But the fruit of the Spirit is love, joy, peace, longsuffering, gentleness, goodness, faith,

23 Meekness, temperance: against such there is no law.

24 And they that are Christ's have crucified the flesh with the affections and lusts.

25 If we live in the Spirit, let us also walk in the Spirit.

26 Let us not be desirous of vain glory, provoking one another, envying one another.

6:1 Brethren, if a man be overtaken in a fault, ye which are spir-itual, **restore such an one in the spirit of meekness; considering thyself, lest thou also be tempted.**

2 Bear ye one another's burdens, and so fulfil the law of Christ.

3 For if a man think himself to be something, when he is nothing, he deceiveth himself.

4 But let every man prove his own work, and then shall he have rejoicing in himself alone, and not in another.

5 For every man shall bear his own burden.

6 Let him that is taught in the word communicate unto him that teacheth in all good things.

7 Be not deceived; God is not mocked: for whatsoever a man soweth, that shall he also reap.

8 For he that soweth to his flesh shall of the flesh reap corruption; but he that soweth to the Spirit shall of the Spirit reap life everlasting.

9 And let us not be weary in well doing: for in due season we shall reap, if we faint not.

10 As we have therefore opportunity, let us do good unto all *men,* especially unto them who are of the household of faith.

NOTES

Blessing of Spiritual Fruit

Lesson Text: Galatians 5:18—6:10

Related Scriptures: Romans 6:1-23; 8:1-17; 13:8-14; Colossians 3:12-17

TIME: probably A.D. 48

PLACE: from Syrian Antioch

GOLDEN TEXT—"The fruit of the Spirit is love, joy, peace, longsuffering, gentleness, goodness, faith, meekness, temperance: against such there is no law" (Galatians 5:22-23).

Introduction

We have seen it many times. A well-known person is caught saying or doing something embarrassing. A public apology is then offered, along with the assurance "That is not who I am." We may have good reason to be skeptical, but it is true that people can sometimes act in ways that are inconsistent with "who they are."

Consider the Apostle Peter. When he first met Jesus, the Lord declared, "Thou shalt be called Cephas" (John 1:42), meaning "stone." Peter's rock-like character and commitment to Jesus were unquestionable, but they needed time to grow and mature as he progressed in his life of following Christ.

Peter's denials, though painful, did not define or reflect his true character.

Like Peter, our intentions as followers of Christ may be commendable, but we are not unblemished. What we do does not always reflect who we really are in Christ. This is why the Bible often reminds us of *who* we are, even as it tells us *what* to do.

LESSON OUTLINE

I. THE CHRISTIAN'S CHARACTER—Gal. 5:18-24

II. THE CHRISTIAN'S CONDUCT—Gal. 5:25—6:10

Exposition: Verse by Verse

THE CHRISTIAN'S CHARACTER

GAL. 5:18 But if ye be led of the Spirit, ye are not under the law.

19 Now the works of the flesh are manifest, which are these; Adultery, fornication, uncleanness, lasciviousness,

20 Idolatry, witchcraft, hatred, variance, emulations, wrath, strife, seditions, heresies,

21 Envyings, murders, drunkenness, revellings, and such like: of the which I tell you before, as I have also told you in time past, that they which

do such things shall not inherit the kingdom of God.

22 But the fruit of the Spirit is love, joy, peace, longsuffering, gentleness, goodness, faith,

23 Meekness, temperance: against such there is no law.

24 And they that are Christ's have crucified the flesh with the affections and lusts.

Led by the Spirit (Gal. 5:18). Paul warned his readers in verse 17, affirming that we believers still struggle with sin and do not always do what we should, even though we desire to honor Christ. Paul reiterated, however, that the answer is not to put ourselves under the old covenant law. To make obedience to that law obligatory only puts us in bondage. The law does not free us from sin's power; it reveals our sin and points us to the One who removes sin and its consequences (3:24).

{Christ has freed us from the bondage of the law (Gal. 3:25; 5:1) and given us the Holy Spirit to lead us and empower us to please God. Thus, a Christian can be characterized as one who is "led of the Spirit" and so is "not under the law" (5:18). This is what we are: free in Christ to live in the realm of the Spirit.}Q1

Not marked by fleshly works (Gal. 5:19-21). {As Christians, our character is also marked by the absence of "works of the flesh."}Q2 Paul proceeded to list some of the more obvious sins that characterize the "lust of the flesh" (vs. 16). Kent noted that "'works' is an apt designation of these productions of the natural man, for they are the result of natural human activity unaided by the Spirit of God" (*The Freedom of God's Sons,* BMH).

The sins listed in Galatians 5:19 are sexual in nature and cover illicit relations among both married and unmarried people. "Uncleanness" extends to one's immoral thoughts, and "lasciviousness" refers to a complete lack of restraint in sexual matters. The next two works of the flesh relate to corrupt religion (vs. 20). "Idolatry" is worshipping images or other things, putting them in the place of God. The word translated "witchcraft" literally refers to the use of drugs, but it came to mean the "preparation and application of magical devices" (Ridderbos, *The Epistle of Paul to the Churches of Galatia,* Eerdmans).

The remaining vices listed in Galatians 5:20-21 are social in nature. "Hatred" gives rise to "variance," which is strife. "Emulations" is misdirected zeal, while "wrath" refers to outbursts of anger. The word translated "strife" seems to indicate selfish displays. "Seditions" refers to divisions that come from conflict, and "heresies" denotes the separate groups that form as a result of divisions. The list ends with "envyings, murders, drunkenness, revellings." The latter refers to drunken parties.

Paul made it clear these sins are representative and not exhaustive. The apostle then stated what he had told his readers before: those who practice such things will never inherit the kingdom of God. These are characterizing marks of those who are unsaved.

This does not mean that such people are beyond hope or that anyone who commits one of these sins is lost. It simply means that anyone whose life is characterized by sins such as these demonstrates that he or she is not a follower of Christ. Christians can sin and can sin quite grievously, but their lives will not be persistently characterized by works of the flesh.

Marked by spiritual fruit (Gal. 5:22- 24). {In contrast to the works of the flesh, Paul listed the fruit of the Spirit. This fruit is produced by the indwelling Holy Spirit. This does not mean we have no role, however, for it is only as we submit to Christ and seek His will that the Spirit produces these qualities in us.}Q3

{The singular form of "fruit" in the Greek language emphasizes the "unity and coherence of the life in the Spirit" (Pfeiffer and Harrison, eds., *The Wycliffe Bible Commentary,* Moody) and may even suggest that these qualities are one fruit consisting of nine elements.}[Q4] They are listed separately, however, and each one should be present and growing in the believer's life.

Christlike love, as Paul explained elsewhere (I Cor. 13), is selfless, unconditional, and unending. It always seeks the good of others. Joy is inner contentment that is unaffected by outward circumstances. Peace is "that inner calmness of emotions and thoughts which rests on the assurance that God is too good to be unkind and too wise to make mistakes" (*Gromacki, Stand Fast in Liberty,* Kress).

Longsuffering is patience, especially in the face of opposition. Gentleness, or kindness, describes one who has a tender regard for the interests and feelings of others. Goodness is very similar to gentleness, though the emphasis seems to be more on generosity. Faith should be understood as faithfulness in following the Lord and being reliable.

Meekness is gentleness in the use of strength. In secular Greek the word was used of taming wild animals (Friedrich, ed., *Theological Dictionary of the New Testament,* Eerdmans). Finally, temperance is self-control.

These Spirit-produced qualities obviously do not need to be restrained by laws, as do the works of the flesh. Those who are Christ's display these qualities in their lives. This is because every true believer has crucified the flesh with its passions and sinful desires. The Christian makes a definitive break with sin when he or she believes in Christ. The believer can still fall into sin, but sin no longer has power over him or her. Rather, the Christian's life is characterized by godly fruit.

THE CHRISTIAN'S CONDUCT

25 If we live in the Spirit, let us also walk in the Spirit.

26 Let us not be desirous of vain glory, provoking one another, envying one another.

6:1 Brethren, if a man be overtaken in a fault, ye which are spiritual, restore such an one in the spirit of meekness; considering thyself, lest thou also be tempted.

2 Bear ye one another's burdens, and so fulfil the law of Christ.

3 For if a man think himself to be something, when he is nothing, he deceiveth himself.

4 But let every man prove his own work, and then shall he have rejoicing in himself alone, and not in another.

5 For every man shall bear his own burden.

6 Let him that is taught in the word communicate unto him that teacheth in all good things.

7 Be not deceived; God is not mocked: for whatsoever a man soweth, that shall he also reap.

8 For he that soweth to his flesh shall of the flesh reap corruption; but he that soweth to the Spirit shall of the Spirit reap life everlasting.

9 And let us not be weary in well doing: for in due season we shall reap, if we faint not.

10 As we have therefore opportunity, let us do good unto all men, especially unto them who are of the household of faith.

Selfless in service (Gal. 5:25-26). Having presented what a Christian is and is not through the lists of works of the flesh and fruit of the Spirit, the apostle now began to issue directives for what Christians are to do. At this point, Paul shifted from an emphasis on doctrinal truth to the application of that truth in daily life. {First, if (or since) we "live in the Spirit," we must also "walk in the Spirit." In other words, we are to conform our conduct to this new life we entered when we were saved.}[Q5] Among other things, this means we are to serve God and others selflessly.

We are not to proudly seek glory for ourselves. We are not to provoke others with a selfish attitude. And we are not to envy those who might be more honored than we are. There is no place for self-centeredness among those who belong to Christ.

Compassion for the needy (Gal. 6:1-3). {Instead of being focused on ourselves, we are to help those in need. "Overtaken in a fault" can mean either that the one overtaken was surprised by the fault itself and did not mean to fall into sin, or it can mean the person was surprised when someone discovered his sin. In either case, the offender is a Christian whom his fellow Christians are to restore.}[Q6]

The word for "restore" in Galatians 6:1 was used of mending nets (cf. Matt. 4:21; Mark 1:19). What is envisioned here is more mature, or spiritual, believers restoring a sinning brother or sister to usefulness in the church. This affirms that Christians do, in fact, fall into sin at times. It also tells us that although all believers should exhibit the fruit of the Spirit, there are various levels of fruitfulness among Christians simply because the Christian life is a continuing process of growth and development of Christlike character.

Those who are more mature in the faith are to look out for those who are struggling with sin, and they are to restore them. {They are to do so in a spirit of meekness. The same word is used for one of the fruits of the Spirit and emphasizes that the restorers must be exhibiting that fruit. The one who restores needs to take heed to himself, being mindful of his (or her) own potential for falling into sin.}[Q7]

The principle stated in Galatians 6:2 may have many applications, but in this context it refers to restoring a sinning brother or sister, relieving that one of the heavy burden he or she bears. When we do this, we demonstrate Christlike love and "so fulfil the law of Christ." "'The law of Christ' is: 'Love one another' (John 13:34; 15:12). Paul has already discussed the 'law of love' (Gal. 5:13-15), and now he is applying it" (Wiersbe, *Be Free,* Victor).

Galatians 6:3 is a warning against pride. Pride or conceit can interfere with Christians acting in a compassionate way to bear the burdens of fellow believers. When they think so highly of themselves that they refuse to help the lowly person trapped in sin, they are deceiving themselves, for they are no better than the sinning brother or sister. In fact, "measured by God's standards, no one amounts to anything" (Barker and Kohlenberger, eds., *The Expositor's Bible Commentary, Abridged,* Zondervan).

Reflective and responsible (Gal. 6:4-5). "Let every man prove his own work" is an implied warning against comparing ourselves to others. We each have our own work to do, and we must "prove," or test, the quality of our work by God's standards, not man's. We are not to take pride in achieving or exceeding the expectations of people. Rather, we are to examine ourselves to see if we are accomplishing what God wants us to do, for that is the only legitimate grounds for rejoicing.

{At first, the call for everyone to "bear his own burden" (vs. 5) seems to conflict with verse 2. Paul used a different word for burden here, however, probably to distinguish this statement from the previous one. Here the burden is not sin or its consequences but the work of verse 4, or the "normal duty which falls upon every man" (Ridderbos). Each person is responsible for his own work before God.}[Q8]

Supportive of leaders (Gal. 6:6-9). {Another duty of Christians is to "communicate" with those who faithfully teach them. The word for "communicate" here means "to share with." This refers to financial support. Those in the church who devote themselves to instructing the saints are worthy of support, as Paul repeatedly stated (cf. I Cor. 9:14; Phil. 4:15-18; I Tim. 5:17-18).}^{Q9}

In the context of all that Paul had previously said in Galatians, the statement in 6:7, "Be not deceived; God is not mocked," probably contained a final warning against honoring the false teachers who were deceiving them while treating faithful teachers of the Word with disdain. To do this was to treat God with contempt. The universal principle that one reaps what he sows is applicable here (cf. I Cor. 9:10-11; II Cor. 9:6). If the Galatians did not generously support honest, faithful teachers, they would reap emptiness and even hardship in their lives.

The principle is restated in Galatians 6:8, where the apostle gives it much wider application; namely, that sowing to the flesh reaps "corruption," while sowing to the Spirit reaps "life everlasting." One who consistently directs his life toward pleasing the flesh will reap corruption, or moral decay. His self-centered life proves he is not a Christian. A Christian should consistently be sowing to the Spirit; that is, he should be directing his life toward the things of God. Such a person proves by the life he lives that he is a follower of Christ and will reap eternal life.

Again, a believer can sin, as we have seen, but he cannot continue in such a lifestyle if he is truly born again. It is important that the Christian make daily choices to sow to the Spirit so that his life reflects who he truly is in Christ.

{The reward of godly living is not always immediately evident, so there is the temptation to grow weary of the commitment to do good. Paul urged his readers to remain diligent in this, realizing that the basic principle of sowing and reaping is unalterable and that the harvest of divine blessing will come in God's good time.}^{Q10}

Doing good to all (Gal. 6:10). The good we do—and the good we reap as a result—is not limited to our treatment of godly teachers. We are obligated to do good to all people as we have the opportunity. Paul added, however, that our first priority is to our own family, the "household of faith." Our loving concern is to be expressed for all people, but our special concern is our fellow Christians.

—Jarl K. Waggoner.

QUESTIONS

1. How does being led by the Spirit differ from being under the law?

2. What did Paul say about Christians and the "works of the flesh" (Gal. 5:19)?

3. How is the fruit of the Spirit produced in Christians?

4. What might be suggested by the fact that the fruit of the Spirit is singular (vs. 22)?

5. What is added by the idea of walking in the Spirit (vs. 25)?

6. What is our duty to Christians "overtaken in a fault" (6:1)?

7. With what attitude should we approach those who are in sin?

8. How does bearing our own burden (vs. 5) differ from bearing one another's burdens (vs. 2)?

9. What is our obligation to those who teach us the Word?

10. How does the law of sowing and reaping relate to not growing weary in doing good?

—Jarl K. Waggoner.

Preparing to Teach the Lesson

As you may be well aware, there is a lot of false and misleading talk about spiritual life. Some gurus and teachers in the world have a totally false idea of what is spiritual and what is carnal, or fleshly, the fruit of a fallen human nature. Part of your responsibility as a teacher is to correct any misunderstandings your students may have about this and to educate them as to what real spiritual life is.

TODAY'S AIM

Facts: to see clearly the elements of refusing the works of the flesh and living in the Spirit.

Principle: to learn to walk in the Spirit each day of our lives.

Application: to daily refuse to do the deeds of the flesh and instead to obey the promptings of the Holy Spirit.

INTRODUCING THE LESSON

As a class, we need to be so aware of true spiritual life and so used to practicing our walk in the Spirit that we can help and encourage one another in its pursuit. The world at large teaches what it calls "spiritual" things. They are really emotional things.

The Scripture is clear that before we trust Christ and are born again, our spirits are fatally flawed. We are "dead in trespasses and sins" (Eph. 2:1). We have emotions and aspirations, even a hunger for spiritual things, but our spirits are dead without Christ. That is the reason so many false religions and philosophies are spawned. We have a hunger for answers, and if we do not get the light of Scripture and the right answers, we invent answers. Inventions from flawed hearts and minds are always sinful and anti-God. We must study the Word of God to receive correct spiritual information. We must respond to that information positively in order to walk in true spiritual life instead of spiritual death.

DEVELOPING THE LESSON

1. Free from the law but not free to sin (Gal. 5:18-21). Notice that it is only when we are "led of the Spirit" that we are free from the law. When the Holy Spirit, resident within us through faith in the Lord Jesus Christ, prompts us to godly activities and thoughts, we do not have to even think about keeping any kind of law or regulation. That does not mean we can violate any of them; it means the Holy Spirit does not lead us to act in any way that God does not approve of. Even though we are saved, we still have indwelling sin, and we can still do that which is wrong. The sins listed in these verses are indicative, not exclusive. The scriptural pronouncement is clear. Those "who are controlled by "such things shall not inherit the kingdom of God."

2. What to expect when walking in the Spirit (Gal. 5:22-26). Notice that the "works of the flesh" (vs. 19) section is in the plural and the "fruit of the Spirit" (vs. 22) section is in the singular. Although nine results of walking in the Spirit are given, it is referred to as the fruit (singular) of the Spirit. When walking in the Spirit, there is a unified way of thinking and feeling, with a resultant way of doing what is truly spiritual. When we have crucified the flesh with its affections and lusts, we are dead to them. They can no longer have any place in our lives.

3. What to do as a Spirit-led believer (Gal. 6:1-6). Sometimes believers behave like unbelievers and violate the rule of the Lord over them. They fall into sin. If you and I are walking in the Spirit and are not in sin ourselves, we are to gently and humbly attempt to help people see their error, repent of it, and submit again to Christ's lordship over them. This may be the hardest thing for any of us to do, but it is essential to the body of Christ, the church. Most of the time, we see Christians criticizing sinning brothers or sisters. Condemning others is a sin, and it certainly does not help solve the problem.

4. In for the long haul (Gal. 6:7-10). We are told not to be deceived; that is, we should not kid ourselves! We should never think that we can somehow get away with sin just because we prayed about it and the temptation to do it did not go away. God expects us to obey the promptings of the Holy Spirit. He will not do for us that which we refuse to do or neglect to do. God will not tie our shoelaces. If we trip and fall because we did not tie them, it is our responsibility, not God's. We will reap what we sow. We will reap later, and we will reap it multiplied. This is a principle that we might wish to overlook or ignore, but doing that will not change its truth,

In God's perfect timing, we will reap a harvest of blessing if we walk in the Spirit. We have no idea what that will be like, but it is a merciful and loving God who is preparing it. He wants to graciously and lavishly bless His children. We will have plentiful opportunities to do good to "all men, especially unto them who are of the household of faith." And Paul encourages us to never give up or get tired of doing good.

ILLUSTRATING THE LESSON

Blessings to others result from walking in the Spirit.

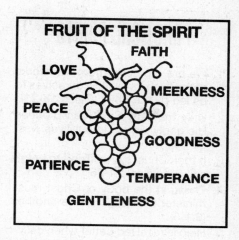

FRUIT OF THE SPIRIT
FAITH
LOVE
MEEKNESS
PEACE
JOY
GOODNESS
PATIENCE
TEMPERANCE
GENTLENESS

CONCLUDING THE LESSON

It is impossible to overstate the importance of this week's theme. The whole point of the Christian life is encompassed here. As we yield our own wills to the prompting of the Lord through His Holy Spirit, we will be living a holy and blessed life free from sin's dominion and the negative works of the flesh. This is part of that for which Christ died. Being saved and going to heaven when we die is wonderful, but so is a life on earth filled with the presence and power of the Lord. This is a life lived for others, not self, just as Christ lived.

There is no higher calling. The humblest Christian can walk in the Spirit just as effectively as the most powerful saint. There are no required qualifications except trusting Christ and obeying His Holy Spirit. No one and nothing can stop any one of us from doing it. All of heaven's resources are behind the one who walks in the Spirit and does not fulfill the lusts of the flesh.

ANTICIPATING THE NEXT LESSON

In our next quarter of study, we will examine how Jesus pleased God the Father.

—Brian D. Doud.

PRACTICAL POINTS

1. We are protected from the works of the flesh if we allow ourselves to be led by the Spirit (Gal. 5:18-21).
2. Only the Holy Spirit can produce His godly virtues in our lives (vss. 22-23).
3. It took Christ's crucifixion to break sin's grip (vss. 24-26).
4. Those in the body of Christ must minister selflessly to one another (6:1-3).
5. Help is received better when delivered with love. We should always act in humility (vss. 4-5).
6. We are all in the same race and should not compete with but help one another to the finish (Gal. 6:6-10; cf. Rom. 12:5).

—Lendell Sims.

RESEARCH AND DISCUSSION

1. The world's population is divided into numerous cultures. Is there any difference from one culture to another in the manifestation of the works of the flesh? Are certain cultures more prone to works of the flesh than others?
2. How can the fruit of the Spirit negate the works of the flesh?
3. Romans 12:2 instructs us to "be not conformed to this world." How can we evangelize those we are supposed to be separated from?
4. How do we see the law of reaping and sowing played out in our own culture?
5. When evangelizing, how do we know whether we are the one planting or watering?

—Lendell Sims.

ILLUSTRATED HIGH POINTS

And such like: . . . against such (Gal. 5:21, 23)

Paul did not limit fleshly works or spiritual fruit to the items he listed in Galatians 5:19-23. This is indicated by the phrases "and such like" and "against such."

A unicyclist got a ticket for riding his unique vehicle on a Coney Island sidewalk. He then filed a three-million-dollar lawsuit, pointing out that the law prohibits bicycles and defines "bicycle" as a two- or three-wheeled device propelled by human power" ("Letter of the Law, Spirit of the Law," www.brooklynspoke.com). Since his vehicle had only one wheel, he reasoned he was not in error.

There are tens of thousands of laws on the books simply because we duck, dodge, and fly through loopholes with the greatest of ease. We could, however, put aside the law volumes if we understood the law of love written on our hearts (cf. Rom. 2:29; I Thess. 4:9).

Ye which are spiritual, restore (6:1)

In a news interview, a Christian mother spoke of her family's grief after the death of their eighteen-month-old son in a hot car. Her husband drove to work and forgot that it was his turn to drop the child off at daycare. Through their pain, the family has pulled together and is even endeavoring to help others. Sadly, a portion of the public has been cruelly judgmental.

This mother understands their reaction from her own reactions in other cases. The reality is that we tend to blame the person when something like this happens to someone else but the circumstances when it happens to us. Let us lean more toward kindness and forgiveness than faultfinding.

—Therese Greenberg.

Golden Text Illuminated

"The fruit of the Spirit is love, joy, peace, longsuffering, gentleness, goodness, faith, meekness, temperance: against such there is no law" (Galatians 5:22-23).

Everything about salvation in Christ shouts to us of living a holy life through the power of the Holy Spirit. The church was born for this. There can be no confusion. As believers we must realize that God has saved us to be holy, and He has provided His Spirit to create the capacity to live a holy, godly, God-pleasing life. What is such a life all about? This text gives us two things to think about.

The first is that a holy life has a manifold expression—it is a multiplicity of virtues. We note that the term "fruit" is singular, but that one fruit has an abundance of expressions in the life of the Christian. All of these expressions should emerge in our lives in a unity. We should see a "fruit cluster," a ninefold expression of the sacred presence of the Spirit in our lives.

The fruit of the Spirit is in contrast to the works of the flesh, each of which is a singular expression of sinful activity. Our sinful nature has many potential expressions of sin. But when the Holy Spirit is in control of our lives, we will see a fullness, a completeness, to our character in Christ.

We should manifest love, the capacity to act in the best interests of others. We should manifest joy, an inner happiness in God that transcends our trials and troubles. We should manifest peace, an abiding tranquillity present in our minds and hearts. We should manifest longsuffering, a patience that is able to endure difficulty without a response of the rebellious flesh.

We should also personify such things as gentleness and goodness, a kindly generosity of spirit toward others. We should show forth faith, or faithfulness—the ability to be steady, committed, and strong throughout all the seasons and challenges of life. And we should exhibit meekness, a humbleness of spirit that is willing to yield rights for the good of others. Last but not least, we should display temperance, or self-control, diligently putting into practice what we are learning from God's Word, and doing it in a disciplined way.

Do you see this "fruit cluster" emerging in your life? As we yield to the Holy Spirit hour by hour and minute by minute, these expressions of holy living will emerge in the life of the true Christian, to the glory of God. It is a wonderful and manifold statement of the difference Christ makes in our lives. These are not standards we achieve by human merit, but rather they are the fruit of the Holy Spirit's presence in our lives.

The second thing to think about from the golden text is that a holy life yields not only this beautiful, manifold expression of fruit; it also constitutes a powerful force. Paul states the firm truth that against this kind of life there is no law. Nothing can be erected to stop it. If the Holy Spirit is producing this fruit, then it does not matter what the enemies of the Christian life do. It does not matter what the world does. This fruit will come. It is intrinsically powerful because it is of God; it comes from the presence of the Spirit. Let us do all we can to nurture the presence of the Holy Spirit within us, that His manifold and powerful fruit may emerge in our lives.

—Jeff VanGoethem.

Heart of the Lesson

What does it mean to live holy lives in the Spirit? First, let us broaden our concept of the word "holy." Holiness is often equated with purity, but it also can be defined as "set apart." God wants us to be holy. He desires that we be literally set apart. In other words, do our words, our actions, and our attitudes differ from those who have not been redeemed by the blood of the Lamb? Sinners are going to act like sinners. It is confusing when the saints are more adept at behaving the way sinners do than they are at behaving the way children of God should.

1. The flesh and the Spirit (Gal. 5:18-26). When we fulfill the desires of the flesh, we find that our hunger for them grows. The more we feed the flesh, the more we learn that we are never able to satisfy the lusts of the flesh. Instead, our moral compass keeps being pushed beyond its limits until one day we have lost our moral perspective completely.

The Apostle Paul provides us with a list of the works of the flesh. This is not an all-inclusive list but rather a summary. If we are able to steer clear of the things Paul speaks about here, chances are that we will not succumb to other temptations.

Just as there are works of the flesh, there is fruit of the Spirit to enable us to overcome temptation. "The fruit of the Spirit is love, joy, peace, longsuffering, gentleness, goodness, faith, meekness, temperance: against such there is no law" (vs. 22). We can indulge in the fruit of God's Spirit without measure. As we partake of the fruit of the Spirit, we are able to live in the Spirit.

As we live in the Spirit, we are also able to walk in the Spirit.

2. Watch (Gal. 6:1-6). If someone falls into sin and begins to walk in his flesh rather than by the Spirit, we are to restore him gently. Why? What if we were tempted by the same issue? What if we fell? Would we not want to be restored? We all need a spiritual realignment now and then. Sometimes we fall into temptation by choice; sometimes we fall into sin through ignorance. Either way, we need to repent and turn away from that sin.

Sometimes we need other people to show us the error of our ways. This can be done by a spiritual leader or by a trusted, godly friend. It is what Paul meant when he said, "Bear ye one another's burdens, and so fulfil the law of Christ" (vs. 2). We are to help our brothers and sisters in Christ overcome the works of the flesh and encourage them to walk in the Spirit.

3. Warning and promise (Gal. 6:7-10). "Be not deceived; God is not mocked: for whatsoever a man soweth, that shall he also reap." There are two ways to look at verse 7: as a warning and as a promise. If we live our lives based solely on selfish desires, with no regard for anyone else, this verse is a warning. However, if we seek God and walk in His Spirit, this verse is a promise. This is why Paul urges us not to get weary in doing good toward others. It is going to pay off!

If we believe that the Bible is true, then we can be assured that God keeps tabs on how we treat one another. God is not mocked. As we strive to be a blessing to others, we will be blessed!

—*Kristin Reeg.*

World Missions

Our God is a God of excellence, lining up every detail of His Word in perfect order. The list of fruit of the Spirit is deliberately sequenced according to how God works in our lives. For example, without a foundation of love, no life will produce fruit. And temperance, or self-control, may appear last because once a person loses it, there may be nothing else to do but to start over with love. God has made this fruit available to us to combat the works of the flesh and to demonstrate His overcoming power in our lives.

Belinda came to a Reach & Rescue Ministries' homeless shelter on the day she was released from prison. Our group was there to provide the weekly chapel service. I brought a rousing message; at least I thought so. Many of the women were moved. Several came up for prayer for salvation, healing, and other issues. Belinda did not budge. Her face was like stone as she stared forward, waiting for the dismissal prayer.

At "amen," she stumbled across a row of stragglers, dashing for the exit. I trotted after her but missed her. She became the object of many of my prayers for the next week. I was determined to make contact with her on the subsequent visit. When I saw Belinda enter the next week, I stopped her at the door, introduced myself, and thanked her for coming. She blandly responded, "They said I had to."

Again Belinda sat through our service, scrambling out the door as soon as we finished. Again, I felt the need to focus on her in my prayers. The third week, I met her again at the chapel door. This time I obeyed the words that had been echoing in my head all day: "Love her." God was letting me know that He would soften her with love. I planned to say hello, but out of my mouth came, "Would it be all right if I hug you?"

Belinda stared at me for a few seconds, appearing to be stunned. "I guess," she said. As the service began, I noticed tears coming from Belinda's eyes. At the conclusion, Belinda came up to me for what I thought would be prayer. She pulled me over to the side and told me about some of the childhood abuse and abandonment she had suffered from her parents and the violence and perverted lifestyle that had resulted from such turmoil in her life.

Then she revealed the shocker. She confessed that because she lived an openly sinful lifestyle, her son's friends would call him names and tease him. At twelve years old, her son could take no more and shot himself in the head. Belinda said she could not forgive herself for his death, but reading the Bible and coming to chapel were helping her feel the love of God. She admitted that her life had been a whirlwind and she had no self-control.

The demonstration of God's love prepared Belinda to be open to the gospel. She became progressively softer to accepting love from the Father and gestures of love from the Christians around her. Belinda surrendered her life to Christ several months later. She rejected her former lifestyle and has been growing in Christ. She is an example of how the Holy Spirit starts with love and develops the fruit that eventually leads to self-control.

Holy living is not ours to accomplish alone. Like Belinda, as we allow the Holy Spirit to bear His fruit in us, He will help us live for Him.

—Beverly Medley Jones.

The Jewish Aspect

In Galatians 5, Paul contrasted the works of the flesh with the fruit of the Spirit. Neither the Jewish people of Paul's day nor Jewish people today who have any allegiance to Judaism would disagree that such acts as adultery, murder, and drunkenness are evils. Their problem, like that of so many morally-minded people, is not identifying evil but rather avoiding it.

Christians, of course, should recognize that the key to godly living is found in the blessings of the new covenant. The Spirit writes God's law upon the hearts of believers. The history of Jewish family life over the last two thousand years illustrates the uphill struggles of trying to live morally without the Spirit's empowerment.

In 1215, the Fourth Lateran Council decreed a quarantine of Jews in every city in what was called the ghetto. Ghettos were locked up each night and closely guarded. In one sense, this was a blessing for the Jews, for it kept families together and reduced the sinful temptations of the Gentiles from contaminating the Jews. Divorce was virtually nonexistent. Man and wife were required to get along. Rabbis said that the chief ingredients of marriage were mutual respect, devotion, chaste conduct, and kindness (Ausubel, *The Book of Jewish Knowledge,* Crown Publishers).

In our Jewish community, a young, unmarried woman came from Eastern Europe and took up residence. She was extremely attractive, and Jewish wives began to complain that she was too flirtatious with their husbands. As a body they complained to the rabbi about the young woman. He threatened to put her out of the community, but she repented and was restored to the community. She eventually married and won general acceptance among the Jews.

Judaism has always placed great value on marriage and families. Much of the law relates to family life, and Israel's history has reinforced the perceived dangers of outside influence and intermarriage with Gentiles.

European Jews always feared for their children, but it was not so in ghetto communities. Mothers were charged with the spiritual formation of children until they could read. Then fathers took over, imbuing them with the tenets of Deuteronomy 6:4-6. The father was released from responsibility when the child reached age thirteen (Ausubel).

After World War II, immigrants swelled the synagogue congregations in most American communities. The Jewish sense of freedom was not without cost, however. It caused the sacred marriage customs of the Jews to be easily ignored. Marriage outside of Judaism has always been a feared consequence of living close to profligate Gentiles. In America, 52 percent of Jewish marriages are contracted with non-Jews. While Reform Jews seem unconcerned, the Orthodox still seek to maintain their Jewish identity and customs and live upright lives.

What our Jewish friends fail to understand is something many Christians also do not seem to grasp. All the effort in the world to avoid evil can never produce a morally upright life. We might avoid the worst influences from outside, but we cannot escape our own sinful human nature. Thus, no one can live a holy life apart from the work of the Holy Spirit, who indwells only followers of Christ and produces in them the spiritual fruit Paul described. Sadly, Judaism offers no personal Holy Spirit who permanently indwells God's people and empowers them to live holy lives.

—Lyle P. Murphy.

Guiding the Superintendent

"Do as I say and not as I do" is a familiar old expression used by some leaders and parents. One of the things this might imply is that authority figures should be unconditionally followed, even though they frequently are not walking according to their words. The fact is that people sometimes give orders or advice without setting a consistent example.

In this week's lesson, we will receive instruction concerning living a holy lifestyle.

DEVOTIONAL OUTLINE

1. Living by the sinful nature (Gal. 5:18-21). Paul told the Galatians about the works of the flesh. He listed the sexual sins of adultery, fornication, uncleanness, and lasciviousness. Sins against God such as idolatry and witchcraft display a lack of godly reverence. Paul also denounced hatred, discord, jealousy, wrath, strife, division, and factions.

Paul said to the Galatians that a life characterized by participation in fleshly activity indicates that a person will not partake of the kingdom of God. They will not receive God's blessings.

2. Fruit of the Spirit-filled life (Gal. 5:22-26). Shifting toward living in the Spirit, Paul provided a listing of attributes connected to a Spirit-filled life. Love is the anchor of the fruit of the Spirit. Joy and peace reflect contentment.

Longsuffering, gentleness, and goodness are proper traits for believers to show in their interactions with others. Faithfulness reflects the tenacity to stay consistent in the Christian walk. Meekness and temperance demonstrate restraint.

Paul called upon those who trust in Christ to put to death evil passions and lusts. Paul further instructed the church to refrain from conceit, jealousy, and provoking one another.

3. Living the Spirit-filled life (Gal. 6:1-10). Paul addressed the Galatian church on how to treat fallen believers. Paul cautioned them not to be demeaning. They were to restore believers with mercy.

Paul wanted the church to display love. The way that could be expressed was by sharing and not becoming conceited. They were not to resort to self-serving comparisons.

Paul next moved the discussion to giving. Paul informed the Galatians that it was their responsibility to share their resources with their teachers. He used the term "communicate" to illustrate his point. Failing to financially support their teachers would result in missing blessings from the Spirit.

Paul encouraged his readers not to allow discouragement to impede their thinking. They would be the beneficiaries of God's blessings if they did not quit.

CHILDREN'S CORNER

It is never too early for children to learn the distinction between right and wrong. Help them aspire to live in a holy manner at all times. Affirm the necessity of listening to God's voice.

Years ago, "What would Jesus do?" was a popular slogan. When tempted, many believers quoted it. Children need to know that the best way of listening to God and learning how to live a holy life that pleases Him is to follow Jesus' example. And the only way to learn what Jesus would do in any situation is to get to know Him through reading His Word. This is a process that will take their whole lives, but they can already be learning now!

—*Tyrone Keith Carroll, Sr.*

our behalf, those whose faith is in Christ can also rejoice and trust that He is with us to bring us through those tough times that would otherwise tempt us to give in to feelings of fear and despair.

Because of the amazing plan He has and the wonderful way in which He works, God even uses trials to bring blessings our way. The idea of rejoicing amid suffering (Jas. 1:2) is likely to leave many Christians scratching their heads. But just as there is more to this idea than being happy about having problems, there is also more to being a Christian than being forgiven of your sins.

The truth of the matter is that the Lord has brought us back to life spiritually and into a relationship and partnership with Himself (Eph. 2:4-10). His desire is to reproduce the life of Christ in us (II Cor. 3:18). He now wants to work through our lives to reach others with the blessing of His salvation and all that it entails.

As we experience and are yielded to the blessing of God working in our lives, He produces godly attributes in us (Gal. 5:22-23). This enables others to see the power of God at work.

God's people are not exempt from having problems and facing struggles. Actually, Jesus promised His first disciples just the opposite when He said, "In the world ye shall have tribulation" (John 16:33). Should those who trust and follow Jesus today expect anything less?

The inability to see the complete panoramic view of all that God is doing at the present time can hinder us from recognizing many of His great blessings for what they truly are. As His people, however, we are called to trust Him no matter what (cf. Rom. 8:37-39; II Cor. 5:7). His power, knowledge, and wisdom know no bounds.

Although the full experience of God's great blessings is yet in our future, He is abundantly blessing us right now— even when we remain completely unaware.

God's Undeniable Glory

Reginald Coats

Stubbing your toe, stepping on a sharp object, or bumping into a wall are all accidents that you are more likely to experience if the lights have been turned off or you have had your vision impaired in some other way. But the brilliant and wonderful way in which God's creation functions ensures that no one *accidentally* fails to see the beauty of how wonderful He and His perfections truly are.

Not only does creation clearly call attention to God's glory (Ps. 19:1-6; Rom. 1:20-23), but the Son of God and

promised Saviour came into the world and made the glory of God known to mankind in the most unmistakable way (John 1:14, 18; Col. 2:9). The full range of God's perfect attributes, such as His love, grace, mercy, righteousness, and justice, could not have been more clearly or completely displayed than when Jesus, who was and is sinless in every way, suffered the full outpouring of God's wrath against sin (Rom. 3:21-26; II Cor. 5:21).

The purpose of glorifying God is embedded within all that He has created, and this purpose is to be embraced by all. Just as the heavens proudly pronounce the glory of God, all of creation shares in this most important of divine callings. Along with the majestic mountains and amazing sunsets that He has brought into existence, God also works through His people when making His own majesty known to the world.

We should not let pride prevent us from glorifying God as we should. Since He is our Creator and Sustainer, we could never accomplish anything without Him (John 15:5; Rom. 11:36). We must therefore see to it that credit is given where credit is due and praise God for all that He accomplishes through us.

John the Baptist is a prime example of someone who did not mistake his place and purpose in God's plan of bringing glory to Himself. John readily recognized and acknowledged his own insignificance in comparison to that of the Lord (John 1:26-27; 3:27-30). His goal was to call attention to the Lord and the arrival of the promised Saviour. He sought no recognition or accolades for himself but instead sought glory for the Lord.

Just as a passerby does not deserve credit for the design and construction of the most fascinating and amazing architectural masterpiece his eyes have ever seen, so no one besides the Lord deserves credit for all that He has done and is doing. As absurd as it would be to congratulate a mere tourist for erecting the edifice that he has come to view, it is even more foolish to fail to praise God alone for His mighty works.

God's faithfulness provides yet another lens through which certain aspects of His glory can be seen. When the Lord sent the angel Gabriel to inform Mary that she was the chosen vessel through whom He would bring the Saviour into the world, it did not mark the start of a new promise but was rather the continuation of an older one that had been made thousands of years earlier in the Garden of Eden (Gen. 3:15). God was faithfully at work during that entire time to make good on His promise to deliver the Deliverer.

The gift of God's salvation comes only through His Son (I John 5:11). Apart from Him taking the initiative to rescue us from sin and its penalty, we would all still be in the same helpless and hopeless situation—"dead in trespasses and sins" (Eph. 2:1). And God's goal for saving those who put their trust in Him is to magnify His own glory (1:12-14).

What an awesome honor and privilege it is to have been brought back to life by God and enlisted by Him to live for His glory. An integral part of being reconciled to God is experiencing the transformational work of His Spirit from within (cf. II Cor. 3:18; Titus 3:5). Those who have trusted Jesus as Saviour are even described in Scripture as being "partakers of the divine nature" (II Pet. 1:4). All that is good within or about us is from God, to whom belongs all of the glory.

In spite of the Lord clearly revealing His glory through His creation, written Word, and Son, there remains opposition and an unwillingness by many to acknowledge Him as God (Rom. 1:18-25; II Cor. 4:3-4). Some desire glory for themselves, while others ascribe the glory that belongs only to the Lord to undeserving and unintelligent created things.

However, the Lord remains undaunted by any such opposition to His glory. He is steadfast in His unwillingness to share the glory that belongs to Him, as God and Creator, with any created thing or being (Isa. 42:8).

The people of God should, therefore, not allow themselves to be discouraged when met with hostility as a result of being ambassadors of Christ.

Jesus assured His followers that they would face opposition and hatred in and from the world (John 15:18-19). He also, however, instructed them to "be of good cheer" because of the victory that is found in Him (16:33). Any and all attempts to suppress the glory of God are doomed to fail.

In the meantime, God continues to equip and work through those whose faith is in Him, and those who oppose Him cannot thwart His plan. The unmistakable truth of the matter is that "the whole earth is full of [God's] glory" (Isa. 6:3), and He will not be denied.

When all is said and done, every person who has ever lived will one day confess and bow in acknowledgement that Jesus is Lord—"to the glory of God the Father" (Phil. 2:11). And all who have trusted Him as Saviour will enjoy His glory forever (Rev. 21:23-24).

TOPICS FOR NEXT QUARTER

PARAGRAPHS ON PLACES AND PEOPLE

BETHLEHEM

This ancient town was first mentioned in Genesis 35 as the burial place for Rachel (Ephrath). Located about six miles south of Jerusalem, its name means "house of bread" or "fruitful," which may be a reflection of the richness of the land and the many crops that were grown in the area. We see that Joshua allocated this land to Judah when it is mentioned as part of that tribe's territory during the time of the judges (Judg. 17:7).

Bethlehem was the hometown to many mentioned in Scripture (Judg. 12:8; Ruth 1:2; 4:11; I Sam. 17:12).

Micah's prophecy calls the area insignificant (Mic. 5:2), but it would have future fame. When asked by King Herod, the religious leaders in Jerusalem understood that the Messiah would be born there (Matt. 2:3-6).

GALATIA

This fertile region of central Asia Minor (modern-day Turkey) was an area inhabited by Gallic (Celtic) tribes. They were known for being skilled at warfare and also for their unpredictability. This general area became a Roman province called Galatia around 25 B.C. and over time hosted many settlements of other peoples, including Jews, making for a culturally diverse region.

Paul visited the region on his first missionary journey, establishing churches in Antioch of Pisidia, Iconium, Lystra, and Derbe (Acts 13—14). When he revisited the area later, he encountered Timothy and possibly Luke, adding them to his missionary team (Acts 16:1, 6, 10). Paul again revisited the area on his second missionary journey, encouraging the believers there (Acts 18:23).

GABRIEL

Gabriel is one of only two angels in Scripture that we learn the names of (Michael being the other). His name means "man of God" or "God is my strength."

We are introduced to Gabriel when he is sent to Daniel to give him the explanation of the vision of the ram and he-goat (Dan. 8:16). Later, he is sent again to give Daniel the seventy-weeks prophecy (9:20-27).

When we meet Gabriel again in Scripture, he is announcing two miraculous births. First, he appears to Zacharias in the temple to announce that he and Elisabeth would have a son (Luke 1:11-19). Gabriel introduces himself as one who stands "in the presence of God." Six months later, he was sent to Nazareth. He gives Mary the news that she would be the one to bring forth the Messiah, Jesus (vss. 26-33).

HIGH PRIEST

This was a position established by God in the Mosaic covenant (Ex. 28:1). The first high priest was Moses' brother, Aaron, and God declared that all high priests after Aaron were to be descendants of him.

The high priests were appointed by God, not man (Heb. 5:4). The primary role of the high priest was to be a representative—of God to the people and of the people to God.

We see in Hebrews that the role of high priest was perfectly fulfilled in Christ as the representative of both God and humanity (2:17). As a "great high priest" (4:14), Jesus provides direct access to God and His mercy.

—*Kelly Hawver.*

Daily Bible Readings for
Home Study and Worship

(Readings are for the week previous to the lesson topics.)

1. December 4. The Promise of Messiah's Forerunner
M — A Promise to Abraham and Sarah. Gen. 18:9-15.
T — God Rescues and Reassures Hagar. Gen. 21:9-21.
W — Leah Bears Four Sons. Gen. 29:31-35.
T — In the Spirit of Elijah. Mal. 4:1-6.
F — The Messenger of the Lord. Matt. 11:9-15.
S — A Deliverer for Israel. Judg. 13:2-24.
S — Promise to Zacharias. Luke 1:8-20.

2. December 11. God's Promise to David
M — The Seed of David. Ps. 89:1-5.
T — David Anointed King. I Sam. 16:1-13.
W — A House for the Lord. I Kgs. 8:12-26.
T — The Lord's Oath to David. Ps. 132:1-18.
F — The Seed of David Endures Forever. Ps. 89:19-37.
S — King over All Israel. II Sam. 5:6-12.
S — An Everlasting Kingdom. II Sam. 7:4-16.

3. December 18. God's Promise of a Saviour
M — A Deliverer Promised. Gen. 3:14-15.
T — The King Will Descend from Judah. Gen. 49:8-12.
W — The House of David. II Sam. 7:25-29.
T — The Righteous Branch. Jer. 23:5-8.
F — The Supremacy of Jesus. Heb. 1:1-8.
S — He Is Immanuel. Isa. 7:10-14.
S — Jesus' Birth Foretold. Luke 1:26-38.

4. December 25. The Birth of the Saviour (Christmas)
M — The Prince of Peace. Isa. 9:6-7.
T — A Light to the Gentiles. Isa. 60:1-4.
W — A Ruler Born in Bethlehem. Mic. 5:1-6.
T — The Fullness of Time. Gal. 4:4-7.
F — The Saviour of the World. I John 4:9-15.
S — You Shall Name Him Jesus. Matt. 1:21-25.
S — A Saviour Is Born to Us. Luke 2:1-17.

5. January 1. Blessing of Reconciliation
M — No Longer Strangers. Eph. 2:11-22.
T — Accepted by Christ. Rom. 15:1-7.
W — Resolve Problems with Others. Matt. 5:23-26.
T — Renewed Relationship with God. Ps. 51:7-17.
F — Jesus—Lord of Redemption. Col. 1:18-23.
S — Peace with God. Rom. 5:1-11.
S — Ministry of Reconciliation. II Cor. 5:11-21.

6. January 8. Blessing of Forgiveness and New Life
M — God Cleanses His People. Ps. 51:1-6.
T— God Redeems His People. Ps. 130:1-8.
W — God Forgives Iniquity. Ps. 103:1-5.
T— Forgiveness Leads to Forgiveness. Mark 11:24-26.
F— Forgiving as God Forgives. Matt. 6:12-15.
S — Guilt of Sin Removed. Ps. 32:1-11.
S — Forgiveness and New Life. I John 1:1—2:5.

7. January 15. Blessing of Intercession
M — Melchizedek Blesses Abraham. Gen. 14:17-20.
T — Jesus Encourages Prayer. Mark 14:32-42.
W — Jesus Earnestly Prays. Luke 22:39-46.
T — Jesus' Every Prayer Is Heard. John 11:32-45.
F — The Future King-Priest. Ps. 110:1-7.
S — Christ Helps Us in Our Weakness. Heb. 2:5-18.
S — Jesus, Our Intercessor. Heb. 4:14—5:10.

8. January 22. Blessing of Liberty in Christ
M — The Sign of Abraham's Covenant. Gen. 17:9-14.
T — Set Free by the Son. John 8:31-36.
W — Freedom in the Spirit. II Cor. 3:12-18.
T — Serve God Above All. I Cor. 7:17-24.
F — Freedom for Gentiles. Gal. 2:1-10.
S — Redeemed from the Law's Curse. Gal. 3:10-14.
S — Spiritual Liberty. Gal. 5:1-17.

9. January 29. Blessing of Belonging in Christ
M — Living in Unity. Ps. 133:1-3.
T — Unity of the Spirit. Eph. 4:1-6.
W — All Receive God's Grace. Eph. 4:7-10.
T — God's Gifts to Bring Unity. Eph. 4:11-16.
F — Gifts to Be Used in Humility. Rom. 12:3-8.
S — All Are One in Christ. Gal. 3:26-29.
S — Many Parts, One Body. I Cor. 12:14-31.

10. February 5. Blessings amid Trials
M — Israel Will Be One Again. Ezek. 37:15-28.
T — Suffering for Doing Good. I Pet. 3:13-18.
W — Faithful in Afflictions. Rev. 2:8-11.
T — Patient Endurance. Rev. 3:7-13.
F — Stand Firm. Jas. 5:7-11.
S — Our Living Hope. I Pet. 1:3-9.
S — The Crown of Life. Jas. 1:1-8, 12-18.

11. February 12. Blessing of God's Comfort
M — God Himself Is Our Comfort. Isa. 51:12-16.
T — God's Compassion Brings Comfort. Isa. 66:10-14.
W — An Abiding Comforter. John 14:15-27.
T — Power in Weakness. II Cor. 12:7-10.
F — Patient Hope. Rom. 8:18-25.
S — Eternal Encouragement. II Thess. 2:13-17.
S — God of All Comfort. II Cor. 1:3-11.

12. February 19. Blessing of Godliness
M — Put On the New Self. Eph. 4:17-24.
T — Put Off the Old Self. Eph. 4:25-32.
W — Called God's Children. I John 2:28—3:3.
T — Renewed by the Spirit. Titus 3:3-8.
F — Imitators of God. I Thess. 1:4-10
S — A Life Worthy of the Lord. Col. 1:9-14.
S — Everything Needed for a Godly Life. II Pet. 1:3-14.

13. February 26. Blessing of Spiritual Fruit
M — Freedom in the Spirit. Rom. 8:1-11.
T — Spirit-Led Sons of God. Rom. 8:12-17.
W — Spirit-Led Behavior. Col. 3:12-17.
T — Slaves to Righteousness. Rom. 6:15-23.
F — The Fruits of Righteousness. Phil. 1:9-11.
S — Spirit-Led Understanding. I Cor. 2:10-16.
S — Walking with the Spirit. Gal. 5:18—6:10.

REVIEW

God's Great Blessings

UNIT I: Blessing of a Saviour

December 4

The Promise of Messiah's Forerunner

1. How did Zacharias react to the angel's appearance?
2. What prayer did the angel say had been heard?
3. What evidence would point to the unique ministry of John in God's plan?
4. What would John's ministry entail?
5. How did Zacharias respond to Gabriel's message?
6. What excuse did Moses offer for not going back to Egypt?

December 11

God's Promise to David

1. How had God lived among His people before David's time?
2. What did God mean when He promised to make David a house?
3. What work did God say David's heir would accomplish?
4. How was it possible for David's dynasty to be eternal?
5. Has Jesus yet fulfilled the Davidic covenant? Explain.

December 18

God's Promise of a Saviour

1. At what particular time was the Angel Gabriel sent to Mary?
2. What was Mary's relationship to Joseph at this time?
3. Was Mary's godly character the key to God's choosing her? Explain.
4. What is meant by the title "Son of the Highest" (Luke 1:32)?
5. What in Gabriel's message proved to Mary that her son would be the Messiah?

December 25

The Birth of the Saviour (Christmas)

1. Why did God arrange for Jesus to be born in Bethlehem?
2. Why is the mention that there was no lodging place for Joseph and Mary important?
3. What was the purpose of swaddling clothes?
4. Why were the shepherds fitting witnesses of Jesus' birth?
5. What is the meaning of the title "Christ," or "Messiah"?

UNIT II: Blessing of the Gospel

January 1

Blessing of Reconciliation

1. Why is it wrong to "glory in appearance" (II Cor. 5:12)?
2. What was the primary motivation for Paul to serve Christ?
3. Because Christ "died for all" (vs. 15), how should we live?
4. What ministry was given to Paul?
5. How can we be "ambassadors for Christ" (vs. 20)?

January 8

Blessing of Forgiveness and New Life

1. Why did the Apostle John emphasize the humanity of Jesus?
2. What does it mean to say that God is light?
3. What does walking in light or walking in darkness mean?
4. By what means can believers be

clean even though sinful?

5. What is the test that reveals whether someone truly knows God?

January 15
Blessing of Intercession

1. Why is it essential that our Great High Priest be both human and divine?
2. How can we as sinners have access to God's throne of grace?
3. From what ancestry did Jewish priests have to come? Why?
4. How does Christ's priesthood differ from that of Jewish priests?
5. In what sense did Christ learn obedience?

January 22
Blessing of Liberty in Christ

1. On what did Paul base his call to the Galatians to stand fast in liberty?
2. What threatened their freedom in Christ?
3. What righteousness do we hope for by faith?
4. What danger did Paul express through the proverb about leaven?
5. How does faith relate to the fact that love fulfills the law?

UNIT III: Blessing of Grace in Christ
January 29

Blessing of Belonging in Christ

1. Why should we welcome the diversity God has given the church?
2. How were the Corinthians destroying the harmony of the church?
3. How can a church of diverse elements present a unified witness?
4. In Paul's list of spiritual gifts, which ones did he rank higher? Why?
5. How was Paul's ranking of gifts a rebuke to the Corinthians?

February 5
Blessings amid Trials

1. What specific thing did James tell his readers to pray for?
2. What is promised to those who endure trials?
3. Does God tempt us? Why or why not?
4. Through what has God begotten us to new life?

February 12
Blessing of God's Comfort

1. What two things did Paul say God was the Father of?
2. What is one of the greatest benefits of receiving comfort from God in hard times?
3. What was steadfast in Paul relative to the Corinthian believers?
4. How did he describe his trial?
5. What did Paul say about prayer and its importance for believers?

February 19
Blessing of Godliness

1. How were farmers in Israel to provide for the poor?
2. Why is mistreatment of the disabled such a serious sin?
3. What two wrongs must be avoided in legal cases?
4. What serious consequences can result from slandering a person?

February 26
Blessing of Spiritual Fruit

1. How does being led by the Spirit differ from being under the law?
2. What did Paul say about Christians and the "works of the flesh" (Gal. 5:19)?
3. What is added by the idea of walking in the Spirit?
4. With what attitude should we approach those who are in sin?